THE LIFE COURSE IN CONTEXT

FIRST EDITION

Edited by Kyong Hee Chee
Texas State University

Bassim Hamadeh, CEO and Publisher
Michael Simpson, Vice President of Acquisitions
Jamie Giganti, Managing Editor
Jess Busch, Senior Graphic Designer
Marissa Applegate, Acquisitions Editor
Monika Dziamka, Project Editor
Natalie Lakosil, Licensing Manager
Mandy Licata, Interior Designer

www.cognella.com   800-200-3908

I thank Kellen Begin for his invaluable assistance with this project.

Contents

Introducing the Life Course Perspective

The goal of this section is to introduce the life course perspective as a dynamic theoretical approach, and to illustrate how it can be applied to studying multiple connections between neighborhoods and the health of individuals. The life course perspective is a relatively new theoretical framework, within which researchers can examine changing human lives in the context of time and place (Elder, 1994). As described by Robert, Cagney, and Weden (2005), main principles or themes of this perspective are life-span development, place and time, timing, linked lives, and agency. The principle of life-span development lies in the assumption that "[h]uman development and aging are lifelong processes" (Elder, Johnson, & Crosnoe, 2003, p. 11). It encourages us to take a long-term perspective on human lives, necessitating an observation of individual experiences over time. The life course perspective also builds on the idea that place and historical time shape human development. The principle of place and time, therefore, helps researchers attend to neighborhood characteristics as sources of advantages or disadvantages for residents' health, while recognizing historical events that expose residents to benefits or risks. The timing principle of the life course perspective refers to the notion that the effects of exposure to risks (or lack of exposure to benefits) differ by the age at which a person experiences exposure (or deficits). The principle of linked lives represents "the notion of interdependent lives" that "[h]uman lives are typically embedded in social relationships with kin and friends across the life span" (Elder, 1994, p. 6). Processes involved with linked lives include socialization and support across the life cycle and across generations (Elder, 1994, p. 6). There are some theories useful for elaborating on linked lives, especially with regard to mechanisms leading to specific behaviors, including, but not limited to, health behaviors. Social network theory concerns the structural aspects of social relations such as the density of social networks, whereas social capital theory often deals with the value, function, or outcomes of social relationships, which may promote or inhibit certain actions. Finally, the principle of agency in the life course perspective emphasizes that individuals make their own life-course choices within the social structure of opportunities and constraints (Elder, Johnson, & Crosnoe, 2004). Encouraging human agency might enhance healthful behaviors for individuals.

Robert, Cagney, and Weden (2005) also apply these life-course principles to neighborhoods, exploring how neighborhoods change over time, and how such changes may influence residents' health. Theoretical models consistent with the principle of life-span development include the ecological perspective, which often focuses on the study of race- and social class-based residential segregation. The place and time principle of the life course is implicit in a political economy perspective, in that it focuses on political and economic factors as causes for differential neighborhood development and the unequal distribution of resources, ultimately determining the health of residents. Persistent racial and economic segregation in U.S. urban neighborhoods reflects historical circumstances and calls for decisions at the societal level to a more equitable distribution of various resources across neighborhoods in order to enhance citizens' health. The life-course principle of timing helps us to see that neighborhoods change as they go through critical periods of their development. A critical point in time for a neighborhood may occur when a neighborhood's distribution of racial and ethnic groups reaches a threshold. The linked-lives principle helps illuminate why there is a high degree of stability at the neighborhood level, even in the midst of high mobility at the individual level. This neighborhood-level continuity is attributable to the fact that the lives of earlier residents tend to shape those of later residents, perhaps through cultural phenomena. Robert, Cagney, and Weden (2005) cite subcultural models to posit residents' noneconomic reasons to remain in place. Whether or not residents maintain enduring relationships with other residents may determine residential mobility and quality of life. The role of agency is also important when it comes to variations in neighborhood characteristics. Some are more resilient than others in responding to disasters, and the source of resilience is social networks (or social capital) at the neighborhood level, which can be mobilized for collective action to deal with neighborhood problems. This ability to mobilize resources for beneficial changes can be termed as collective efficacy. Robert, Cagney, and Weden (2005) conclude that more research needs to employ life-course principles to understand the dynamics of neighborhood changes and the effects of those changes on individual- and neighborhood-level health, so as to intervene to decrease health disparities. Overall, the life course perspective is a multifaceted theoretical approach, useful for addressing continuity and changes involved with diverse human life paths that vary by place and time.

REFERENCES

Elder, Glen H. Jr. 1994. "Time, Human Agency, and Social Change: Perspective on the Life Course." *Social Psychology Quarterly* 57(1):4–15.

Elder, Glen H. Jr., Monica Kirkpatrick Johnson, and Robert Crosnoe. 2003. "The Emergence and Development of Life Course Theory," pp. 3–19. In *Handbooks of Sociology and Social Research: Handbook of the Life Course*. J. T. Mortimer and M. J. Shanahan, Eds. New York: Kluwer Academic/Plenum Publishers.

Robert, Stephanie A., Kathleen A. Cagney, and Margaret M. Weden. 2005. "A Life-Course Approach to the Study of Neighborhoods and Health," pp. 124–143. In *Handbook of Medical Sociology*, 6th ed. C. E. Bird, P. Conrad, and A. M. Fremont, Eds. Nashville, TN: Vanderbilt University Press.

A Life-Course Approach to the Study of Neighborhoods and Health

By Stephanie A. Robert, Kathleen A. Cagney, and
Margaret M. Weden

Renewed attention to the importance of neighborhood context to health and well-being (Entwisle 2007; Sampson et al. 2002) has led to insight and innovation in health research over the last decade. While biomedical research has focused on how processes within our bodies affect health, and much social science and public health research has emphasized how the behavioral and psychosocial characteristics of individuals affect health, research on neighborhoods reminds us that individuals live in a variety of social and spatial contexts, and that these contexts are important to shaping health and well-being.

We argue that most research on neighborhoods and health has been hampered by considering individuals and neighborhoods as static entities. Little research has examined how neighborhoods affect the health of individuals over time, how neighborhoods themselves change over time, and how the life courses of individuals and neighborhoods interact to impact individual and population health.

A life-course approach "guides research on human lives within context" (Elder, Johnson, and Crosnoe 2004, 10) and is therefore a natural approach for studying the impact of neighborhoods on health. This approach highlights issues of age and time to pinpoint critical periods when neighborhood might be most important to health in a person's life course, and which aspects of neighborhood might matter at different times. A life-course approach can also point to the dynamic nature of neighborhoods, and how neighborhood

Stephanie A. Robert, Kathleen A. Cagney and Margaret M. Weden, "A Life-Course Approach to the Study of Neighborhoods and Health," *Handbook of Medical Sociology*, Sixth Edition, pp. 124–143. Copyright © 2010 by Vanderbilt University Press. Reprinted with permission.

stability and change over time can contribute to the health and well-being of residents. While most life-course research examines the life course of *individuals*, we argue that studying the life course of *neighborhoods* might significantly expand our understanding of the impact of neighborhoods on health.

FIVE PRINCIPLES OF THE LIFE COURSE APPLIED TO INDIVIDUALS

The life course is described variously as a theoretical orientation, a perspective, and a framework (Mortimer and Shanahan 2004). We highlight five general principles common to most life-course approaches: life-span development, place and time, timing, linked lives, and agency (for more thorough summaries, see, e.g., Elder, Johnson, and Crosnoe 2004; Mortimer and Shanahan 2004). We provide examples of how the principle has been applied to improve our understanding of how neighborhood context affects the health of individuals as they age, then describe how the principles might be applied to better understand the life course of *neighborhoods*, and how the neighborhood life course might affect health.

Life-Span Development

The principle of life-span development emphasizes taking a long-term perspective on individual development and how it is shaped by experiences throughout life (Elder, Johnson, and Crosnoe 2004). Although this principle suggests that the impact of neighborhoods on health should be examined over people's entire life span, much of the literature has examined the relationship between neighborhood context and health at one point in time. Although such cross-sectional analyses provide useful insights into the relationship between neighborhood context and health, they cannot test whether neighborhood context has contemporaneous, lagged, or cumulative effects on health.

As notable exceptions, several studies have simultaneously tested the relevance of lagged and contemporaneous influence of neighborhoods on health, exploring the influence of early life neighborhood exposures on health at different points later in the life course (Curtis et al. 2004; Wheaton and Clarke 2003; Naess et al. 2008). For example, Wheaton and Clarke (2003) found that childhood neighborhood socioeconomic disadvantage had a lagged effect on early adult mental health over and above the effects of adult neighborhood context.

Neighborhood context also may have a cumulative impact on health over time. Living in a disadvantaged neighborhood context may instigate a chain of risk (Kuh et al. 2003; Ferraro and Shippee 2008)—a sequence of events that accumulate over the life course to produce poor health. From this perspective, neighborhood context affects not only clusters of risk and protective factors, but chains of risk or protective factors that compound over time to produce cumulative advantage or disadvantage that affects health (Dannefer 2003; O'Rand 1996). For example, research examining an index of cumulative neighborhood disadvantage over decades finds that cumulative neighborhood disadvantage is associated with subclinical atherosclerosis in women (Carson et al. 2007; Lemelin et al. 2009).

The principle of life-span development also suggests that we conceptualize how neighborhoods can have both direct and indirect effects on health over time. While much research demonstrates that neighborhood context has an *independent* impact on health over and above individual socioeconomic status (Robert 1999; Pickett and Pearl 2001; Kawachi and Berkman 2003), research has not sufficiently examined how neighborhood context indirectly affects health *through* its impact on individual SES—that is, by shaping individual educational, occupational, and economic achievement, which then have more proximal effects on health.

Scholars have tested various aspects of these relationships rather than considering entire pathways. For example, research demonstrates that neighborhoods impact schooling and educational achievement of children. Sampson, Sharkey, and Raudenbush (2008) showed that among black children in Chicago, living in severely disadvantaged neighborhoods very early in life had a lagged effect on lower verbal ability a number of years later. The magnitude of this relationship was approximately equal to missing a year or more of schooling. Theoretically, these neighborhood effects on verbal ability might subsequently impact health through a number of pathways, such as children's ability to succeed in school; to secure a good job, income, and health insurance in adulthood; and to make healthy lifestyle choices (Mirowsky and Ross 2003).

In sum, the principle of life-span development highlights the idea that neighborhoods may have lagged, cumulative, and contemporaneous effects on individual health over a person's life span. Longitudinal studies are needed to understand the complex pathways linking neighborhoods to health as people age.

Place and Time

The principle of place and time highlights the idea that both place and historical context matter to a person's health. Indeed, the primary strength of research on neighborhoods and health is that it emphasizes how one of the places we are exposed to in our daily lives—our neighborhood—shapes our health. Research on neighborhoods shifts our understanding of health from a state determined only by individual and family processes to one promoted or constrained by the physical, social, economic, and service environments of the neighborhoods in which we live and work.

Health outcomes have been linked to multiple aspects of neighborhood context—neighborhood socioeconomic status (Diez Roux et al. 2004; Pickett and Pearl 2001; Robert 1999), social capital (Cagney and Browning 2004; Carpiano 2007), age structure (Cagney 2006), the built environment (Freedman et al. 2008), and crime (Sundquist et al. 2006; Morenoff, Sampson, and Raudenbush 2001).

Aspects of larger place contexts have also been linked to health (Osypuk and Galea 2007)—county or state-level income inequality (Lynch et al. 2001; Wen, Browning, and Cagney 2003; Kawachi, Kennedy, and Lochner 1997), county- or state-level policies and services (Kaplan et al. 1996), and racial residential segregation at metropolitan area, city, and county levels (Lee and Ferraro 2007; Robert and Ruel 2006; Subramanian, Acevedo-Garcia, and Osypuk 2005; Walton 2009).

Moreover, research has highlighted the importance of neighborhood context in understanding racial and ethnic disparities in health—disparities in hypertension (Morenoff et al. 2007), obesity (Robert and Reither 2004), self-rated health (Cagney, Browning, and Wen 2005; Browning, Cagney, and Wen 2003; Robert and Ruel 2006; Robert and Lee 2002; Subramanian, Acevedo-Garcia, and Osypuk 2005), asthma prevalence (Rosenbaum 2008; Cagney and Browning 2004), and mortality (Yao and Robert 2008).

An understanding of the importance of neighborhood to a range of economic and quality of life outcomes led to implementation of and research on the effects of housing relocation programs such as the Moving to Opportunity (MTO), Gautreaux, and Yonkers experiments. These housing mobility experiments are directly relevant to examining how changing a family's neighborhood place might effect changes in physical and mental health outcomes over the life course. Research on these programs provides some evidence that moving out of high-poverty neighborhoods improves the mental health (Leventhal and Brooks-Gunn 2003) and physical health (Fauth, Leventhal, and Brooks-Gunn 2008) of movers compared to stayers, though these effects are modest and are generally stronger for adults than for children.

Although housing relocation experiments provide some evidence of the impact of neighborhoods on health and other outcomes, neighborhoods can impact health and well-being over the life course in ways that cannot be overcome by housing relocation alone (Ludwig et al. 2008; Sampson, Sharkey, and Raudenbush 2008; Sharkey 2008). For example, because childhood neighborhood context has a lagged effect on the mental health of young adults (Wheaton and Clarke 2003), moving young adults out of poor neighborhoods may not overcome the lagged impact of childhood poverty residence on their mental health. Similarly, if exposure to poor neighborhoods is particularly critical in childhood, then children in housing relocation programs have already been exposed to poor neighborhoods—exposures that a residential move may not easily overcome (Sampson, Sharkey, and Raudenbush 2008). However, the housing relocation too may produce either lagged or cumulative benefits to mental and physical health that will appear much later. For example, Fauth, Leventhal, and BrooksGunn (2008) find that adults randomly assigned to move to lower-poverty neighborhoods experienced improvements in self-reports of collective efficacy and safety and improvements in weak social ties, while maintaining strong social ties outside their neighborhood. These beneficial aspects of their new neighborhood may have a lagged or cumulative impact on the physical and mental health of these adults and their children over a longer period of time.

Although the literature on neighborhoods and health has emphasized well the place aspect of the life-course principle of place and time, less attention has been paid to time (cohort and period effects). Yet the cohort and period effects of historical events have been examined in some economic and demographic research to evaluate the influence of exposures at different points along the life course. For example, historical disasters like famine and pandemics have been used to study the long-lasting effects of early life exposures on later life health and longevity of the survivors of these events (Susser and Lin 1992; Preston, Hill, and Drevenstedt 1998; Almond 2006; O'Connor 2003).

Age, period, and cohort characteristics can also converge to produce different environments that affect health. For example, Small (2004) conducted ethnographic work in a low-income Puerto Rican enclave, documenting how residents resisted relocation efforts. He showed that the initial migratory generation was more invested than the younger generations in neighborhood-level social capital and in maintaining the enclave; younger generations did not feel the same sense of social ties or belonging. He illustrates how age and cohort converged to shape expectations about neighborhood.

Though clearly the life-course principle of place and time is the underpinning of most neighborhood research on health, almost all the recent research has focused on urban areas to the exclusion of rural areas, even though rural residents have worse health on a number of outcomes (Hartley 2004). Indeed, racial disparities in health are often more severe in rural areas (Probst et al. 2004), but get overlooked in the recent neighborhood research, including racial-segregation research, which focuses on urban and suburban areas (Robert and Ruel 2006).

Moreover, the recent resurgence of attention to neighborhoods and health has been predominantly quantitative in nature, building upon the strength of a number of large national and regional surveys. However, a number of qualitative approaches have been advanced to fill gaps in our understanding of the meaning that residents place on their neighborhoods, and to describe people's spatial and social interactions in their neighborhoods (Airey 2003; Altschuler, Somkin, and Adler 2004; Israel et al. 2005; Patillo 1999). For example, Carpiano (2009) utilized the "go-along" interview (Kusenbach 2003) to better understand the meaning people assign to the "action space" (Cummins et al. 2007) of the neighborhoods in which they interact. Dennis and colleagues (2008) introduced participatory photo mapping (PPM) to study the implications of place for the health of children. They involved children living in a low-income neighborhood in a project in which children took photos of aspects of their neighborhood environments related to their health, provided narratives about the meaning of the photos, and participated in mapping their experiential data along with other existing neighborhood-level data using GIS mapping technologies. Such approaches are needed to help us better understand how people experience and interpret their spatial and social spaces, variations in these experiences and interpretations across residents, and the implications for individual and neighborhood health and well-being.

Timing

The life-course principle of timing suggests that the timing of an exposure or experience can be important in determining health, as Elder, Johnson, and Crosnoe explain: "The developmental antecedents and consequences of life transitions, events, and behavioral patterns vary according to their timing in a person's life" (2003, 12). For example, critical-period models in epidemiology emphasize the importance of the timing of health risks or exposures, often focusing on how exposures during particular biological or social developmental stages can have long-lasting health impacts (Lynch and Davey Smith 2005).

The principle of timing raises the question of whether neighborhood context is particularly important to health at specific ages, as some theory and evidence suggests may be true for childhood (Brooks-Gunn et al. 1993; Jelleyman and Spencer 2007) or for older adulthood (Robert and Li 2001; Glass and Balfour 2003). For example, young children and older adults may have greater physiological vulnerability to environmental exposures in poor neighborhoods than do young adults and adults in midlife. On the other hand, young and middle-aged adults may experience more immediate direct exposure to the stressful aspects of high unemployment in disadvantaged neighborhoods. Researchers studying the Chicago heat wave found that the higher mortality of older adults could be attributed not only to their greater physiological vulnerability to temperature, but also to their being the most likely to live in areas hardest hit by commercial decline (Browning et al. 2006). Further research is needed to explore which dimensions of neighborhoods are more or less important to people at specific ages or critical periods in their development.

Other aspects of timing can be explored to understand neighborhood effects on health. For example, Wen, Cagney, and Christakis (2005) studied older adults in Chicago who had experienced hospitalizations and examined the impact of neighborhood on their subsequent mortality. Their findings suggest that during a critical period of illness, older adults (or perhaps people of all ages) are more vulnerable to their neighborhood environments, with some neighborhoods being more facilitative of recovery than others.

Using a life-course approach to examine how timing of neighborhood exposure affects health also requires attention to how the timing of neighborhood exposure may have impacts on different measures of health. Naess and colleagues (2008) examined the relative contribution of neighborhoods on mortality risk along the life course of different cohorts for different causes of death. They found that for the youngest age group, area of residence close to death is most strongly related to mortality for psychiatric and violent causes of death. However, determinants of cardiovascular mortality included area of residence in both childhood and adulthood.

The principle of timing suggests that we explore whether exposures to neighborhood may be more or less salient at different points during an individual's development, or during critical events, such as illness or pregnancy, and whether such exposures affect different health outcomes at different ages.

Linked Lives

The life-course principle of linked lives, as conceived by Elder, suggests that "each generation is bound to fateful decisions and events in the other's life course" (1985, 40). This principle of linked lives is consistent with a body of research that examines social networks and social capital as particularly important aspects of the neighborhood context that promote or constrain health (Wen, Cagney, and Christakis 2005). Although the social network and social capital literatures have developed separately, the combination of these theoretical approaches provides great promise for improving our understanding of how neighborhoods affect health over the life course.

Social network theory highlights the social structure of social networks, which can shape a range of outcomes, including health. Wellman and Frank (2001) conceptualize multiple levels in which networks take root, highlighting the interdependence of individual, dyadic, and larger network characteristics. Network analysis, then, provides a structure to which we can apply theoretical ideas regarding how individuals, network ties, and network properties might interact at different levels to produce health within and between neighborhoods (Berkman and Glass 2000; Smith and Christakis 2008; Luke and Harris 2007).

While social network theory focuses on the structure of social networks, social capital theory focuses on their function. Social capital is conceptualized either as the resources that result from social structure (Burt 2001; Bourdieu 1986) or as a function of social structure that is beneficial to those who hold it (Coleman 1990). Lin, Cook, and Burt (2001) define social capital as resources embedded in a social structure that are accessed, mobilized, or both in purposive actions.

To further understand how linked lives within neighborhoods affect health, we should consider neighborhood social networks and the social capital that flows through them in ways that promote and constrain health. Although dense social networks might protect health through social support mechanisms (Berkman and Glass 2000), they might simultaneously promote unhealthy behaviors. For example, Carpiano (2007) found that higher neighborhood-level social support was associated with greater odds of individual level daily smoking and binge drinking, controlling for neighborhood socioeconomic conditions and social cohesion.

Indeed, social networks and the social capital that flows through them to affect health may function differently depending on other characteristics of the neighborhood context. As summarized by Berkman and Clark: "It would seem that one must differentiate between the existence of networks and their capacity to provide resources" (2003, 299). For example, although being socially isolated is generally detrimental to individual health (Berkman and Glass 2000), some suggest that social isolation might be protective when people live in hazardous neighborhood environments. Caughy, O'Campo, and Muntaner (2003) found that, in poor neighborhoods, children whose parents reported knowing few of their neighbors had lower levels of internalizing problems than those whose parents knew many of their neighbors. Being part of a dense social network can also place excess demands on network members (Portes and Sensenbrenner 1993). Schieman and Meersman (2004) found that the association between neighborhood problems and physical health problems among older men was exacerbated for men who contributed greater levels of support, suggesting that the demands of living in challenging neighborhoods may tap individual health resources.

The life-course principle of linked lives may be particularly relevant when examining the positive and negative health effects of living in neighborhood ethnic enclaves.

Although most of the literature on racial segregation and health focuses on the negative impact, particularly economically, of living in neighborhoods with high concentrations of ethnic minorities, some research on ethnic enclaves suggests that their social networks can serve to constrain and promote positive health behaviors, distribution of health-system knowledge, and good health and well-being (Eschbach et al. 2004; Lee and Ferraro 2007). Studies have found that living in neighborhoods with a high proportion of Hispanic residents is protective of selfrated health and of depressive symptoms among older Mexican American adults (Patel et al. 2003; Ostir et al. 2003). Other research found that the health advantage of living in a high-density Mexican American neighborhood outweighed the health disadvantages of even high-poverty residence for Mexican American older adults (Eschbach et al. 2004).

Future research on neighborhoods and health would benefit from attention to the structure of social networks within and between neighborhoods, the social capital that flows through them in different types of neighborhoods, and the ways that these networks and capital support or constrain health over time.

The life-course principle of linked lives also draws on the vertical notion of the life course; that is, that our life trajectories are shaped by generations before and after us (O'Rand 1996). This leads us to ask about intergenerational characteristics, interactions, or relationships, and the extent to which they matter for the way in which neighborhood social context affects health over the individual life span. Sharkey (2008) recently demonstrated that neighborhood socioeconomic context has much continuity from one generation to the next. Indeed, his results suggest that although family income, education, and occupational status all contribute to a child's later neighborhood type, the characteristics of the child's neighborhood of origin have even stronger effects on later neighborhood type (see also Jackson and Mare 2007). Moreover, Sharkey (2008) found that this intergenerational transmission of neighborhood context was particularly strong for African Americans and that among children born in the poorest U.S. neighborhoods, 70 percent of African Americans were still living in poor neighborhoods as adults, compared to 40 percent of white adults born into the poorest neighborhoods—findings consistent with Crowder, South, and Chavez's (2006) determination that blacks have less locational return on their social, economic, and educational attainment.

Such intergenerational transmission of neighborhood context, and racial differences in this transmission, suggests that a cross-sectional estimate of adult neighborhood context is likely to be correlated with lifetime neighborhood context (Jackson and Mare 2007; Sharkey 2008), and that this correlation is likely stronger for African Americans (Sharkey 2008). Future research should consider the duration of exposure to neighborhoods over one's life span (Quillian 2002, 2003; Clampet-Lundquist and Massey 2008) as well as a measure of intergenerational transmission of neighborhood context (Sharkey 2008) when examining how neighborhood context might affect health. Such an approach may be particularly crucial to understanding racial disparities in health.

Agency

The life-course principle of agency suggests that individuals "construct their own life course through the choices and actions they take within the opportunities and constraints of history and social circumstance" (Elder, Johnson, and Crosnoe 2004, 11). This may be the life-course principle least attended to in contemporary research on neighborhoods and health (Entwisle 2007). Much of the recent neighborhood research has taken a primarily structuralist approach, examining how neighborhoods constrain individual opportunities in a fairly deterministic way, with less attention to how individuals impact neighborhoods in return.

One exception is research that examines residential mobility—how individuals sort into different neighborhoods based on their individual and neighborhood preferences and characteristics, thereby affecting the context of their neighborhoods (e.g., Charles 2001; Harris 1999; Krysan 2002; Moffit 2001; Quillian 2002). Yet mobility in and out of neighborhoods is only one way in which individuals can change their neighborhoods.

Almost no attention has been paid to variation in how individual residents make choices or react (other than moving), given the same neighborhood constraints, and the individual, family, and group characteristics that may buffer the impacts of neighborhood constraints on health. Research focusing on mean health effects of living in a disadvantaged neighborhood virtually ignores the variance in health among people in disadvantaged neighborhoods. Why do some residents of disadvantaged neighborhoods remain healthy in the face of neighborhood constraints and challenges?

Although directly improving the neighborhood context—reducing neighborhood constraints or shoring up neighborhood assets—might be the best long-term approach to reducing the detrimental impact of disadvantaged neighborhood environments on health (Osypuk and Galea 2007; Link and Phelan 1995; Schulz et al. 2002), steps could be taken to buffer the impacts of disadvantaged neighborhoods on poor health. Stress and coping theories (Pearlin 1999; Thoits 1995; Turner, Wheaton, and Lloyd 1995), as well as risk and resilience theories (Ryff et al. 1998; Rutter 1990), can be applied to examine how individual and neighborhood factors may buffer the effects of exposure to neighborhood stressors and risks. For example, Krause (1998) found that religious coping style buffered the association between living in dilapidated neighborhoods and self-rated health among older adults. Schieman and Meersman (2004) found that the relationship between neighborhood problems and depression among older women was buffered by the support that women received. Opportunities for future research include the exploration of individual and neighborhood characteristics that might buffer the impact of neighborhood disadvantage on poor health.

Public health interventions often attempt to support and encourage aspects of human agency that can be health enhancing, such as providing tools and resources for people to choose and implement healthy behaviors despite constrained resources (Bird and Rieker 2008). But there are few examples of theory applied to empirically examine the role of human agency in reciprocal exchange with the neighborhood—examining how individual agents attempt to actively change their environments through social organization, social networks, and social action in ways that promote health.

Yet sociology provides many theories about social movements (Della Porta and Diani 1999; McAdam, McCarthy, and Zald 1996; Meyer and Whittier 1994; Poletta and Jasper 2001) that could help us understand how individuals and groups interact with their neighborhoods in ways that might improve individual and neighborhood health. Small (2002) applied social organization theory to examine structure, culture, and neighborhood participation and change in a Puerto Rican housing project in Boston and found that how different cohorts frame the same neighborhood can affect their participation. While having a positive frame can sustain willingness to participate in the neighborhood, those who have less positive frames need mechanisms to incite neighborhood participation such as an exogenous threat or a momentary crisis, both of which can transform cultural perceptions of neighborhoods and reconfigure the conception of neighborhood participation as important. Other promising research examines the active role of community organizations as transformative agents in neighborhoods through which individuals can express agency and action, perpetuating or transforming the neighborhood environment (Swaroop and Morenoff 2006; Stoll 2001).

A view of human agency as a force of neighborhood change has been applied fruitfully in the social movements literature regarding environmental health movements and neighborhood reactions to environmental challenges (Brown and Mikkelsen 1990; Bullard 1994; Szasz 1994), but rarely regarding the social movements literature on health more generally. However, Brown and colleagues (2004) have presented a new theoretical conceptualization of "health social movements" with a framework that could be applied to social movements that occur within and across neighborhoods and that may improve individual and population health.

The growing attention to community-based participatory research is partly based on an understanding that individuals are active agents— they can come together to either respond to or proactively change their environments (e.g., Israel et al. 2005). Participatory research provides promise for generating knowledge that is deemed useful by communities and for instigating processes that may more effectively lead to the application of that knowledge to social change that could promote health.

Future research should build upon theories of social organization and social movements to expand our understanding of the role of individuals and community organizations in inciting participation and bringing about neighborhood change to improve individual and population health.

FIVE PRINCIPLES OF THE LIFE COURSE APPLIED TO NEIGHBORHOODS

Most theoretical approaches to the life course focus on the life course of individuals, not the life course of neighborhoods. Similarly, research on neighborhoods and health has been slow to examine how neighborhoods themselves change over time, and how their life course may affect residents (Sampson, Morenoff, and Gannon-Rowley 2002). Yet sociologists and other social scientists have a range of rich theories about neighborhood change, though such theories are not commonly applied to individual and population health outcomes.

Approaches to neighborhood change have been explored through research in sociology, human ecology, political science, population studies, and economics. Studies have considered various dimensions of neighborhood change, addressing the evolving U.S. landscape determined by industrialization, urbanization, and the patterns of migration and segregation. Here we highlight key approaches either that have been used to look at health outcomes, or that appear particularly fruitful in this regard.

Life-Span Development

The principle of life-span development encourages us to examine how neighborhoods themselves change over time, and how neighborhood trajectories impact the lives of residents. Theoretical models of neighborhood stability and change can be differentiated by whether they focus more on the role of the characteristics or interactions of individuals in shaping neighborhood change (the ecological and subcultural perspectives) or more on institutional factors external to the neighborhood that significantly shape its characteristics and processes (the political economy perspective) (Schwirian 1983; Temkin and Rowe 1996).

A dominant approach to thinking about neighborhood change over time is the ecological perspective, closely linked with the Chicago School of sociological theory, which emphasizes individual environment interactions (Schwirian 1983; Temkin and Rowe 1996). A seminal example is Park's (1952) invasion-succession model of neighborhood change, in which neighborhoods are viewed as comprising "ecological niches" that are more or less favorable to habitation by different types of people. Essentially, individuals vote with their feet to determine where they will live, and the sum of these choices determines how neighborhoods take shape and change over time—affecting the life course of neighborhoods.

Duncan and Duncan (1957) and Taeuber and Taeuber (1965) derived racial residential succession models to explain the residential resettlement and segregation of blacks in the 1950s and 1960s. More recent iterations include locational attainment theory (Alba and Logan 1993) and spatial assimilation theory (South and Crowder 1997, 1998; South, Crowder, and Chavez 2005b), both focusing on how people determine whether to remain in or leave a neighborhood depending on their human capital and assessment of the neighborhood's suitability to their own social and economic characteristics. This approach highlights the life-span development of neighborhoods while integrating the life-course principle of individual agency, as individuals choose to select into or out of neighborhoods, though the constraints on these choices may be uneven.

An important focus in ecological perspectives on neighborhood change has been dimensions of neighborhood change and stability related to race and social class, particularly in the study of residential segregation, gentrification, and urban decline (Massey 1990; Alba and Logan 1993; South and Deane 1993; Jargowsky 1997; South and Crowder 1997; Gotham 1998; Iceland, Sharpe, and Steinmetz 2005; Scopilliti and

Iceland 2008). Duncan and Duncan (1957) created neighborhood change typologies describing the succession of neighborhoods through economic and racial change. These typologies for neighborhood succession have been updated and applied to outcomes in health and social development (Massey, Condran, and Denton 1987; Ruel and Robert 2009).

For example, Massey, Condran, and Denton (1987) examined changes in neighborhood racial context over time and categorized neighborhood census tracts as either white, black entry, black transitioning, black established, or declining. They found that living in black transition or established black census tracts is associated with higher crime rates, high school dropout rates, infant mortality rates, and adult mortality rates. Ruel and Robert (2009) extended this work using a dynamic typology of neighborhood racial residential history between 1970, 1980, and 1990. Using a national longitudinal survey of U.S. adults, they examined whether living in neighborhoods with different racial histories was associated with individual self-rated health and mortality. Results showed that racial disparities in health and mortality are explained by neighborhood racial residential history, neighborhood poverty level, and individual socioeconomic factors. Some results suggest that living in an established black neighborhood or in an established interracial neighborhood may actually be protective of health, once neighborhood poverty is controlled. They conclude that examining the dynamic nature of neighborhoods contributes to an understanding of health outcomes generally and racial health disparities more specifically.

Additional research is needed to examine how the life span of neighborhoods affects the health of residents. It may be important to understand not only how people's neighborhood experiences change when they move, but also how neighborhoods change around the people residing within them, and the effects on individual and population health.

Place and Time

Not only are neighborhoods places themselves but also they are located within larger places (cities, counties, states, countries) that shape their nature. Attention to the life-course principle of place attends to the dynamics of neighborhood change in the context of changes to surrounding neighborhoods. For example, Crowder and South (2008) demonstrate that individuals' mobility decisions were based not only on neighborhood racial composition, but also on the racial composition of surrounding areas, resulting in mobility that affected patterns of segregation. The literature on racial residential segregation considers the nesting of spatial residence, since racial segregation indices are created by comparing the racial composition among smaller residential units (i.e., census tracts) to create the racial-segregation index of a larger residential unit (e.g., city or county). But additional research should capitalize on recent innovations in geographic information systems (GIS), mapping, and spatial statistics to relate changes in one neighborhood to those in others. This may be particularly important in light of current national trends in immigration, growth of the Latino population, and changing economic circumstances, which will all likely distribute people and resources unevenly across place, with unclear implications for individual and population health.

In contrast to ecological perspectives on neighborhood change, which focus on how individual residential mobility shapes neighborhood contexts, a political economy perspective focuses upstream on the political, economic, and social factors that produce or reinforce differences across neighborhoods in the first place (Navarro 2002). Such upstream factors affect the neighborhood conditions and resources that then have a more proximal impact on residents' health (Osypuk and Galea 2007; Link and Phelan 1995).

The political economy perspective places neighborhood change in the context of an overarching system in which economic, political, and social forces external to neighborhoods guide neighborhood dynamics (Schwirian 1983; Temkin and Rowe 1996). Central themes of the political economy approach are social conflict, power, and the role of macroeconomic forces in shaping local conditions (Logan and Molotch 1987). From a political economy perspective, the dynamics of neighborhood change and the distribution of individuals and resources across neighborhoods do not reflect only the attributes of individual residents who vote with their feet to change neighborhoods, but rather the interests of external power structures.

Neighborhood research consistent with this approach includes research on inequality that views cities and metropolitan areas as the context within which housing, employment, and education markets develop in ways that segregate people and resources into different neighborhoods (e.g., Jargowsky 1997; Wilson 1987). Galea, Freudenberg, and Vlahov (2006) suggest that three municipal-level factors are important determinants of health: government, markets (e.g., housing and labor), and civil society (e.g., community organizations). Altschuler, Somkin, and Adler (2004) find evidence that politicians may be more responsive to white and more affluent neighborhoods than to black and poor ones, potentially shaping the availability of healthproducing resources in neighborhoods. LaVeist (1993) demonstrated that neighborhoods with greater black political empowerment had lower levels of infant mortality. Each of these examples highlights the embeddedness of neighborhoods in a larger social, political, and economic context that shapes them.

Again, the life-course principle of place and time encourages us to consider the importance of not only place but also historical time when examining the life course of neighborhoods. Here, it seems relevant to highlight the January 2009 volume of the *Annals of the American Academy of Political and Social Science* that addressed the relevance of the 1965 Moynihan report to our present-day understanding of urban neighborhoods and the persistence of racial and economic residential segregation in urban America. Clearly, historical circumstances that led to racial and economic residential segregation in the United States have been perpetuated rather than interrupted by more recent social, economic, and political periods (Sampson 2009). As we move to redress such segregation, an ecological approach to neighborhood change might suggest that we need to better understand how to create individual incentives and neighborhood environments that will promote a distribution of individuals across neighborhoods that might promote health for individuals and populations. A political economy perspective would suggest a focus on understanding the societal-level decisions and structures that need to change in order to distribute economic, social, political, and human resources more equitably across neighborhoods. Both approaches need to incorporate a more thorough understanding of how social networks within and across neighborhoods might facilitate either a different distribution of residential mobility or a different distribution and flow of resources through the networks.

Timing

Just as individuals may experience neighborhood characteristics as more salient to their health at different critical periods in their life, neighborhoods may be affected by events during critical periods of their development. Early work by Schelling (1978) examined thresholds or "tipping points" at which a neighborhood reaches a racial or ethnic composition that motivates residents to begin to leave. The event in this case is the outmigration of select residents during a tipping point stage of neighborhood racial/ethnic composition. Recent studies have provided further insight about the pace and progression of racial and economic neighborhood change, addressing the timing of neighborhood changes (Frankel and Pauzner 2002) and the potential role of threshold effects (Quercia and Galster 2000). However, most recent research demonstrates that despite much individual mobility in and out of neighborhoods, neighborhoods themselves remain fairly stable in their socioeconomic and racial characteristics over time—individual mobility serves only to replicate the economic and racial segregation of neighborhoods (Bruch and Mare 2006; Sampson and Sharkey 2008).

Although most of this research has not yet been applied to examining the role of individual or neighborhood health as either a determinant of individual moves or as a neighborhood-level outcome of the sum of individual moves, this line of research may be fruitful. In particular, agentbased models have been suggested as a promising approach to examining the dynamic nature of individuals, neighborhoods, and health (Entwisle 2007; Auchincloss and Diez Roux 2008). Agentbased models are an example of systems dynamics models that provide simulations of how microentities (i.e., people) change over time when interacting with other microentities and in response to characteristics of the environment (i.e., neighborhoods). Agent-based computer simulations might be used to produce representations of the individual-level and neighborhood-level health outcomes of these dynamic interactions between individuals and neighborhoods over time (Auchincloss and Diez Roux 2008; Entwisle 2007).

Also addressing the life-course principle of timing, the timing and geographic spread of public health programs, medical technology, and economic development have been used to identify the relative contribution of social, economic, medical, and public health factors in the timing and pace of changes in the causes of mortality within a population—specifically, the declines in infant mortality and infectious disease in the United States and Western European countries (McKeown 1976; Szreter 2004; Fogel and Costa 1997).

Linked Lives

The principle of linked lives, highlighting that those before and after us shape our life trajectories (O'Rand 1996), can be applied to neighborhoods as well. Sampson and Sharkey (2008) demonstrated the durability of neighborhood characteristics over time in terms of neighborhood income and racial structure. Although there is much mobility on an individual level, with individuals moving into and out of neighborhoods for a variety of economic and racial preference reasons (Quillian 2002), an ecological approach to neighborhood change demonstrates that the resulting individual choices in residential mobility culminate in stunning stability of neighborhood characteristics over time, at least in terms of stable neighborhood income and racial structure (Sampson and Sharkey 2008; Sampson 2009).

One criticism of the ecological perspective on neighborhood change is that it over-emphasizes economic competition for land and resources as the drivers of individual mobility and resulting neighborhood change (Temkin and Rowe 1996). Ecological models have also been criticized for their "value-free" assumptions regarding the nature of individual-environment interactions (Beatty 1988), and for emphasizing residential mobility as an efficient redistribution of people rather than as a cultural and social phenomenon.

One resolution offered for this criticism entails developing models with greater attention to the historical, cultural, and social exchange processes involved in neighborhood change and stability. "Subcultural models" are often seen as a type of ecological perspective that focuses on the role of cultural forms (like social networks and symbolism) in neighborhood dynamics. From this perspective, subcultural models more directly address the life-course principles of historical embeddedness and linked lives that are less developed in many ecological models.

Consistent with this approach, Logan, Alba, and Zhang (2002) find that, among immigrant groups in New York and Los Angeles, living in ethnic enclaves was a choice many made, unrelated to economic constraints. Similarly, Spilimbergo and Ubeda (2004) found that racial differences in residential mobility between whites and African Americans were explained by local ties to family members. Such research highlights noneconomic reasons for ties to place, consistent with theory on the social and psychological ties that connect people to neighborhoods (Altman and Low 1992; Gerson, Stueve, and Fischer 1977).

Subcultural models are also interested in residents' relationships with one another and how these relationships lead to neighborhood attachment and cohesion (Schwirian 1983; Temkin and Rowe 1996). This stickiness of relationships that can prevent residential mobility can affect health in both positive and negative ways. On the one hand, a subcultural approach is consistent with an active area of research on the role of neighborhood social and cultural capital and cohesion (Putnam 2000; Bourdieu and Wacquant 1992; Carpiano 2006; Sampson, Morenoff, and Gannon-Rowley 2002), usually seen as positive and protective of health, while their absence can lead to "social disorganization," increasing the risk of exposure to violence, of poor social well-being, and of death (Sampson, Morenoff, and Gannon-Rowley 2002). On the other hand, the presence of social capital and cohesion is not always positive for neighborhoods. Strong neighborhood social cohesion may inhibit neighborhood racial and ethnic change, and thereby be implicated in explicit or implicit neighborhood conditions that increase race- or class-based segregation and discriminatory housing policies or practices (Schwirian 1983). Examples include local efforts to block in-migration of minorities (Cutler, Glaeser, and Vigdor 1999). A subcultural model suggests that we examine how the social networks of neighborhoods can perpetuate or change neighborhoods over time. A political economy perspective would further suggest that we examine the political and economic social structures that might serve to preserve or change these networks, or to infuse resources through them in ways that may improve health and reduce health disparities within and between neighborhoods.

Agency

Despite the differences in focus between the subcultural and ecological perspectives, both recognize a role for individual agency, focusing on how individual factors interact with neighborhood factors to produce individual residential mobility that leads to neighborhood stability or change. However, this is a limited view of agency in the neighborhood context, as there may be other neighborhood characteristics that bring about neighborhood change and affect individual and population health.

When examining the dynamic nature of neighborhoods, we might consider variations in the resilience of neighborhoods to weather challenges. Although the concept of resilience is most often applied to the protective factors that individuals marshal to adapt to risk (Ryff et al. 1998; Rutter 1990), neighborhoods can be seen as resilient as well. The best theoretical and empirical work explicitly addressing neighborhood resilience has been conducted in the area of disaster readiness and response (Pais and Elliott 2008), examining the characteristics of neighborhoods that affect their ability to adapt in the face of a disaster (see Norris et al. 2008).

However, we can also view collective action supported by neighborhood social and cultural capital as providing an opportunity for neighborhood-level resilience—developing and employing neighborhood social capital which can be employed for advancing the health and social well-being of neighborhood residents even in the face of other neighborhood constraints and stressors. Swaroop and Morenoff (2006) demonstrate that neighborhoods both affect and are affected by neighborhood participation in complex ways. One of their important findings was that rates of participation in local social organizations for expressive purposes were higher in stable neighborhoods, but rates of participation in local social organizations for instrumental purposes were higher in disadvantaged neighborhoods. Neighborhoods produce conditions that create action and are in turn changed by the actions they invoked. More work is needed to examine the ways in which neighborhood participation and organization can buffer the impacts of neighborhood disadvantage on the health of individuals and populations.

Other theories of social capital and collective efficacy can also be invoked to examine neighborhood-level agency. Whereas social capital refers to the resources that result from social structure (Burt 2001; Bourdieu 1986), collective efficacy is about converting those relationships into beneficial action. In high collective-efficacy neighborhoods, residents are willing to intervene on each other's behalf, even if they do not know one another. Sampson, Raudenbush, and Earls's (1997) articulation of the collective-efficacy concept emphasizes neighborhood social capital in the form of mutual trust and solidarity (social cohesion) and expectations for action (informal social control) in explaining the impact of neighborhood context on residents' well-being. As applied to health, collective-efficacy theory suggests that neighborhoods vary in the density and size of their social networks and their associated levels of social cohesion and informal social control— the neighborhood's capacity to mobilize existing social resources (network ties and neighborhood attachments) toward beneficial ends (Cagney, Browning, and Wen 2005; Wen, Hawkley, and Cacioppo 2006). Interestingly, most of this work examines the individual-level outcomes of collective efficacy, not how collective efficacy changes other aspects of neighborhood context. In theory, collective efficacy should eventually lead to the mobilization of resources that benefit and change a neighborhood's social and economic context over time.

It is the very idea of creating change from within neighborhoods that has inspired much of the recent participatory approach to research on neighborhoods and health. Communitybased participatory research (CBPR) projects are used to mobilize individual and neighborhood resources to produce both knowledge and social change (Israel et al. 2005). Therefore, they explicitly consider issues of agency, sometimes at the neighborhood level, and can be used to create neighborhood change and improve individual and population health. However, we know of no research that has systematically examined the cumulative impact of CBPR projects on changing the trajectories of neighborhoods over time.

SUMMARY

This chapter offers the life-course perspective as a lens through which to view research on neighborhoods and health; its application can help us creatively integrate old and new theories and methods for their study, encouraging us to attend to not only the life course of individuals within their neighborhood context, but also to the life course of neighborhoods themselves—examining how the neighborhood contexts in which we live, work, and play change over time, and the implication of those changes for individual and population health.

Incorporating life-course principles can help us better understand the dynamic effects of neighborhoods on health over the individual life course. In particular, research is needed to examine the contemporaneous, lagged, and cumulative effects of neighborhoods on health over the individual life span. Research must distinguish age, period, and cohort effects, and attend to the timing of particular neighborhood exposures at specific ages or stages of development. The overlooked principle of agency can illuminate not only how neighborhoods affect individuals, but also how individuals interact with and change their neighborhoods in ways that affect individual and population health. A variety of research methods are needed to address these questions, including longitudinal analysis of individuals across diverse neighborhoods, qualitative analyses to understand people's experiences within and interpretations of their neighborhoods, and participatory approaches that help us both understand and support action to create change.

Understanding how neighborhood networks and social capital affect health over the life course requires a dynamic approach that goes beyond characterizing networks and social capital at one point in time to examining how they evolve over time within particular neighborhoods and historical periods. Research should examine how networks produce different types and amounts of social capital depending on the neighborhood context, and how this relates to individual health at different ages and developmental stages. Insight into how individuals engage with networks and neighborhoods to both draw on and produce social capital is needed to understand how these interactions can be either protective of or detrimental to health.

The limited body of health research that has examined neighborhood change has focused on how neighborhood contexts change when people move, but not on how neighborhoods change around residents. Ecological, subcultural, and political economy perspectives help us think about how future research might consider the life course of neighborhoods in conjunction with the life course of individuals. Recent research on neighborhood change has sought to integrate one or more of these theoretical perspectives to consider the demographic, cultural, and institutional forces at play in the temporal dynamics of neighborhoods. Integrated consideration of individual and neighborhood dynamics will be instructive to understanding the relevance of neighborhood change for individual and population health. Agent-based models may provide one method of examining the intersecting dynamics of individuals, neighborhoods, and health over time.

Given both the persistence of neighborhood income and racial segregation over time, and the intergenerational transmission of neighborhood context to individuals, it is imperative that we gain a better understanding of the individual and neighborhood-level factors that continue to perpetuate racial and income inequality, and the mechanisms through which they affect individual and population health. Moreover, we need to understand not only the factors that have perpetuated social and economic inequalities and disparities in health, but to identify and understand the outliers. What are the individual and neighborhood-level protective factors that have produced individual and neighborhood resilience in the face of adversity? What aspects of individual and neighborhood-level agency could be promoted to bring about neighborhood change within and across neighborhoods in ways that promote and protect health? What aspects of our political economy might be effectively changed to restructure the individual incentives and barriers to neighborhood selection and mobility, and what are the societal resources that could be redistributed across neighborhoods in ways that would promote heath? Addressing these questions will be crucial not only to improving mean health, but also to reducing health disparities along racial and economic dimensions.

REFERENCES

Airey, Laura. 2003. "Nae as Nice a Scheme as It Used to Be: Lay Accounts of Neighbourhood Incivilities and Well-Being." *Health and Place* 9:129–37.

Alba, Richard D., and John R. Logan. 1993. "Minority Proximity to Whites in Suburbs: An Individual Level Analysis of Segregation." *American Journal of Sociology* 98:1388–1427.

Almond, Douglas. 2006. "Is the 1918 Influenza Pandemic Over? Long-Term Effects of IN Utero Influenza Exposure in the Post-1940 U.S. Population." *Journal of Political Economy* 114(4): 672–712.

Altman, Irwin, and Setha M. Low, eds. 1992. *Place Attachment, Human Behavior, and Environment: Advances in Theory and Research.* Vol. 12. New York: Plenum.

Altschuler, Andrea, Carol P. Somkin, and Nancy E. Adler. 2004. "Local Services and Amenities, Neighborhood Social Capital, and Health." *Social Science and Medicine* 59:1219–29.

Auchincloss, Amy H., and Ana Diez Roux. 2008. "A New Tool for Epidemiology: The Usefulness of Dynamic-Agent Models in Understanding Place Effects on Health." *American Journal of Epidemiology* 168(1): 1–8.

Barber, Jennifer S., Lisa D. Pearce, Indra Chaudhury, and Susan Gurung. 2002. "Voluntary Associations and Fertility Limitation." *Social Forces* 80(4):1369–1401.

Beatty, John. 1988. "Ecology and Evolutionary Biology in the War and Post-War Years." *Journal of Historical Biology* 21:245–63.

Berkman, Lisa F., and Cheryl Clark. 2003. "Neighborhoods and Networks: The Construction of Safe Places and Bridges." In *Neighborhoods and Health*, ed. Ichiro Kawachi and Lisa F. Berkman, 288–302. New York: Oxford University Press.

Berkman, Lisa F., and Thomas Glass. 2000. "Social Integration, Social Networks, Social Support, and Health." In *Social Epidemiology*, ed. Lisa F. Berkman and Ichiro Kawachi, 137–73. Oxford: Oxford University Press.

Bird, Chloe E., and Patricia R. Rieker. 2008. *Gender and Health: The Effects of Constrained Choices on Social Policies.* New York: Cambridge University Press.

Bourdieu, Pierre. 1986. "The Forms of Social Capital." In *Handbook of Theory and Research for the Sociology of Education*, ed. John G. Richardson, 241–58. New York: Macmillan.

Bourdieu, Pierre, and Loïc J. D. Wacquant. 1992. *An Invitation to Reflexive Sociology.* Chicago: University of Chicago Press.

Brooks-Gunn, Jeanne, Greg Duncan, Pamela Klebanov, and Naomi Sealand. 1993. "Do Neighborhoods Influence Child and Adolescent Development?" *American Journal of Sociology* 99:353–95.

Brown, Phil, and Edwin J. Mikkelsen. 1990. *No Safe Place: Toxic Waste, Leukemia, and Community Action.* Berkeley: University of California Press.

Brown, Phil, Stephen Zavestoski, Sabrina McCormick, Brian Mayer, Rachel Morello-Frosch, and Rebecca Gasior Altman. 2004. "Embodied Health Movements: New Approaches to Social Movements in Health." *Sociology of Health and Illness* 26(1):50–80.

Browning, Christopher R., Kathleen A. Cagney, and Ming Wen. 2003. "Explaining Variation in Health Status across Space and Time: Implications for Racial and Ethnic Disparities in Self-Rated Health." *Social Science and Medicine* 57:1221–35.

Browning, Christopher R., Seth L. Feinberg, Danielle Wallace, and Kathleen A. Cagney. 2006. "Neighborhood Social Processes, Physical Conditions, and Disaster-Related Mortality: The Case of the 1995 Chicago Heat Wave." *American Sociological Review* 71:661–78.

Bruch, Elizabeth E., and Robert D. Mare. 2006. "Neighborhood Choice and Neighborhood Change." *American Journal of Sociology* 112(3):667–709.

Bullard, Robert D., ed. 1994. *Confronting Environmental Racism: Voices from the Grassroots.* Boston: South End Press.

Burt, Ronald S. 2001. "Structural Holes versus Network Closure as Social Capital." In *Social Capital: Theory and Research*, ed. Nan Lin, Karen Cook, and Ronald S. Burt, 31–56. New York: Aldine de Gruyter.

Cagney, Kathleen A. 2006. "Neighborhood Age Structure and Its Implications for Health." *Journal of Urban Health* 83(5):827–34.

Cagney, Kathleen A., and Christopher R. Browning. 2004. "Exploring Neighborhood-Level Variation in Asthma and Other Respiratory Diseases: The Contribution of Neighborhood Social Context." *Journal of General Internal Medicine* 19(3):229–36.

Cagney, Kathleen A., Christopher R. Browning, and Ming Wen. 2005. "Racial Disparities in Self-Rated Health at Older Ages: What Difference Does the Neighborhood Make?" *Journal of Gerontology: Social Sciences* 60B: S181–90.

Carpiano, Richard M. 2006. "Toward a Neighborhood Resource-Based Theory of Social Capital for Health: Can Bourdieu and Sociology Help?" *Social Science and Medicine* 62(1): 165–75.

———. 2007. "Neighborhood Social Capital and Adult Health: An Empirical Test of a Bourdieu-Based Model." *Health and Place* 13(3): 639–55.

———. 2009. "Come Take a Walk with Me: The 'GoAlong' Interview as a Novel Method for Studying the Implications of Place for Health and Well-Being." *Health and Place* 15:263–72.

Carson, April P., Kathryn M. Rose, Diane J. Catellier, Jay S. Kaufman, Sharon B. Wyatt, Ana V. DiezRoux, and Gerardo Heissl. 2007. "Cumulative Socioeconomic Status across the Life Course and Subclinical Atherosclerosis." *Annals of Epidemiology* 17(4): 296–303.

Caughy, Margaret, Patricia J. O'Campo, and Carles Muntaner. 2003. "When Being Alone Might be Better: Neighborhood Poverty, Social Capital, and Child Mental Health." *Social Science and Medicine* 57(2): 227–37.

Charles, Camille Zubrinsky. 2001. "Processes of Residential Segregation." In *Urban Inequality: Evidence from Four Cities*, ed. Alice O'Connor, Chris Tilly, and Lawrence Bobo, 217–71. New York: Russell Sage Foundation.

Clampet-Lundquist, Susan, and Douglas S. Massey. 2008. "Neighborhood Effects on Economic SelfSufficiency: A Reconsideration of the Moving to Opportunity Experiment." *American Journal of Sociology* 114(1): 107–43.

Coleman, James S. 1990. *The Foundations of Social Theory.* Cambridge, Mass.: Belknap Press.

Cornwell, Benjamin, Edward O. Laumann, and L. Philip Schumm. 2008. "The Social Connectedness of Older Adults: A National Profile." *American Sociological Review* 73(2): 185–203.

Crowder, Kyle, and Scott J. South. 2008. "Spatial Dynamics of White Flight: The Effects of Local and Extralocal Racial Conditions on Outmigration." *American Sociological Review* 73(5): 792–812.

Crowder, Kyle, Scott J. South, and Erick Chavez. 2006. "Wealth, Race, and Inter-Neighborhood Migration." *American Sociological Review* 71:72–94.

Cummins, Steven, Sarah Curtis, Ana V. Diez-Roux, and Sally Macintyre. 2007. "Understanding and Representing 'Place' in Health Research: A Relational Approach." *Social Science and Medicine* 65(9): 1825–38.

Curtis, Sarah H. Southall, P. Congdon, and B. Dodgeon. 2004. "Area Effects on Health Variation over the Life-Course: Analysis of the Longitudinal Study Sample in England Using New Data on Area of Residence in Childhood." *Social Science and Medicine* 58:57–74.

Cutler, David M., Edward L. Glaeser, and Jacob L. Vigdor. 1999. "The Rise and Decline of the American Ghetto." *Journal of Political Economy* 107(3): 455–506.

Dannefer, Dale. 2003. "Cumulative Advantage/ Disadvantage and the Life Course: Cross Fertilizing Age and Social Science Theory." *Journal of Gerontology: Social Sciences* 58B: S327–37.

Della Porta, Donatella, and Mario Diani. 1999. *Social Movements: An Introduction.* Malden, Mass.: Blackwell.

Dennis, Samuel F., Suzanne Gaulocher, Richard M. Carpiano, and David Brown. 2008. "Participatory Photo Mapping (PPM): Exploring an Integrated Method for Health and Place Research with Young People." *Health and Place* 15(2): 466–73.

Diez Roux, A. V., L. N. Borrell, M. Haan, S. A. Jackson, and R. Schultz. 2004. "Neighbourhood Environments and Mortality in an Elderly Cohort: Results from the Cardiovascular Health Study." *Journal of Epidemiology and Community Health* 58(11): 917–23.

Duncan, Otis Dudley, and Beverly Duncan. 1957. *The Negro Population of Chicago.* Chicago: University Press.

Elder, Glen H., Jr. 1985. "Perspectives on the Life Course." In *Trajectories and Transitions, 1968–1980,* ed. Glen H. Elder Jr., 23–49. Ithaca, N.Y.: Cornell University Press.

Elder, Glen H., Jr., Monica Kirkpatrick Johnson, and Robert Crosnoe. 2004. "The Emergence and Development of Life Course Theory." In *Handbook of the Life Course,* ed. Jeylan T. Mortimer and Michael J. Shanahan, 3–22. New York: Springer.

Entwisle, Barbara. 2007. "Putting People into Place." *Demography* 44(4): 687–703.

Eschbach, Karl, Glenn V. Ostir, Kushang V. Patel, Kyriakos S. Markides, and James S. Goodwin. 2004. "Neighborhood Context and Mortality among Older Mexican Americans: Is There a Barrio Advantage?" *American Journal of Public Health* 94:1807–12.

Fauth, Rebecca C., Tama Leventhal, and Jeanne Brooks-Gunn. 2008. "Seven Years Later: Effects of a Neighborhood Mobility Program on Poor Black and Latino Adults' Well-Being." *Journal of Health and Social Behavior* 49:119–30.

Ferraro, Kenneth F., and Tetyana Pylypiv Shippee. 2008. "Black and White Chains of Risk for Hospitalization over 20 Years." *Journal of Health and Social Behavior* 49:193–207.

Fogel, Robert W., and Dora L. Costa. 1997. "A Theory of Technophysio Evolution, with Some Implications for Forecasting Population, Health Care Costs, and Pension Costs." *Demography* 34(1): 49–66.

Frankel, David M., and Ady Pauzner. 2002. "Expectations and the Timing of Neighborhood Change." *Journal of Urban Economics* 51(2): 295–314.

Freedman, Vicki A., Irina B. Grafova, Robert F. Schoeni, and Jeannette Rogowski. 2008. "Neighborhoods and Disability in Later Life." *Social Science and Medicine* 66:2253–67.

Galea, Sandro, Nicholas Freudenberg, and David Vlahov. 2006. "A Framework for the Study of Urban Health." In *Cities and the Health of the Public*, ed. Nicholas Freudenberg, Sandro Galea, and David Vlahov, 3–18. Nashville: Vanderbilt University Press.

Gerson, Kathleen, C. Ann Stueve, and Claude S. Fischer. 1977. "Attachment to Place." In *Networks and Places: Social Relations in the Urban Setting*, ed. Claude S. Fischer, Robert M. Jackson, C. Ann Stueve, Kathleen Gerson, Lynne McCallister Jones, and Mark Baldassare, 139–61. New York: Free Press.

Glass, Thomas A., and Jennifer L. Balfour. 2003. "Neighborhoods, Aging, and Functional Limitations." In *Neighborhoods and Health*, ed. Ichiro Kawachi and Lisa F. Berkman, 303–34. New York: Oxford University Press.

Gotham, Kevin Fox. 1998. "Blind Faith in the Free Market: Urban Poverty, Residential Segregation, and Federal Housing Retrenchment, 1970–1995." *Sociological Inquiry* 68(1): 1–31.

Harris, David R. 1999. "'Property Values Drop When Blacks Move in, Because . . .': Racial and Socioeconomic Determinants of Neighborhood Desirability." *American Sociological Review* 64:461–79.

Hartley, David. 2004. "Rural Health Disparities, Population Health, and Rural Culture." *American Journal of Public Health* 94(10): 1675–78.

Iceland, John, Cicely Sharpe, and Erika Steinmetz. 2005. "Class Differences in African American Residential Patterns in U.S. Metropolitan Areas: 1990–2000." *Social Science Research* 34(1): 252–66.

Israel, Barbara A., Eugenia Eng, Amy Schulz, and Edith A. Parker, eds. 2005. *Methods in Community-Based Participatory Research for Health*. San Francisco: Jossey Bass.

Jackson, Margot I., and Robert D. Mare. 2007. "Cross-Sectional and Longitudinal Measurements of Neighborhood Experience and Their Effects on Children." *Social Science Research* 36:590–610.

Jargowsky, Paul A. 1997. *Poverty and Place: Ghettos, Barrios, and the American City*. New York: Russell Sage Foundation.

Jelleyman, T., and N. Spencer. 2007. "Residential Mobility in Childhood and Health Outcomes: A Systematic Review." *Journal of Epidemiology and Community Health* 62:584–92.

Kaplan, George A., Elsie R. Pamuk, John W. Lynch, R. D. Cohen, and Jennifer L. Balfour. 1996. "Inequality in Income and Mortality in the United States: Analysis of Mortality and Potential Pathways." *British Medical Journal* 312(7037): 999–1003.

Kawachi, Ichiro, and Lisa F. Berkman, eds. 2003. *Neighborhoods and Health*. New York: Oxford University Press.

Kawachi, Ichiro, Bruce P. Kennedy, and Kimberly Lochner. 1997. "Social Capital, Income Inequality, and Mortality." *American Journal of Public Health* 87(9): 1491–98.

Krause, Neil. 1998. "Neighborhood Deterioration, Religious Coping, and Changes in Health during Late Life. *Gerontologist* 38:653–64.

Krysan, Maria. 2002. "Community Undesirability in Black and White: Examining Racial Residential Preferences through Community Perceptions." *Social Problems* 49:521–43.

Kuh, D., Y. Ben-Shlomo, J. Lynch, J. Hallquvist, and C. Power. 2003. "Life Course Epidemiology." *Journal of Epidemiology and Community Health* 57:778–83.

Kusenbach, Margarethe. 2003. "Street Phenomenology: The Go-Along as Ethnographic Research Tool." *Ethnography* 4(3): 455–85.

LaVeist, Thomas A. 1993. "Segregation, Poverty and Empowerment: Health Consequences for AfricanAmericans." *Milbank Quarterly* 71(1): 41–64.

Lee, Min-Ah, and Kenneth F. Ferraro. 2007. "Neighborhood Residential Segregation and Physical Health among Hispanic Americans: Good, Bad, or Benign?" *Journal of Health and Social Behavior* 48(2): 131–48.

Lemelin, Emily T., Ana V. Diez Roux, Tracy G. Franklin, Mercedes Carnethon, Pamela L. Lutsey, Hanyu Ni, Ellen O'Meara, and Sandi Shrager. 2009. "Life-Course Socioeconomic Positions and Subclinical Atherosclerosis in the Multi-Ethnic Study of Atherosclerosis." *Social Science and Medicine* 68:444–51.

Leventhal, Tama, and Jeanne Brooks-Gunn. 2003. "Moving to Opportunity: An Experimental Study of Neighborhood Effects on Mental Health." *American Journal of Public Health* 93:1576–82.

Lin, Nan, Karen S. Cook, and Ronald S. Burt. 2001. *Social Capital: Theory and Research*. New York: Aldine de Gruyter.

Link, Bruce G., and Jo C. Phelan. 1995. "Social Conditions as Fundamental Causes of Disease." *Journal of Health and Social Behavior*, extra issue: 80–94.

Logan, John R., Richard D. Alba, and Wenquan Zhang. 2002. "Immigrant Enclaves and Ethnic Communities in New York and Los Angeles." *American Sociological Review* 67:299–322.

Logan, John R., and Harvey L. Molotch 1987. *Urban Fortunes: The Political Economy of Place*. Los Angeles: University of California Press.

Ludwig, Jens, Jeffrey B. Liebman, Jeffrey R. Kling, Greg J. Duncan, Lawrence F. Katz, Ron C. Kessler, and Lisa Sanbonmatsu. 2008. "What Can We Learn about Neighborhood Effects from the Moving to Opportunity Experiment?" *American Journal of Sociology* 114(1): 144–88.

Luke, Douglas A., and Jennie K. Harris. 2007. "Network Analysis in Public Health: History, Methods, and Applications." *Annual Review of Public Health* 28:69–93.

Lynch, John, and George Davey Smith. 2005. "A Life Course Approach to Chronic Disease Epidemiology." *Annual Review of Public Health* 26:1–35.

Lynch, John, George Davey Smith, Marianne Hillemeier, Mary Shaw, Trivellore Raghunathan, and George Kaplan. 2001. "Income Inequality, the Psychosocial Environment, and Health: Comparisons of Wealthy Nations." *Lancet* 109(35): 194–200.

Massey, Douglas S. 1990. "American Apartheid: Segregation and the Making of the Underclass." *American Journal of Sociology* 96:329–58.

Massey, Douglas S., Gretchen A. Condran, and Nancy A. Denton. 1987. "The Effect of Residential Segregation on Black Social and Economic WellBeing." *Social Forces* 66(1): 29–56.

McAdam, Doug, John D. McCarthy, and Mayer N. Zald, eds. 1996. *Comparative Perspectives on Social Movements: Political Opportunities, Mobilizing Structures, and Cultural Framings*. Cambridge: Cambridge University Press.

McKeown, Thomas. 1976. *The Modern Rise of Population*. New York: Academic Press.

Meyer, David S., and Nancy Whittier. 1994. "Social Movement Spillover." *Social Problems* 41:277–98.

Mikolajczyk, Rafael T., and Mirjam Kretzschmar. 2008. "Collecting Social Contact Data in the Context of Disease Transmission: Prospective and Retrospective Study Designs." *Social Networks* 30(2): 127–35.

Mirowsky, John, and Catherine E. Ross. 2003. *Education, Social Status, and Health*. New York: Aldine de Gruyter.

Moffit, Robert. 2001. "Policy Interventions, LowLevel Equilibria, and Social Interaction." In *Social Dynamics*, ed. Steven N. Durlauf and H. Peyton Young, 45–82. Boston: MIT Press.

Morenoff, Jeffrey D., James S. House, Ben B. Hansen, David R. Williams, George A. Kaplan, and Haslyn E. Hunte. 2007. "Understanding Social Disparities in Hypertension Prevalence, Awareness, Treatment, and Control: The Role of Neighborhood Context." *Social Science and Medicine* 65(9): 1853–66.

Morenoff, Jeffrey D., Robert J. Sampson, and Stephen W. Raudenbush. 2001. "Neighborhood Inequality, Collective Efficacy, and the Spatial Dynamics of Urban Violence." *Criminology* 39(3): 17–60.

Mortimer, Jeylan T., and Michael J. Shanahan, eds. 2004. *Handbook of the Life Course*. New York: Springer.

Moynihan, Daniel P. 1965. *The Negro Family: The Case for National Action*. Washington, D.C.: Office of Policy Planning and Research, U.S. Department of Labor.

Naess, O., B. Claussen, G. Davey Smith, and A. H. Leyland. 2008. "Life Course Influence of Residential Area on Cause-Specific Mortality." *Journal of Epidemiology and Community Health* 62:29–34.

Navarro, Vincente. 2002. *The Political Economy of Social Inequalities*. Amityville, N.Y.: Baywood Publishing.

Norris, Fran H., Susan P. Stevens, Betty Pfefferbaum, Karen F. Wyche, and Rose L. Pfefferbaum. 2008. "Community Resilience as a Metaphor, Theory, Set of Capacities, and Strategy for Disaster Readiness." *American Journal of Community Psychology* 41:127–50.

O'Connor, Thomas G. 2003. "Natural Experiments to Study the Effects of Early Experience: Progress and Limitations." *Development and Psychopathology* 15(4): 837–52.

O'Rand, Angela M. 1996. "The Precious and the Precocious: Understanding Cumulative Disadvantage and Cumulative Advantage over the Life Course." *Gerontologist* 36(2): 230–38.

Ostir, Glenn V., Karl Eschbach, Kyriakos S. Markides, and James S. Goodwin. 2003. "Neighbourhood Composition and Depressive Symptoms among Older Mexican Americans." *Journal of Epidemiology and Community Health* 57:987–92.

Osypuk, Theresa L., and Sandro Galea. 2007. "What Level Macro? Choosing Appropriate Levels to Assess How Place Influences Population Health." In *Macrosocial Determinants of Population Health*, ed. Sandro Galea, 399–435. New York: Springer.

Pais, Jeremy F., and James R. Elliott. 2008. "Places as Recovery Machines: Vulnerability and Neighborhood Change after Major Hurricanes." *Social Forces* 86(4): 1415–53.

Park, Robert A. 1952. *Human Communities*. Glencoe, Ill.: Free Press.

Patel, Kushang V., Karl Eschbach, Laura L. Rudkin, M. Kristen Peek, and Kyriakos S. Markides. 2003. "Neighborhood Context and Self-Rated Health in Older Mexican Americans." *Annals of Epidemiology* 13(9): 620–28.

Pattillo, Mary E. 1999. *Black Picket Fences: Privilege and Peril among the Black Middle Class.* Chicago: University of Chicago Press.

Pearlin, Leonard I. 1999. "The Stress Process Revisited: Reflections on Concepts and Their InterRelationships" In *Handbook of the Sociology of Mental Health*, ed. Carol S. Aneshensel and Jo C. Phelan, 395–416. New York: Kluwer Academic/ Plenum.

Pickett, K. E., and M. Pearl. 2001. "Multilevel Analysis of Neighbourhood Socioeconomic Context and Health Outcomes: A Critical Review." *Journal of Epidemiology and Community Health* 55:111–22.

Poletta, Francesca, and James M. Jasper. 2001. "Collective Identity and Social Movements." *Annual Review of Sociology* 27:283–305.

Portes, Alejandro, and Julia Sensenbrenner. 1993. "Embeddedness and Immigration: Notes on the Social Determinants of Economic Action." *American Journal of Sociology* 98:1320–50.

Preston, Samuel H., Martha E. Hill, and Gregory L. Drevenstedt. 1998. "Childhood Conditions That Predict Survival to Advanced Ages among African-Americans." *Social Science and Medicine* 47(9): 1231–46.

Probst, Janice C., Charity G. Moore, Sundra H. Glover, and Michael E. Samuels. 2004. "Person and Place: The Compounding Effects of Race/Ethnicity and Rurality on Health." *American Journal of Public Health* 94(10): 1695–1703.

Putnam, Robert D. 2000. *Bowling Alone: The Collapse and Revival of American Community.* New York: Simon and Schuster.

Quercia, Roberto G., and George C. Galster. 2000. "Threshold Effects and Neighborhood Change." *Journal of Planning Education and Research* 20:146–62.

Quillian, Lincoln. 2002. "Why Is Black-White Residential Segregation So Persistent? Evidence on Three Theories from Migration Data." *Social Science Quarterly* 31:197–229.

———. 2003. "How Long Are Exposures to Poor Neighborhoods? The Long-Term Dynamics of Entry and Exit from Poor Neighborhoods." *Population Research and Policy Review* 22:221–29.

Robert, Stephanie A. 1999. "Socioeconomic Position and Health: The Independent Contribution of Community Socioeconomic Context. *Annual Review of Sociology* 25:489–516.

Robert, Stephanie A., and Kum Yi Lee. 2002. "Explaining Race Differences in Health among Older Adults: The Contribution of Community Socioeconomic Context." *Research on Aging* 24:654–83.

Robert, Stephanie A., and Lydia W. Li. 2001. "Age Variation in the Relationship between Community Socioeconomic Status and Adult Health." *Research on Aging* 23:233–58.

Robert, Stephanie A., and Eric N. Reither. 2004. "A Multilevel Analysis of Race, Community Disadvantage, and BMI." *Social Science and Medicine* 59(12): 2421–34.

Robert, Stephanie A., and Erin Ruel. 2006. "Racial Segregation and Health Disparities between Black and White Older Adults." *Journal of Gerontology: Social Sciences* 61B: S203–11.

Rosenbaum, Emily. 2008. "Racial/Ethnic Differences in Asthma Prevalence: The Role of Housing and Neighborhood Environments." *Journal of Health and Social Behavior* 49(2): 131–45.

Ruel, Erin, and Stephanie A. Robert. 2009. "A Model of Racial Residential History and Its Association with Self-Rated Health and Mortality among Black and White Adults in the U.S." *Sociological Spectrum* 29(4): 1–24.

Rutter, Michael. 1990. "Psychological Resilience and Protective Mechanisms." In *Risk and Protective Factors in the Development of Psychopathology*, ed. Jon Rolf, Ann S. Masten, Dante Cicchetti, Keith H. Nuechterlein, and Sheldon Weintraub, 181–214. Cambridge: Cambridge University Press.

Ryff, Carol D., Burt Singer, Gail D. Love, and Marilyn J. Essex. 1998. "Resilience in Adulthood and Later Life: Defining Features and Dynamic Processes." In *Handbook of Aging and Mental Health: An Integrative Approach*, ed. Jacob Lomranz, 69–100. New York: Plenum Press.

Sampson, Robert J. 2009. "Racial Stratification and the Durable Tangle of Neighborhood Inequality." *Annals of the American Academy of Political and Social Science* 621:243–59.

Sampson, Robert J., Jeffrey D. Morenoff, and Thomas Gannon-Rowley. 2002. "Assessing 'Neighborhood Effects': Social Processes and New Directions in Research." *Annual Review of Sociology* 28:443–78.

Sampson, Robert J., Stephen W. Raudenbush, and Felton Earls. 1997. "Neighborhoods and Violent Crime: A Multilevel Study of Collective Efficacy." *Science* 227:918–23.

Sampson, Robert J., and Patrick Sharkey. 2008. "Neighborhood Selection and the Social Reproduction of Concentrated Racial Inequality." *Demography* 45(1): 1–29.

Sampson, Robert J., Patrick Sharkey, and Stephen W. Raudenbush. 2008. "Durable Effects of Concentrated Disadvantage on Verbal Ability among African-American Children." *Proceedings of the National Academies of Science* 105:845–52.

Schelling, Thomas C. 1978. *Micromotives and Macrobehavior*. New York: W. W. Norton. Schieman, Scott, and Stephen C. Meersman. 2004. "Neighborhood Problems and Health among Older Adults: Received and Donated Social Support and the Sense of Mastery as Effect Modifiers." *Journals of Gerontology: Psychological Sciences and Social Science* 59: S89–97.

Schulz, Amy J., David R. Williams, Barbara A. Israel, and Lora B. Lempert. 2002. "Racial and Spatial Relations as Fundamental Determinants of Health in Detroit." *Milbank Quarterly* 80:677–707.

Schwirian, Kent P. 1983. "Models of Neighborhood Change." *Annual Review of Sociology* 9:83–102.

Scopilliti, Melissa, and John Iceland. 2008. "Residential Patterns of Black Immigrants and Native-Born Blacks in the United States." *Social Science Quarterly* 89(3): 551–73.

Sharkey, Patrick. 2008. "The Intergenerational Transmission of Context." *American Journal of Sociology* 113(4): 931–69.

Small, Mario Luis. 2002. "Culture, Cohorts, and Social Organization Theory: Understanding Local Participation in a Latino Housing Project." *American Journal of Sociology* 1:1–54.

———. 2004. *Villa Victoria: The Transformation of Social Capital in a Boston Barrio*. Chicago: University of Chicago Press.

Smith, Kristin P., and Nicholas A. Christakis. 2008. "Social Networks and Health." *Annual Review of Sociology* 34:405–29.

South, Scott J., and Kyle D. Crowder. 1997. "Escaping Distressed Neighborhoods: Individual, Community, and Metropolitan Influences." *American Journal of Sociology* 102(4): 1040–84.

———. 1998. "Leaving the 'Hood: Residential Mobility between Black, White, and Integrated Neighborhoods." *American Sociological Review* 63:17–26.

South, Scott J., Kyle D. Crowder, and Erick Chavez. 2005a. "Exiting and Entering High-Poverty Neighborhoods: Latinos, Blacks, and Anglos Compared." *Social Forces* 84(2): 873–900.

———. 2005b. "Migration and Spatial Assimilation among U.S. Latinos: Classical versus Segmented Trajectories." *Demography* 42:497–521.

South, Scott J., and Glenn D. Deane. 1993. "Race and Residential Mobility: Individual Determinants and Structural Constraints." *Social Forces* 72:147–67.

Spilimbergo, Antonio, and Luis Ubeda. 2004. "Family Attachment and the Decision to Move by Race." *Journal of Urban Economics* 55:478–97.

Stoll, Michael A. 2001. "Race, Neighborhood Poverty, and Participation in Voluntary Associations." *Sociological Forum* 16:529–57.

Subramanian, S. V., Dolores Acevedo-Garcia, and Teresa L. Osypuk. 2005. "Racial Residential Segregation and Geographic Heterogeneity in Black/White Disparity in Poor Self-Rated Health in the U.S.: A Multilevel Statistical Analysis." *Social Science and Medicine* 60:1667–79.

Sundquist, Kristina, Holger Theobald, Min Yang, Xinjun Li, Sven-Erik Johansson, and Jan Sundquist. 2006. "Neighborhood Violent Crime and Unemployment Increase the Risk of Coronary Heart Disease: A Multilevel Study in an Urban Setting." *Social Science and Medicine* 62(8): 2061–71.

Susser, Ezra S., and Shang P. Lin. 1992. "Schizophrenia after Prenatal Exposure to the Dutch Hunger Winter of 1944–1945." *Archives of General Psychiatry* 49(12): 983–88.

Swaroop, Sapna, and Jeffrey D. Morenoff. 2006. "Building Community: The Neighborhood Context of Social Organization." *Social Forces* 84(3): 1665–85.

Szasz, Andrew. 1994. *Ecopopulism: Toxic Waste and the Movement for Environmental Justice.* Minneapolis: University of Minnesota Press.

Szreter, Simon. 2004. "Industrialization and Health." *British Medical Bulletin* 69:75–86.

Taeuber, Karl E., and Alma R. Taeuber. 1965. *Negroes in Cities.* Chicago: Aldine.

Temkin, Kenneth, and William Rowe. 1996. "Neighborhood Change and Urban Policy." *Journal of Planning Education and Research* 15:159–70.

Thoits, Peggy A. 1995. "Stress, Coping, and Social Support Processes: Where Are We? What Next?" *Journal of Health and Social Behavior* 36, extra issue: 53–79.

Turner, R. Jay, Blair Wheaton, and Donald A. Lloyd. 1995. "The Epidemiology of Social Stress." *American Sociological Review* 60:104–25.

Walton, Emily. 2009. "Residential Segregation and Birth Weight among Racial and Ethnic Minorities in the United States." *Journal of Health and Social Behavior* 50:427–42.

Wasserman, Stanley, and Katherine Faust. 1994. *Social Network Analysis: Methods and Applications.* New York: Cambridge University Press.

Wellman, Barry, and Kenneth Frank. 2001. "Network Capital in a Multilevel World: Getting Support from Personal Communities." In *Social Capital: Theory and Research*, ed. Nan Lin, Karen S. Cook, and Ronald S. Burt, 233–73. New York: Walter de Gruyter.

Wen, Ming, Christopher R. Browning, and Kathleen A. Cagney. 2003. "Poverty, Affluence, and Income Inequality: Neighborhood Economic Structure and Its Implications for Health." *Social Science and Medicine* 57(5): 843–60.

Wen, Ming, Kathleen A. Cagney, and Nicholas A. Christakis. 2005. "Effect of Specific Aspects of Community Social Environment on the Mortality of Individuals Diagnosed with Serious Illness." *Social Science and Medicine* 61:119–34.

Wen, Ming, Louise C. Hawkley, and John T. Cacioppo. 2006. "Objective and Perceived Neighborhood Environment, Individual SES and Psychosocial Factors, and Self-Rated

Health: An Analysis of Older Adults in Cook County, Illinois." *Social Science and Medicine* 63(10): 2575–90.

Wheaton, Blair, and Philippa Clarke. 2003. "Space Meets Time: Integrating Temporal and Contextual Influences on Mental Health in Early Adulthood." *American Sociological Review* 68:680–706.

Wilson, William Julius. 1987. *The Truly Disadvantaged.* Chicago: University of Chicago Press.

Yao, Li, and Stephanie A. Robert. 2008. "The Contributions of Race, Individual Socioeconomic Status, and Neighborhood Socioeconomic Context in the Self-Rated Health Trajectories and Mortality of Older Adults." *Research on Aging* 30(2): 251–73.

Section Two

Examining Early Years Through a Multicultural Lens

As demonstrated in Section One, the life course perspective attends to the context of place and time in order to investigate diverse human lives. This makes the life course perspective compatible with a multicultural perspective, which underscores the role of cultural context in differentiated life course outcomes. This section of the book incorporates a multicultural perspective in order to elucidate the early years of the life course. The three studies that follow this introduction also address life-course transitions in a global context. People experience life-course transitions when their social roles change. Social roles represent expected behaviors for a given status, and are linked to social identities.

Smith's (2005) qualitative study of Mexican immigrants in New York examines transnational life as they transition into adolescence, young and early adulthood, and retiree and grandparent roles. For adolescents who belonged to the transnational Ticuani Youth Group, their experience of going to Ticuani, Mexico, and the importance of Ticuani in their lives were distinguished by how quickly they entered early adulthood. The immigrant bargain to them meant that their parents sacrificed so as to see their children finish school and achieve upward mobility. During the progression into adulthood, participation in transnational life becomes less active, partly because of the busy work and family life. According to Smith's (2005) observation, many retired women who are pioneer migrants still return frequently to Ticuani with their third generation. This pattern reflects the evident role of linked lives in continuing the Ticuani identity across multiple generations.

Whereas Smith's (2005) work stresses the influence of places in the lives of Mexican American immigrants in a global era, Berger's (2011) study provides insights into period effect—that is, the effects of historical times—on his Jewish American family members who endured and survived the trauma of the Holocaust in Poland when younger, not owing to luck, but because of their personal agency, which was related to earlier family socialization, as well as individual attributes. Through his analysis of life histories, Berger (2011) wants to examine variations within a cohort sharing the same historical time and place. Berger (2011) discusses important methodological concerns involved with the life history study.

The third study introduced in this section documents Roksa's (2012) quantitative research on inequalities in college completion rates. The author used longitudinal data collected from youth in the United States in order to find if transitioning into roles associated with adulthood (e.g., employment, marriage, and parenthood) helps explain lower degree completion rates for students from disadvantaged backgrounds and racial or ethnic minority groups. This study suggests not only racial/ethnic and class differences in the timing of transitions, but also what those differences signify in terms of educational disparity and cumulative disadvantages across generations.

Thinking about the transition from adolescence to adulthood, we tend to assume a change from a dependent status to an independent status, coinciding with leaving home for education or employment. As documented in the aforementioned studies, this transition is becoming more variable, depending on place and time, timing, and agency.

REFERENCES

Berger, Ronald J. 2011. "Agency, Structure, and Jewish Survival of the Holocaust: A Life History Study," pp. 1–27. In *Surviving the Holocaust: A Life Course Perspective*. R. J. Berger, Ed. New York: Routledge.

Elder, Glen H. Jr. 1994. "Time, Human Agency, and Social Change: Perspective on the Life Course." *Social Psychology Quarterly* 57(1):4–15.

Roksa, Josipa. 2012. "Race, Class, and Bachelor's Degree Completion in American Higher Education: Examining the Role of Life Course Transitions," pp. 51–70. In *Social Class and Education: Global Perspectives*. L. Weis and N. Dolby, Eds. New York: Routledge.

Smith, Robert Courtney. 2005. "'I'll Go Back Next Year': Transnational Life Across the Life Course," pp. 186–206. In *Mexican New York: Transnational Lives of New Immigrants*. R. Smith, Ed. Berkeley: University of California Press.

"I'll Go Back Next Year"

Transnational Life Across the Life Course

By Robert C. Smith

Over time, I noticed changes in my informants' attitudes toward Ticuani and the frequency of their visits. Meeting Alicia in Ticuani in 1999 as she crowned her successor as Queen of the Mass was quite a surprise, given how much she had hated Ticuani five years earlier. At that time she had told me she was uncomfortable there because her Spanish was not good and she missed eating at McDonald's, though she did enjoy Ticuani parties. Born and raised in Brooklyn, Alicia had gone from disliking even going to Ticuani to seeking and gaining the highest honor it can bestow on a young woman. At the same time, I noticed that Alicia's sister Juana and her Ticuani Youth Group friends were returning to Ticuani less frequently and for shorter periods than they had in the early 1990s: jobs, children, spouses, and other adult responsibilities inhibited their ability to go. And some pioneer migrants, especially women such as Doña Maria, were now returning more frequently and for longer periods and taking their third-generation grandchildren. After retirement they had more freedom to return and had assumed child-care responsibilities for their grandchildren. I noted these changes partly because changes in my own life—getting my first job as a professor and the birth of my children—had also limited my ability to travel. I realized that as I was watching the Ticuanenses and their children grow up and grow older, I was doing so myself.[1]

The common thread in these stories is something that social scientists call the life course. Life-course studies analyze the social meaning of passage through life stages, from birth through childhood, adolescence, young adulthood, adulthood, old age, and death. Some studies focus on how historical events such as war or the Great Depression affect the whole life course, whereas others examine the social causes and effects of specific personal transitions, such as marriage.[2] Here I analyze how life-course transitions affect the practices and meanings of transnational life.[3] First, I tell Alicia's story to illustrate how the passage into adolescence leads some youths to participate more in Ticuani life and to make it a key part of their identity. Second, I use the examples of Juana and the Ticuani Youth Group to analyze how the passage into young and early adulthood changed their participation in transnational life.[4] Third, I examine how the transition of pioneer migrants into retirement and the passing of their children into full adulthood has brought these grandchildren back to Ticuani with their pioneer grandmothers. Examining the effect of life-course changes on transnational life requires assessment of settlement conditions in New York, including the limited incomes and day-care options of many second generation parents. Finally, I reflect on possibilities for and limits on creating a lasting local-level transnational life.

THE REINA, ADOLESCENCE, AND MEXICAN IDENTITY

Alicia's story illustrates how transnational life evolves over the life course and how this evolution can be bound up with other processes, such as racial and ethnic identity formation. A long line of research, from Erik Erikson in the 1950s and 1960s to Marcelo and Carola Suarez-Orozco today, documents the strong need during adolescence for a secure ethnic identity that also locates one's social position.[5] Ticuani has become a site for adolescent rituals confirming authentic Mexican identity, especially for adolescents who are becoming increasingly aware of the racial and ethnic challenges they face in New York. Ticuani's adolescent rituals provided Alicia a vehicle by which to change from being a "lockdown girl" in New York to being the Queen of the Mass in Ticuani.

After Alicia handed over her crown to her successor in Ticuani in 1999, I interviewed her at home in Brooklyn. When asked why she did not like Mexico before, she said she was a "lockdown girl" there before becoming the Reina. She could go out only with her older sister, who would not take her because she felt Alicia was too young to go to parties. Being old enough to become Reina meant she could attend key adolescent social functions that Ticuani provides in abundance.

> RS: So when you were thirteen—at your sister's interview—you didn't like Mexico?
>
> ALICIA: I guess because I was younger, I was more with my parents.
>
> My sister didn't want me out [with her] because she was older, and I really had to be stuck there with my parents. And
>
> I guess once I got older, like she started taking me out, and I started going to Mexican parties, and it was fun. … [And] I didn't like the food, the hot foods. My mother don't usually cook Mexican food

because me and my sister would hardly eat it. But now, I guess we learned more. We're older. ...

RS: Before you were the Reina and you went to Mexican parties, how did you feel?

A: I was bored. ... And then my sister was teaching me to dance *cumbia,* so that also changed.

Being invited to compete and then being chosen as Reina was "a big thing" for Alicia. She had seen her cousin compete and "loved the idea" of being Reina because all the Ticuanenses in Ticuani and New York know who the Reina is. It allowed her to socialize with the girls from Ticuani and become more involved in events there. She recalled that it was the "tenth anniversary [of the pageant] and they wanted girls from New York to compete. But there was a problem ... so it was only me and my cousin from New York" and ten girls from Ticuani. Her recollections show how her participation made her feel more Ticuanense and gave her a place there but also raised issues of how "New York" she felt there. She felt honored to compete to be the Reina but also something of an outsider:

I remember once my cousin ... competed for it. I always wanted to [also]. ... So when they told me [I was invited to participate], I was like, "Yeah." ... It was real fun because we're from here and we got to socialize more with girls from over there. So, we got to know them. ... I wanted to know what it felt like to be in a little pageant, and just to have fun. I didn't really go to win, 'cause, you know, the girls from over there had more rights to win than we did. 'Cause we were born here. ... They're more involved with Ticuani than we are. We live here, [so] any activity that [we] would have to be invited [to], it's hard for us to go because I had school. And they were born over there.

While she says that the local girls had "more rights" to be Reina because they are from Ticuani, later she also says she is "just as" Ticuanense as they are, but "also New York." She went on in the interview to describe what being Reina meant, linking it with her growing up.

RS: What did it mean to you to be Reina?

A: It meant a lot. I was born here and then to have the chance to be Reina—it's big. ... I got to meet more people. ... I think that kinda changed the way I am. Before I was way shy. ... [Being the Reina,] I got more involved with the girls and ... It's something I wanted to do when I was younger. Everyone knows who the

Reina is. Every year they come back—

RS: Did you think what would it be like to have everyone think, "Alicia is the Reina"?

A: Yeah, it was fun. I loved the idea. ...

RS: And do you feel like part of this was like a way of growing up or something?

A: Yeah, I think it was. … It changed … who I was. … I used to hate being shy. … [Being Reina,] I realized where I came from, that I loved being Mexican. That I was proud. … [Before] I wasn't really into it, as I am now. I was younger. … Back then I didn't like going to Mexican parties, and over there you like feel the music, you know? … You just get there and you're happy to be there, and it's just a good feeling to feel. I mean, that's where your parents are born, that's who you are.

RS: Do you feel like there's no other place where you're as much yourself as when you're there?

A: No, … 'cause when you're over there, it's not like being here. Here you have to rush … your routine. … Over there, you're on vacation. That's where you're from. … Over there, to whoever, you probably don't know them and you could say good morning, *buenas noches, buenas tardes*. … And here, you talk to a stranger, it's like you're gonna do something to them. Here I don't have time to go to church. Over there … you get there, you feel everything. You feel closer to God. You feel more Mexican. … [My parents] were proud to know I was born here and that I didn't really like Mexico, and then to say I wanted to be the Reina and then, you know [be chosen]—I remember my mother, that the next day she wanted to go tell my grandfather. And he was proud.

Alicia's experience of being the Reina eased her passage into and through adolescence. It helped her to overcome her shyness and fear of being rejected, enabling her to be more social in Ticuani and New York. Afterward she enjoyed going to Mexican parties in New York, which had "bored" her before. These changes were steps in becoming an adolescent. Her Ticuani coming-of-age narrative is reinforced by the positive response from her family. The pride expressed by her mother and her grandfather make her feel more authentically Mexican. This pride and recognition also led to greater adult privileges. After she was crowned Reina, her parents did not give her a curfew in Ticuani, and they allowed her to go out without her sister in New York. Hence, Ticuani's adolescent rituals, especially the Reina pageant, became important parts of Alicia's adolescent experience and narrative. Ticuani pulled her into its adolescent rituals, fostering a more intimate link with Mexico and ushering her from a shy, preteen existence into a more socially active adolescent one.

THE TICUANI YOUTH GROUP

If Alicia's passage through adolescence made Ticuani more important to her, the passage into early adulthood for her older sister Juana and other members of the Ticuani Youth Group had more complicated effects. Scholars such as Frank Furstenberg and

Jeffrey Arnett have identified a new phase in the life course: "early adulthood," usually placed at ages eighteen to twenty-five and distinguished from adolescence and from full adulthood. Early adults typically have achieved some of the milestones of adulthood, such as finishing their education, living independently from their parents, and working full-time, but not others, such as marrying and having children. Although some members of the Ticuani Youth Group move more quickly through early adulthood than others, their entry into that phase of life set off changes in how they relate to Ticuani and transnational life. We can think of the Youth Group as an adolescent invention that endured but changed irrevocably in early adulthood. This point becomes clearer from an examination of the Youth Group's history.

Juana and her friends thought of the Ticuani Youth Group as their version of the adult men's Ticuani Solidarity Committee. During its heyday in the early 1990s, the Youth Group raised money for public works in Ticuani. Its members spoke openly and enthusiastically about their dreams of going back to Ticuani to work. Carolina, for example, was studying nursing and dreamed of going back to work on public-health projects; Juana dreamed in a similarly public-spirited though less specific way. The Youth Group was their attempt to form a second-generation transnational institution. They ultimately failed to realize their larger dream, mainly because early adulthood changed their priorities. But the group did support the establishment of long-term connections to Ticuani and helped cement primary friendships, with return to Ticuani a key shared activity.

The Youth Group became part of its members' coming-of-age story and helped them with two kinds of assimilation work as they moved from adolescence into early adulthood. It first did "racialization work" in helping them differentiate themselves from Blacks and Puerto Ricans. Relatedly, it did "generational work" by showing their parents that they were keeping the immigrant bargain and justifying by their own success the parents' sacrifice in leaving home. To the Youth Group, this bargain meant being successful in work and school, keeping up Ticuani and family customs, and demonstrating that they were not like other Mexicans who were choosing "the wrong path." They also engaged with racialization when they attempted to create, through such events as sports tournaments and parties, safe Mexican spaces in which second-generation Mexicans could learn Mexican ways, in contrast to what they saw as the unsafe spaces and ways of Puerto Ricans and Blacks. Youth Group members showed their devotion to Padre Jesús and Ticuani by raising almost twenty thousand dollars between 1991 and 1993 for fixing a chapel dedicated to Padre Jesús and for the kindergarten in Ticuani. Abraham described the group's purpose to me in a 1997 interview in New York:

> More than anything, the group was to try to support the pueblo [Ticuani]. By contributing a little bit, so that the older people would notice that we young people had our eyes open. That we wanted to do something for our pueblo. That we had desire. Because we are all Ticuani citizens, it does not matter if you were born here. (Spanish, translated by the author)

Youth Group members went farther educationally and professionally than most of their peers, all either continuing with their education—many earning associate's degrees, some bachelor's degrees, and one a master's degree—or doing well at work, some opening their own businesses. Such success became important during the later 1990s, when the fates of increasing numbers of Mexicans looked bleaker than they had before. Juana explained her rationale for belonging to the group in terms that resonate with the immigrant bargain and with distancing herself from her less successful counterparts:

> You're young, you can do it; you should take advantage of this ... your parents worked so hard, why should you go in the wrong path? ... A lot [of] ... our generation, instead of taking ... education—[they] get married, have kids, and stop going to school. And it's the same circle over and over, and we're never gonna get out of that ... we haven't probably gotten to where we wish we were, but we've gone a lot further ... and I think we should be proud. ... We all have decent jobs, we all work—comfortably ... not in factories like our parents ... we can travel. ... That's what they wanted ... what they worked so hard for, so we wouldn't do the same thing. ... I did okay.

Later in the same interview, I asked Juana and Eliana (Mia's sister, another daughter of Don Emiliano and Doña Selena) what the immigrant bargain represented for them; what was their understanding of the "deal" with their parents? Juana answered, about her parents: "I guess they've never asked anything from us. But just to go to school, you know, and that was it. ... Like my mother used to tell me, 'Finish school, get yourself something that, whatever happens to you, you'll be able to take care of yourself, to get a job. Then after that, you could marry.'" Eliana described it more simply: "To get an education for us. To be able to survive." These are apt descriptions of how Youth Group members fulfilled various aspects of the immigrant bargain. The group helped them to achieve their educational goals and created a context in which they could talk explicitly about upward mobility and link it with their parents' sacrifice. Through it they could prove that they had taken the right path.[6] Membership in the group also showed that they had not lost their essential *ticuanensidad*, because they also worked and sacrificed for the pueblo and revered Padre Jesús, whom they credited with the group's successes.

The Shrinking of the Ticuani Youth Group: The View from 2002

Ten years later, the Youth Group has not become the enduring transnational institution some had hoped. Although its members will not say it is actually dead, they have not organized an event in years and are too busy to revive it. Members and their contemporaries return less frequently to Ticuani now, making a trip every several years instead of one or more per year, as before. Yet they still participate in transnational life, and the group plays a role in it. And the cohort, or "class" of teens, coming behind them have also begun to enter into a transnationalized adolescence, for the same reasons.

Why and how did the Ticuani Youth Group lose steam? One reason its members give was the relationship with the men's Committee, which wanted the group to function as a Committee auxiliary, under its authority. For example, the group balked when the Committee asked them to do a census of all Ticuanenses in New York, which they felt "had nothing to do with anything!" They felt the Committee members did not understand the time constraints they faced as youths who "had their own business or were in the university or had a profession." They also believed people would treat them badly when they went to their houses seeking information, according to Abraham. Another fear, especially keen among the teen migrants, or "-1.5ers," who were born in the United States but grew up partly in Ticuani, was that working with the Committee would involve them in what they saw as Ticuani's corrupt, undemocratic, and violent politics. With their futures looking bright in the United States, why enter into that? Speaking before the 1998 election (which broke the tight link between the *municipio* and the Committee), a Youth Group member described how he thought the Committee and the municipal authorities were "working together" and the problems this created for cooperation with the group:

> They collect the cooperations here and send the money there. ... What they do, only they know. They ... never include anyone, including the people in Ticuani. ... We want democracy on a world level, and in Ticuani ... there is no vote. ... Five or six people decide who will be president. ... We would not work ... with the president of Ticuani. We were definitely apart ... neutral. ... With no one. (Spanish, translated by the author)

Group members distinguished between their unwillingness to work with the Committee and *municipio* and their eagerness to work for the pueblo "very independently."

Group members also saw the Committee as "very *machista*." They contrasted the progressive structure of their organization with the macho structure of the Committee—all men, with the same president throughout its history. They also saw the departure of Marla Lanita—the only woman to serve in a responsible position on the Committee, as treasurer—as a macho expulsion of a woman who had tried to be independent, though she herself refuses to characterize it this way. Several members of the group described their relations with the Committee in a 2001 interview:

> They're older men and they think different. ... Don Manuel, he didn't think we were capable. It [the Committee] was mostly men, and we [the group] were mostly women. ... They were always opposing our ideas. Marla Lanita— they pushed her out because she was a woman. *Ellos son muy poco liberal.* [They are not very liberal.] Don Manuel didn't even let Eliana [the Youth Group's female president] finish her sentences! ... Yeah, he would finish her sentences! ... We had too much respect. But my father woulda smacked me for disrespecting an older man. The Committee is very *machista*. ... We had a woman and a man president. ... We all had very strong attitudes. ... But *no dejamos dominar por el hombre* [we did not let the men dominate].

The group also fell victim to life-course changes as its members grew older and became weighed down by adult responsibilities. It was formed when most of its members were in or just out of college, in their late teens to mid-twenties. Most have since married and had children; a number have jobs with inflexible hours and demanding time commitments. These changes have focused their lives more on marriage, raising children, and working in New York. In 2001, group members described the group's loss of momentum this way:

> At first, every Saturday or Sunday we had meetings, and we'd plan events for the summer. For two years. Then the group started to disintegrate. Two people married outside Ticuani. … It was harder to get together than when we were all single. … Gradually, less people came to the meetings. … We all said, even when we get married and have children, we won't stop coming. … But people started leaving the group. Ana married someone from another pueblo, and since you usually follow your husband's group, they were gone.

These problems reflect conflicts between the elements of adolescent transnational life and those of adulthood, settlement, and assimilation. The aspirations, lack of time, and autonomous ambition in the second generation that enabled them to keep the immigrant bargain with their parents conflicted with the demands of their previous level of transnational activity. The New York Committee has not institutionalized and reproduced itself across generations; it has neither drawn large numbers of the second generation in nor worked out other ways to cooperate with them. And the New York focus of Youth Group members makes Ticuani less central in their imagination of their futures. Most are coming to see it as a place mainly for vacation and ethnic renewal.

The changing gender bargains in the second generation limit the extent to which the Committee can serve as a model for the Youth Group. While most of the first-generation wives of Committee members work, most also take nearly complete responsibility for domestic duties, freeing up the men to do Ticuani public service. But most second-generation women have renegotiated this division of labor, and many second-generation men want change too, with the result that most are unwilling to sacrifice as much time for Ticuani as their parents did. The women, in particular, do not feel that they also serve by staying home and waiting. Neither is honor among Ticuanenses as powerful a motivation for many in the second generation, because Ticuani itself occupies so much less of their imagined future. Hence, assimilation and transnationalization can work in complementary ways, as shown by the greater interest and ability of upwardly mobile second-generationers to participate in transnational life, but they can also conflict, with the goal of upward mobility allowing this group less time and inclination for transnational life.

Lasting Effects of the Ticuani Youth Group and Other Second-Generation Return

That adult obligations consume much of the time formerly dedicated to the Youth Group does not prevent its former members from participating in transnational life in other ways. Many second-generationers who are now married, with children and jobs, still return to Ticuani to experience the closeness to God, to see their relatives, and for special events, such as baptizing a child. The devotion to Padre Jesús that emerges in adolescence among many persists into young adulthood. Eliana, who endured a very difficult pregnancy, had promised Padre Jesús that she would baptize her child in Ticuani if he was healthy. She described her experience:

> I made a promise to Padre Jesús that if everything would be fine, I would do Xavier's christening again [in Ticuani]. ... Also, when we come back here we feel a lot closer to God ... the first thing you do when you come, you thank God that you're here. It's just—like going to church in New York is a lot different. ...I was concerned that maybe Xavier would be disabled, because that was one of the risks [of the medications]. The doctor ... even suggested ... an abortion. ...I was like, I'm gonna have the baby, and I'm just gonna pray to Padrecito, and hopefully everything will be fine. And that's when I promised that I would bring Xavier [to Ticuani].

When she was blessed with a healthy child, the entire family and many friends traveled to Ticuani for Xavier's baptism. Although a baptism is not an event that recurs, as was Eliana's adolescent return, it helped cement her own and her son's and her family's links with Ticuani.

Many friendships that developed in the Youth Group have remained central to the friends' lives. This is partly due to the intensity of the experiences the members shared in Ticuani and partly because they shared them as teenagers, when such identity-affirming friendships become especially compelling. Juana observes: "I got really good friendships out of it. These are still my main friends. Carolina's mother called me her *mugre*. ... I see her [Carolina] almost every day." Their friendship was characterized by activities suggesting a close extended family: "I mean, we see them, like if we're ready to go out, we'll see them, or like I said, when they cook [a meal for everyone] in their house, we'll see them, or when there's a birthday, we all get together. We still pass Christmas together. Yeah, over Christmas, we all get together, and stuff like that." Calling Juana Carolina's *mugre* was a gentle way of teasing her about how close the friends were; *mugre* is the Spanish word for the dirt under one's fingernails. This emergence of primary, enduring friendship groups has been seen, with similar dynamics, in studies of the effects of Jewish and Protestant religious camps and programs on the enduring importance of religion and ethnicity in participants' lives, and anecdotally in the effects of Jewish summer camps in the Catskills.[7]

Ticuani also offers young adults the chance to see friends they do not see often in New York because their lives are now so busy. Young adults can return each year to Ticuani and know they will find friends; they may even have a small reunion. Now twenty-six years old, employed full-time, and living with her boyfriend, Juana described her feelings about Ticuani after a three-year absence in a 2001 interview there: "It means a lot ... to come back. ... For three years, I used to see all my people come back, and I would stay [in New York], and that felt horrible. But now, I'm ecstatic. That night that I flew here, I didn't want to stop [in] Puebla [or] Mexico [City]. I came straight from the airport." Juana did not have these intense emotional attachments to Ticuani and Mexican friends as a child but rather formed them by participation in Ticuani's adolescent rituals and the Ticuani Youth Group.

Young adult returnees play important roles in the adolescent rituals of their younger relatives who return to Ticuani. Carolina teaches local girls who wish to participate in Ticuani's beauty pageant to walk in the appropriate way, put on their makeup, and speak in public, offering an older New York woman's reassurance. Single men and women return to Ticuani to meet prospective mates. And most returnees derive great satisfaction from participating in the religious and civic rituals and ceremonies for Padrecito.

RETIREMENT AND THE TRANSNATIONALIZATION OF CHILD CARE

Just as adult responsibilities have affected early adults' relationships with Ticuani, older people find that their changing situations, and those of their grown children, have altered their transnational life. These circumstances in turn create the transnational life of the third generation. Retired pioneer women in New York become the primary caregivers for their U.S.-born grandchildren and bring them back to Ticuani for extended periods. Some pioneer migrants retire to live in Ticuani, and their second-generation children leave the grandchildren with them for periods of time. The links between these three generations are forged both in the conditions of life in New York and the evolving links with Ticuani and Mexico, partly determined by migrants' movement through the life course.

During the 1990s, many pioneer migrant women retired with small pensions from the garment workers' union or other unions to which they had belonged, and, as naturalized U.S. citizens, began receiving Social Security or Supplemental Security Income. Like Doña Maria, Doña Florencia is retired and cares for her grandchildren full-time while her adult children spend long hours at work and study. Often, second-generation adult children take over a cheap apartment lease the pioneer parents have held for many years, or the two generations purchase a home together. Having grandparents take care of the children enables the family to save on childcare expenses. Moreover, parents feel that their children are safer and better taken care of by their own parents than by strangers in institutional day care.[8] And since grandmothers are thereby relieved of the need to spend much of their limited income on rent, they can afford to travel to Ticuani more often.

This arrangement supports evolving relationships with Ticuani that are also driven by the first generation's life-course changes. Many of these retired pioneers spend a couple of months at a time in Ticuani, especially in the winter, when they and their grandchildren would be stuck indoors in New York. Moreover, many of them have inherited houses in Ticuani from their deceased parents or other relatives, and hence must return to Ticuani to maintain the property, which they see as vital to their future security. Doña Florencia inherited a house that she says she keeps for her children and herself. She now has a tenant who lives in an outbuilding on the property, keeps an eye on things, and turns the light on for her when she comes to Ticuani. In an interview in New York, she told me why she goes back despite no longer having relatives in Ticuani:

> This is your own property. We are not going to sell it. ... Having all the children there, one goes to relax a little, one in one's own house. Here, the weather does me harm—asthma—and I go to my house [in Ticuani]. And there one does not pay rent. ... It is not just for me, but rather that all my children go to rest ... in August, in January, well, they have somewhere to go, their house. (Spanish, translated by the author)

Doña Florencia sees owning a house—her "own property"—as giving emotional security, a good vacation spot, and also, she later commented, refuge from the uncertain environment in the United States. This conversation took place in 1997, the year after Congress had greatly restricted immigrants' access to a variety of services and benefits, including Social Security, unemployment insurance, and Supplemental Security Income. As a result, Doña Florencia told me, she was applying for U.S. citizenship, because "I am not going to let them take that Social Security away from me."[9] She saw her house in Ticuani as a safety net: if she became unable to survive in New York, she would move back to Ticuani. She also enjoys enhanced status by living in her Ticuani house without paying rent. Economically successful families in New York often build huge houses in Ticuani not only so that returning grandparents and their third-generation charges can live in a more spacious and less stressful environment than in New York, but to provide tangible proof of their hard work and virtue in New York.

In New York, Doña Maria lives with her daughter and son-in-law, who entrust her with the care of their five children, aged five to fourteen (in 2001). Both parents leave for work very early and get back after dinner. She described their schedules this way:

> He leaves ... at five in the morning. ... The mother leaves at seven-thirty. ... The whole day ... they are with me, the kids. And I take care of them ... I get them up and ready and fed, and they don't want to go, but ... they go to school. ... At three the little one finishes and the big ones come, and they are with me all afternoon. And I give them something to eat, if there is anything. (Spanish, translated by the author)

Commenting on taking the children to Ticuani, she notes that the fourteen-year-old wants to have her *quinceñera,* or "sweet fifteen" party, there:

> DOÑA MARIA: [The five-year-old] has come four or five times [to Ticuani].
> ... She was two months the first time I brought her; she was really little. I brought her bottle, her medicine, her carrier, and her stroller. ...
>
> RS: How are you teaching them the customs of here? ...
>
> DM: I explain to them all the customs, and the food ... and they eat. I teach them how to make the sauce, how to use *chile,* but

> only a little. Not too rich, but they eat their *tapas,* their tacos. … And [the big ones,] they went on the Antorcha. … For this, they come too because they like the pueblo, the Feast, the customs. And [the fourteen-year-old] told me, "I want to marry a Ticuanense." … She is going to celebrate her *quinceñera* party here. (Spanish, translated by the author)

Doña Maria spends a month or two in Ticuani during the winter and two months in the summer. She finds life easier and better for her and the grandchildren in Ticuani, commenting that in New York the children are closed up in the house ("the poor things" from chapter 7), while in Ticuani they can run around freely. Moreover, in New York, the family lives in a small apartment in a walk-up building down the street from the elementary school the children attend. The apartment's four rooms are not enough for eight people, though they are always full of the good smells of Doña Maria's cooking and the noise of the children's play or the (too-loud) television. In Mexico, they live in two houses—Doña Maria's own house, which she inherited from her parents, and the new house her daughter and son-in-law have built next door. Her house is a now-standard construction, a one-floor cinderblock house with four large rooms laid out in an L shape. It has a large yard, about thirty by seventy yards, where chickens, pigs, and other animals range and in which the children are free to run, dig, and otherwise enjoy themselves or to take naps in the hammock strung under the large tree in the middle of the yard. Outside their house is a walking path that leads in one direction to the church and in the other to the zocalo. There is no traffic. The new house, which sits only a few yards from hers in the same yard, is a state-of-the-art returning migrant house. It has two floors, a pitched roof (unlike the old cinderblock houses), and darkened glass windows on the upper floors to keep out the heat.[10] The children have three or four bedrooms to themselves instead of one bedroom and the living room, as in New York, and there is a large kitchen with modern appliances and an adult sitting room with sliding glass doors that open into the yard. Air conditioning is planned.

Doña Maria also described how the children learn about Ticuani customs and religious practices, such as devotions to Padre Jesús and the Antorcha. I saw them participate in a variety of religious processions and Masses, as well as attend secular activities, such as the dances and the rodeo, and the amusements (such as video games, carnival rides, and table soccer) that come to town during the Feast. In my conversations with them, they seemed to be thoroughly acquainted with and eager to participate in all these activities.

Although it is most common for grandmothers to bring preschoolers to Ticuani, older children also visit. Doña Monica's oldest grandchild, Nestor, a high school senior in New York, brought his seventeen-year-old girlfriend to live with his family for two and a half months in Ticuani in the middle of his senior year. Interestingly, they were treated not as errant teens but rather as a young couple. The girlfriend's mother approved of the trip, and Doña Monica spoke of Nestor and Marlena, who was Puerto Rican, as if they were already married and Marlena was part of the family. The couple,

Figure 15: Luxurious two-story house, Ticuani, 2004. Note the images of Jesus and Mary in the second-story windows.

who had been together for three years at that point, participated in many Ticuani rituals together, and she was warmly received.

Bringing grandchildren to Ticuani for long periods of time results directly from the converging life-course changes of the first-generation pioneers and their second-generation children. The latter need time to work and study and hence need help in taking care of their children. The former have the time to travel and the freedom to live in a place that offers them and their grandchildren more freedom and safety than they have in New York.

Some third-generation children spend longer periods in Ticuani with resident grandparents or other relatives. Xavier, the five-year-old son of Youth Group members Eliana and Lazaro and the grandson of Don Emiliano and Doña Selena, is one of these. After Eliana's hard pregnancy, Xavier had some health problems. Even after these cleared up, he was seen to be "too skinny" and was sent to live for several months with his grandparents in Ticuani to "fatten him up" on a Mexican diet. They believed eating more meat would strengthen him. Since then he has visited Ticuani at least once a year, and he sometimes goes with an aunt but without his parents. Second-generation parents may send their children on extended visits for a variety of reasons: to improve their health, to teach them Mexican and Ticuani culture, to keep a *promesa* to Padre Jesús, or to enable a parent to finish schooling in New York. Parents are most likely to send children on long visits if they lived in Ticuani for a time during their own youth.[11]

The conversation below shows how Ticuani has become a regular, normal part of Xavier's experience.

ELIANA: I told him, "Xavier, we're going to Mexico *para el 25 de enero* [for the twenty-fifth of January]," and he's jumping like, "Oh, Mommy, I want to go *a la procesión* [in the procession]—I wanna dance *como los Tecuanis* [like the Tecuanis]." … He's following our culture—that's another, a new generation. Hopefully he'll get to come when he's older. … That's my hope, but … I'm gonna let Xavier live his life. … Of course, I will always lead him to the right stuff. …

RS: Twenty years from now, what do you want his life to be, in relation to this place?

E: I want him to be educated, have a good degree, a good career. … To Ticuani—to keep our traditions, to do something for his pueblo—not his pueblo, but his family's pueblo. … He's growing up with that idea that ever since he was born, he's been coming to Ticuani, especially for the *fiesta de Padre Jesús*. … He loves it, he lives it. Do you know how many times he watches his christening? He's like, "Wow, Mami, that was in Ticuani, with Padre Jesús," and you know, he's really happy about that. Yeah, he remembers.

RS: And how often does he watch the tape?

E: Every weekend, two times. … He loves it, he just loves it. … One thing that he must do, on the twenty-fifth, he must come with me on the procession and walk all the way to the church. … He knows that's one of the main things we came here for.

That Xavier walks in the procession extends his mother's promise to Padre Jesús during her difficult pregnancy. This procession is a six-hour walk at night through and around the town, with many people carrying heavy candles, crosses, or other objects of worship. The men take turns carrying the heavy icon of Padre Jesús on his throne, encased in glass. I have twice walked in this procession with Xavier, Eliana, and their family, and he does indeed seem to be excited about and devoted to Padre Jesús. (I carried him on my back for part of the procession not because he complained, but because I missed my own son.) He also talks about Padre Jesús in New York. For him, spending time in Ticuani is as natural as it is for any small child to visit his grandparents and other relatives. It seems likely that for Xavier and others like him, Ticuani will always be a second home. Even if he does not continue to go, Ticuani has already strongly influenced how he thinks of himself and about what being Mexican means. If he does return regularly, Ticuanense transnational life may persist into the fourth generation.

Victoria, Eliana's sister, has embarked on another transnational childrearing strategy quite similar to the one her own parents used. She has left her two young children with her parents in Ticuani while she finishes her master's degree in New York. As things were, she could not make enough money to pay for both day care and her schooling, leaving her the painful choice between finishing her degree and keeping her children with her. She felt a great deal of pressure from her family to finish the degree, as it would be a symbol of the family's success. Indeed, Don Emiliano expressed disappointment that she had had children before finishing her degree, even confessing in one extreme moment that he felt his daughter had betrayed and made fools of her parents by doing this. Her parents' offer to take care of the children and their emotional investment in her success, combined with her own desire to finish the degree and her exhaustion at trying to do it all, convinced her to leave her two children in Ticuani until she finished.

CONTEXTS FOR COMPARISON

These stories document how three life-course transitions—from childhood to adolescence, from adolescence to early adulthood, and from middle age to retirement—affect transnational life. Return to Ticuani and participation in its rituals have different meaning at different stages in life. Many children use Ticuani and its safe space and rituals to help them forge a positive Mexican identity in adolescence. As adolescents pass into adulthood, they participate less actively in transnational life, both because they have settled many of the adolescent identity questions that animated their earlier participation and because of the demands of jobs and children. Yet most still return to Ticuani and maintain the close friendships forged through Ticuani. And as pioneer migrants, especially women, retire, they are free to spend more time in Ticuani and often bring along the third generation, for whom they are primary caregivers. In Ticuani the children enjoy more open space and freedom, and they learn Ticuani religious and civic customs, including the devotion to Padrecito that can persist through life. Ticuani is not just a family story passed down through generations, as are so many Americans' links with their ancestral lands, but rather a lived experience.

I raise two questions to provide comparative context, to which I will return in the book's conclusion. The first concerns enduring effects of participation in transnational life. I have documented some effects over the course of fifteen years, but longer-term effects are probable. One source of comparison is the Jewish summer camps that brought up to a million Jewish children from the New York area into the Catskills each summer from the postwar period to the early 1970s, as documented by the sociologist Phil Brown.[12] Another is the National Conference of Synagogue Youth (NCSY), created by the Union of Orthodox Jewish Congregations in America in 1959 as a way of stemming the exodus of young people from Orthodox Judaism. According to my former Barnard College colleague, the late Nathalie Friedman, the techniques and practices of this organization included youth camps in Israel, weekend-long observations of the Sabbath called *shabbaton,* and organized prayer meetings. Special efforts focused on the high school and college years, which were seen as "make or break" years for shaping Jewish identity and practice. Results of the NCSY efforts included increased religious observance in adulthood and marriage between observant Jews.[13] The long-term effect of the *shabbaton* was heightened, especially for those attending public schools, by the high level of activity,[14] the company of friends, and opportunity to move into leadership positions working with younger adolescents.

Similarly, those reflecting on their Catskills experiences report that their annual summer-camp experience there was an important part of their journey into young adulthood. Former camper Alan Stamm relates how his time in the Catskills camps affected him and his generation:

> Without articulating it, we took meaningful steps … toward discovering what we enjoyed, what we did well, who we were, what we might like to be when we grew up. We got to test ourselves in the security and relative freedom of an alternative world without homework, music lessons, assigned reading … and other strictures. … But we'd carry the values—honesty, respect, teamwork, love of family—that were reinforced as we put on musicals, competed in color wars, listened to Sholem Alecheim morality tales and learned lifelong lessons. We value our camp months as a clear, dramatic transition time from adolescence to young adulthood and who we have become now. More than school, the concentrated and intense eight-week crucible was the first place we thrived, explored, experimented and maybe rebelled a tiny bit outside the nest. Such a bargain our folks got for the price.[15]

This quote evokes the continuing emotional importance of the writer's Catskills experiences in middle age and beyond and captures the same notions of belonging and adolescent transition expressed by secondgeneration Ticuanenses. The summer camps and NCSY experiences resonate with those of returning children of Ticuanense migrants. The eightweek camp sessions correspond roughly to the annual sojourn of many returning Ticuanense youths. Ticuanense youths also participate in an intense set of rituals, religious and communal, with returning friends. Judging by the NCSY data, the company of friends should make more enduring the influence of Ticuani on their identity. The metaphor of a "crucible" that helped shape the writer's transition from adolescence to adulthood is an apt one and is perfectly pitched to my argument. The extent to which the returnees enjoy the Antorcha and related events is evidence that something important is happening, and, by the participants' own reckoning, it involves their coming of age as Mexicans both in New York and, in key ways, in Ticuani.

Comparing (not equating) these Jewish and Ticuani experiences is instructive. While I doubt that the New York area will ever send a million teenagers back to Mexico every summer, with more than twenty million Mexicans and Mexican Americans in the United States, it seems quite likely that at least a million Mexicans go back to their own or their parents' communities of origin every year or two. Even assuming that Ticuani exerts a stronger influence than most, such return must affect identity and promote some transnational practices. A growing literature documents similar transnational practices by migrants from most migrant *municipios* in Mexico. With more than 600 hometown associations registered with the Mexican government in the late 1990s—prima facie evidence of transnational activity—and about 2,200 *municipios* in all of Mexico (some of which have more than one hometown association), transnational life seems widespread. Although it probably does not include all migrants, that it includes many in the second generation seems hard to dispute.

Moreover, given that the transnationally active tend to also be most active in public life in the United States—in politics, business, and even gangs—even limited participation can have significant effects. In New York City, for example, there were more than 300,000 Mexicans in 2000, over half of whom were under age twenty-five. Taking a pessimistic view, even if only 5 percent are transnationally active, that means 7,500 youths. And the likelihood is that more than 20 percent of second-generation Ticuanenses participate in transnational life, and perhaps more.

A second issue is whether transnational life itself persists over time and generations. The failure to institutionalize the Ticuani Youth Group reflects the second generation's imagination of their futures mainly in New York and not in Ticuani, the demands of their assimilated lives in New York, and the Committee's failure to involve younger people. Hence settlement and transnationalization often work at cross-purposes among young adults, though they reinforce each other among adolescents. Yet the issue is complex, and the forms and functions of transnational life vary by contexts of reception, the quality and frequency of transnational life, and historical epoch. The sociologist Cecilia Menjivar argues that obstacles to movement, poverty, and being indigenous result in few return visits by second-generation Guatemalans in the United States. As a consequence, the chances are greatly reduced that they will maintain ties to their parents' home country.[16] When I compared local-level Swedish transnational life from the 1850s to the 1930s with that of Ticuani today, I found that second-generation Swedes lived more "Swedish" lives—speaking Swedish in school and in public, marrying other Swedes, and living in mainly Swedish communities—than Ticuanenses in New York live "Mexican" lives.[17] But second-generation Swedes had almost no transnational activity (such as travel to the home country or sending remittances) even when their parents did, whereas second-generation Ticuanenses had transnational activity their Swedish counterparts could not have imagined. Similarly, a study of Italian migrants shows a great deal of second-generation immersion in Italian enclaves in the United States, and a great deal of first-generation return to Italy, but not a great deal of documented second-generation return or other active transnational life.[18]

Other cases, less well known, show important second- and latergeneration transnational life. Prior to World War I, Polish migrants pursued exile politics, with Nationalist, Communist, civil, and even religious organizations lobbying to have the international community restore Poland's territory and sovereignty. During World War I, Polish nationalist organizations intensified this lobbying campaign. Poles in the United States even organized the Polish "Kosciusko Army" on American soil (but under French auspices), for which some 38,000 U.S.-born Polish Americans volunteered and some 22,000 served (out of a total force of 90,000 in the Polish army). These Polish Americans accounted for half of Poland's casualties in the war, and many others later fought in the Polish-Soviet war of 1920.[19] That Polish Americans volunteered to fight and die for Poland in such numbers shows the importance of second- and later-generation diasporic links.[20] Similarly, during the 1990s, second- or later-generation children of immigrants have returned from the United States to the Balkans to fight in its wars and to former Soviet states such as Estonia to participate in its politics.[21]

CONCLUSION

Forms of transnational involvement change with the life course, attenuating and intensifying at different stages. Among Ticuanenses, the prospects for third-generation transnational life are still uncertain. The extent to which it will continue to matter to individuals will depend on many factors, including level of outmigration from places like Ticuani, relative levels of development in the home and host countries, the extent to which the Mexican government and Mexican American organizations create diasporic links with the Mexican American population, and the reaction of the United States government and others to such links.

Jewish Survival of the Holocaust

A Life Course Perspective

By Ronald Berger

M y subject is survival, or more specifically survival of the Holocaust—
the Nazi's genocidal campaign that took the lives of about six
million Jews, *Shoah* in Hebrew (for catastrophic destruction) and
what the Nazis called the Final Solution.[2] The question of survival has been
a long-standing preoccupation of literature and popular culture, whether it
is the story of Robinson Crusoe castaway on a remote tropical island or the
artificially constructed competition of the "reality" TV show *Survivor*. In
his book *Deep Survival: Who Lives, Who Dies, and Why*, Laurence Gonzales
purports to describe "the art and science of survival, ... whether in the
wilderness or in meeting any of life's great challenges."[3] According to
Gonzales, "every survival situation is the same in its essence"—it is one
in which the individual is "annealed in the fires of peril, ... looking death
in the face." More recently, in *The Survivors Club: The Secrets and Science
that Could Save Your Life*, Ben Sherwood defines a survivor as "anyone who
faces and overcomes adversity, hardship, illness, or physical or emotional
trauma," including "the friends and family who stand beside them," noting
that "everyone is a survivor."[4]

Surely it is a stretch to say that "every survival situation is the same in
its essence" and that "everyone is a survivor." Is the experience of Auschwitz
really the same as being stranded in the wilderness? It is one thing to portray
genuine victims of terror as "survivors" (such as survivors of rape, domestic
violence, and childhood sexual abuse, or even survivors of life-threatening

illnesses), but it is quite another to portray the crises and challenges of everyday life (such as surviving a divorce, surviving college, getting a job, or keeping a job) as akin to surviving the Holocaust. Nevertheless, popular culture is replete with such injudicious comparison,[5] which include using the Holocaust, Nazism, and Nazi concentration camps as metaphors to describe such diverse phenomena as the condition of women in society, abortion, the AIDS epidemic, the Israeli-Palestinian conflict, the experience of adult children of alcoholics, and the exploitation of animals.[6]

Clearly, if we are going to consider survival of the Holocaust as an object of serious scholarly inquiry, the concept requires more rigor. As far as I can tell, outside of some early studies of human behavior in the concentration camp, which treated the prisoners more as passive *victims* than as survivors,[7] as well as the genre of the Holocaust memoir itself, of which Elie Wiesel's *Night* and Primo Levi's *Survival in Auschwitz* stand out as classics,[8] Robert Jay Lifton (1967) was perhaps the first scholar to bring the concept of the survivor into the social and behavioral sciences, beginning with his work on the survivors of Hiroshima.[9] Later in his essay "The Concept of Survivor," Lifton aimed to delineate "common psychological responses of survivors" without implying that the events themselves—Hiroshima, Auschwitz, or a devastating flood—could be equated.[10] His focus was the "*total disaster*: the physical, social, and spiritual obliteration of a human community," and he defined the survivor in this context as "one who has encountered, been exposed to, or witnessed death, and has himself of herself remained alive."[11]

During the period in which Lifton was working on this topic, Terrence Des Pres published his important treatise, *The Survivor: An Anatomy of Life in the Death Camps*.[12] Des Pres defined the *context* of survival as a "condition of extremity" that persists beyond one's "ability to alter or end," where "there is no escape, no place to go except the grave." The survivor, according to Des Pres, is one who sustains unimaginable physical and psychic damage and yet "manages to stay alive in body *and* in spirit, enduring dread and hopelessness without the loss of will to carry on in human ways." He is not a hero but "a protagonist in the classic [literary] sense, for by staying alive he becomes an effective agent in the fight against evil and injustice."[13]

The topic of survival is immensely personal to me because it involves members of my family who survived the Holocaust in Nazi-occupied Poland. When I say members who survived, I should not exaggerate, because there were *only two* members of our Polish family who had not emigrated before the war who eluded the death grip of the Nazis: My father, Michael Berger, was interned in several concentration camps, including the Auschwitz camps at Birkenau and Monowitz; and my uncle, Sol Berger, escaped the camps by passing as a Catholic Pole with a construction crew, the Polish Partisans, and the Soviet army. In my book, I recount their story of Holocaust survival and interpret their experiences—before, during, and after the war—using the tools of sociological analysis. In particular, I use a *life course* perspective to interpret the trajectories of my father and uncle's lives, enhancing this approach with insights from *agency-structure* and *collective memory* theory.

The concept of the life course refers to an age-graded sequence of socially defined roles and events that individuals enact over time.[14] A basic premise of this approach is that human lives are shaped by a person's unique location in historical time and place. While being concerned with how people live "their lives in changing times and across various contexts," life course theory postulates that early life experiences have a significant impact on later life outcomes.[15] For our purposes, it draws attention to the prewar experiences of Jewish survivors that maximized or minimized, as the case may be, their chances of eluding the Nazi's death grip and enduring their condition of trauma. Such a view, as we shall see, challenges the conventional wisdom about "luck" or randomness as the preeminent feature of survival. It also gives us a way of accounting for survival without relying on psychological theorizing that has dominated the scholarly literature, which assumes that survival was a matter that was endogenous to individuals.

Life course theory characterizes human action as consisting of the dynamic interplay between *personal agency* and *social structure*, which agency-structure theory posits as the two foundational or presuppositional categories of *all* sociological discourse.[16] Personal agency entails a person's capacity for self-direction, an ability to make decisions and exercise a degree of control over their life, even transform the social relations in which they are enmeshed. Social structure, on the other hand, establishes the external parameters of human action, which enhance and/or limit opportunities and life outcomes. With regards to the Holocaust, one might ask: Didn't a social structure as powerful and ruthless as the Nazis', which appeared beyond one's ability to alter of end, negate the human capacity for agency? Indeed, doesn't the circumstance of the Jews in this context illustrate, as Lawrence Langer observes, "what it meant (and means) in our time to exist *without* ... human agency"?[17] Life course and agency-structure theory will help us grapple with such complex questions of futility and resistance to social structures of extremity in a way that avoids dichotomous characterizations of Jews as overly passive or overly heroic.

An additional focus of the life course perspective entails the concept of *life trajectories*, or life pathways, a sequence of social roles and experiences that are marked by significant events, transitions, and turning points; as well as the concept of population *cohorts*, which is akin to the notion of generations, which consist of individuals who share the experience of particular historical events at particular points in their lives.[18] Whereas *transitions* are more or less orderly or gradual, *turning points* are marked by disruptions, which are generally unexpected, that propel one into a dramatically different life trajectory. The Holocaust was, of course, a dramatic turning point in the lives of European Jews, which fundamentally altered the trajectory of their lives, if they lived at all. Moreover, the trauma of the ordeal was something that survivors reckoned with for the rest of their lives, whether they tried to express or repress their anguish. This trauma was cultural, as well as personal, as it left an indelible mark on later cohorts of Jews who did not live through the event themselves.[19] It had a particular impact on the "second generation" children of survivors, like myself, who have played a special role in helping our elders explore their past and narrate that past to broader audiences,[20] which illustrates the life course axiom about linked or interdependent lives, whereby "sociohistorical influences are expressed through [a] network of shared relationships."[21] This cross-generational practice of "collective witness," as Stephen Couch calls it,[22] has been a bonding experience for the first and second generation and has symbolically substituted for the "rituals of mourning" and the absence of "graves, headstones and burial places which were so cruelly denied to the victims" and their families.[23]

This brings us to the third theoretical orientation, which focuses on the phenomenon of collective memory, of which the practice of collective witness is a part. Collective memory entails the ways in which historical events are recollected in group context, if they are recollected at all, for collective memory entails both the remembering and the forgetting of the past.[24] While collective memory is constructed, in part, by members of the group that lived through an event, it is also constructed by members of subsequent generations who experience the event vicariously through books, films, memorials, museums, and so forth. Indeed, most of us learn about the past through cultural representations and social institutions that infuse disparate individual memories with common symbolic meaning, creating a sense of shared values and ideals that persists across cohorts and provides the foundation for social solidarity and a unified polity. As we shall see, however, the manner in which the Holocaust was remembered in the postwar years was not self-evident from the trauma of the event itself, and alternative or multiple collective memories of the Holocaust have competed with each other for social recognition as the "master narrative" of the past.

Collective memory

BREAKING THE SILENCE

The Holocaust was a traumatic experience for the individuals who died and lived through it, but it was also a collective trauma, not only for Jews, but for the entire world. In the early postwar years, however, it was not explicitly recognized as such, and silence permeated the cultural air. As a member of the postwar "baby boom" cohort, growing up in Los Angeles, California, in the 1950s and 1960s, I actually knew very little about the Holocaust and about what had happened to my father and our European family during World War II. When I was much older, after the veneer of silence had been lifted, my father told me that after he immigrated to the United States in 1946, no one, even Jewish relatives, was particularly interested in hearing about his ordeal. People would say things like, "We suffered too. Did you know that we couldn't get sugar [during the war] and that gasoline was rationed?" So my father and other survivors like him stopped talking about their experiences. At that time the idea of the Holocaust "survivor" who was held in awe as a witness to history had yet to be constructed. The world was not ready to listen to their stories, to say nothing of embracing them as revered figures. They were viewed as "displaced persons," "refugees," "greenhorns."[25]

When I was six or seven years old, my father later reminded me, I asked him why I had grandparents only on my mother's side of the family while all my friends had two sets of grandparents. At that time all he said was that they had died. When I was a little older, he did tell me about being in a concentration camp and about his agony over losing his parents. At that age, however, I do not think I really understood what being in a concentration camp entailed. Back then, it seemed to me, the only observable trace of his ordeal was the blue number 160914 tattooed on his left arm.

Moreover, I cannot recall any attention given to the subject during all my years in public school or later even in college at UCLA. Nor can I recall it mentioned in Hebrew school during the period of my life I was preparing for my bar mitzvah. Quite frankly, my most vivid images of World War II came not from the Holocaust but from movies about the experiences and heroics of American soldiers. My first serious encounter with the Holocaust, if you can call it serious, did not occur until the 1978 airing of the television miniseries Holocaust, a docudrama based on the Gerald Green screenplay about two fictional families, one Jewish and one German, which was viewed by some 120 million viewers in the United States alone.[26]

I was raised in a workingand middle-class Jewish enclave on the west side of Los Angeles. It was my mother's decision that we should live there. Her parents, who were also Jewish, had immigrated to the United States between the two World Wars and had settled in Glendale, California, just outside the borders of Los Angeles proper. This is where my mother was raised. It was an anti-Semitic community, home of the John Birch Society. My mother never experienced violence because of her Jewish identity, but neither did she think it was an environment in which she wanted to raise her own children.

Until I was eight years old, we lived next door to the family of one of my father's friends, a man who was also a Holocaust survivor. Richard Stewart had been in one of the same concentration camps as my father, Auschwitz-Monowitz, the Auschwitz subsidiary that provided slave labor for I.G. Farben, a German petrochemical corporation.[27] There were other survivors (as well as prewar European immigrants) in our social network and extended family. I did not, however, realize any of this at the time. I was surrounded by people with European accents, which seemed completely natural to me, and I had no idea of the implications of all this.

The public schools I attended in Los Angeles had large Jewish populations. It was not uncommon for classrooms to be virtually empty on the Jewish holidays of Rosh Hashanah and Yom Kippur. At Christmastime I did not feel left out or envious of Christian children because my parents were successful at deluding my brother and me that the practice of receiving gifts over an eight-day period for Hanukkah was much better than a one-day holiday. Only later did I discover that many Christian children enjoy a veritable orgy of gifts on that one day that far surpasses anything we received during our week-long celebration.

My parents' religious beliefs could best be described as agnostic, although they always self-identified as Jews and held strong nationalist sentiments toward Israel. For us, being Jewish was more of an ethnic-cultural identity than a theological faith. During my childhood, we did observe all of the major Jewish holidays, and it was assumed that at thirteen years of age I would have my bar mitzvah, which I did. But further Jewish education was not obligatory, although I did study Hebrew for another six months. Because I was raised in a liberal Jewish milieu, I felt as though I were an assimilated American. And that was fine with me. I did not believe that being Jewish made me an outsider until I moved to southeastern Wisconsin in 1981 upon accepting a teaching position at the University of Wisconsin-Whitewater (UW W).

UW W is located in a small college town between Madison and Milwaukee, about two hours by car from Chicago. In Whitewater and the neighboring small towns in which I lived for several years, there are few, if any, Jews. Most of the people in these communities are either Catholic or Lutheran who have little contact with people from non-Christian backgrounds. Within a month or two after I first arrived, I was invited to dinner at a faculty member's house. After dinner the conversation somehow turned to religion, and our hostess said, in what seemed like a non sequitur, "Those Jews have a lot of nerve thinking they are the chosen people!" Then there was the little seven-year-old, a neighbor of mine, who expressed confusion to her parents when she found out I was Jewish because she thought that all "Jews had horns." Several years later, a 12-year-old friend of my stepson casually remarked, "Jews are bad people."

At other times I heard comments pertaining to people who would "Jew you down." The first time I heard this was from our elderly departmental secretary. She spoke with no vehemence, as though the idiom were not steeped in prejudice. A few years later, after I married into an extended family of Wisconsin Synod Lutherans, a rather conservative and theocratic lot, my father-in-law made the "Jew you down" remark. I thought of saying something to him but decided to let the matter rest. Later, when my sister-in-law used the phrase, I did intervene, explaining why I thought it was an offensive comment. I found it rather amusing that she had been complaining about her failed efforts to negotiate a reduction in price from a local carpet dealer. Apparently she thought it was the carpet dealer, not she, who was the one doing the "Jewing down." Recently, a colleague, a professor of sociology, used the term to describe his own miserly habits. I did not say anything to him.

There also was the time I was in a liquor store buying a bottle of wine or some beer, when the salesclerk told an anti-Semitic joke to the customer he seemed to know who was standing next to me. I do not even remember the specifics of the joke; it was something about a Jewish businessman who committed arson insurance fraud and moved to Florida. The clerk, of course, did not know I would find the joke objectionable, but again I said nothing. This particular battle I did not need to fight. But I did feel as though I were invisible. I began to realize how people of color must feel when they go into a store in a white community. All eyes are on them. If being Jewish were something you could see on my face, they would be watching me too.

It is not that I am complaining about all this. These little affronts to my ethnic ancestry pale in comparison to the real thing. But they are part of the life trajectory that was leading to my encounter with my family's story of the Holocaust.

Oddly enough, at this time I was unaware of the growing collective consciousness among second-generation children of survivors, which first gained national recognition through Helen Epstein's 1977 *New York Times Magazine* article, "Heirs to the Holocaust," which was followed by the publication of her book *Children of the Holocaust: Conversations with Sons and Daughters of Survivors* in 1979.[28] Eva Fogelman traces the second-generation movement, in part, to the more general cultural interest in familial "roots" and genealogy that emerged in the United States in the mid-1970s,[29] an interest that gained momentum after the 1977 broadcast of the television miniseries *Roots*, based on Alex Haley's epic novel about a fictional African American family,[30] which was followed the next year by the *Holocaust* miniseries. Together, these popular and widely viewed docudramas caused people of various ethnic stripes to become more interested in learning about their ethnic-familial pasts. Life course theory describe this phenomenon in general terms as a *period effect*, an historical event that has a relatively uniform impact across different cohorts in a society.[31]

My own interest in exploring my father's past, however, was piqued at a lecture I attended at the university in 1987. Robery Clary, the actor most known for his role as Louis LeBeau in the television sitcom *Hogan's Heroes*, spoke to a standing-room-only audience of over 800 people. The TV show was rather popular at the time, and I had never seen so many people turn out for a non-sporting event at the university. Clary's topic was the Holocaust and his survival of it. He explained that for most of his postwar life he had kept still about his experience to avoid the painful remembering of his "thirty-one months of hell." But as he turned sixty, he said, he began to realize that soon there would no longer exist living testimony to the Holocaust. Clary added that he was particularly concerned about the so-called Holocaust "revisionists," including those with scholarly credentials, who continue to deny that the atrocities occurred.[32]

During the audience question-and-answer period that followed Clary's speech, a young woman stood up, identified herself as twenty-five-years-old, and said that she was outraged that she had not been taught about or "heard of the Holocaust" before Clary's lecture. The audience, including myself, was taken aback by her comment. However, what also soon struck me was how little I knew about the Holocaust and in particular about what had happened to my father and his family. This led to an immediate phone call back home. "We have to record your story," I told my father. And he seemed pleased. He was ready for someone to ask, and happy that he would be able to, in his words, "leave a legacy for my family."

What started out as a family project blossomed into something more. Through my previous work as a sociologist, I had been concerned with questions of class, race, and gender. (At that time religious ethnicity, among other categories of social difference, had not been let into this holy trinity.) But now, as I began to feel a sense of "nostalgic allegiance" to my ethnic origins,[33] I was struck by how much I had failed to inquire into my own heritage and realized that the topic of Holocaust survival could be a legitimate object of sociological inquiry.[34]

To be sure, I approached this topic with some trepidation. I became aware that there were Jews, like Elie Wiesel, who believed that the Holocaust was "a sacred and essentially incomprehensible event" that was beyond the analytical capacities of social science, or any literary narrative for that matter.[35] I found myself, like Gerald Markle and colleagues, scrutinizing the experience of survivors with some discomfort, fearing unintentional "trivialization and disrespect."[36] At the same time, I was encouraged by those scholars who argued against mystifying the Holocaust as beyond intellectual discourse.[37] Shamai Davidson, an Israeli psychiatrist who worked extensively with Holocaust survivors, suggested that the accumulation of many oral histories may make possible a perspective that was even "denied some individual survivors as they were preoccupied by the bitter drama of their own battle for survival."[38]

EMBRACING JEWISH PARTICULARITY

"In the beginning," writes Jeffrey Alexander, "the Holocaust was not the 'Holocaust'. … In the torrent of newspaper, radio, and magazine stories reporting the discovery by American infantrymen of the Nazi concentration camps, the empirical remains of what had transpired were typified as 'atrocities,'" part of the general horror of war.[39] The particularity of Jewish victimization and the suffering of Jewish survivors were opaque; and the photographic and film images that were taken by the Allies presented the victims (dead and alive) as a "petrified, degrading, and smelly" depersonalized mass of misery that generated revulsion rather than compassion.

At the Nuremberg trials following the war, Jewish victimization was certainly acknowledged, but it was subsumed under the broader categories of "war crimes" and "crimes against humanity" and soon half forgotten.[40] The word "Jew" was not even mentioned in Alain Resnais's otherwise brilliant 1955 documentary film *Night and Fog*.[41] And William Shirer's *The Rise and Fall of the Third Reich*, a 1960 bestseller, devoted just two to three percent of its some 1,200 pages to the Jewish genocide.[42] In this context, most Americans came to view World War II in terms of what Alexander calls the "progressive narrative" of the war, the belief that the evil of Nazism had been overcome and "relegated to a traumatic past whose darkness [had been] obliterated" in favor of a forward-looking vision of a more humane and democratic age.[43] In doing so, the collective memory of the Final Solution was effaced.

In the current period—when books and films about the Holocaust abound, and when the United States has a memorial museum dedicated to the genocide adjacent to the nation's other venerated monuments—it is difficult to imagine the public's disinterest in the Holocaust during the early postwar years. In his autobiography, for example, the eminent Holocaust historian Raul Hilberg recalls how difficult it was to find a publisher for *The Destruction of European Jews*, his ground-breaking account of the bureaucracy that implemented the Final Solution. Eventually he found Quadrangle Books, a small independent company, which agreed to publish the book in 1961 after a Jewish-survivor family promised to subsidize the project with $15,000 to pay for books that would be donated to libraries.[44]

Even classic works such as Elie Wiesel's *Night* and Anne Frank's diary had inauspicious beginnings. Wiesel reports that his book, pared down from a much longer version that was first published in Yiddish, was at first considered too slender or too depressing for an American audience; and when it was eventually published in 1960 by Hill & Wang, it was not a commercial success.[45] And were it not for *The Diary of Anne Frank* screenplay written by Frances Goodrich and Albert Hackett, which was made into a highly acclaimed Broadway play in 1955 and an Academy Award caliber film in 1959, Anne's diary, first published in Dutch in 1947, might have lingered in obscurity for many more years.[46]

The case of Goodrich and Hackett's version of Anne's diary is especially noteworthy for undermining Jewish particularity. In order to appeal to broader Christian audiences, the screenplay downplayed Anne's Jewishness and turned her into a universal representative of martyred innocence. Anne's longer mediations on Jewish persecution and anti-Semitism were not included in the theatrical productions, and instead remarks were substituted that do not even appear in the diary: "We're not the only people that've had to suffer. There've always been people that've had to ... sometimes one race ... sometimes another." Thus one reviewer wrote that *The Diary of Anne Frank* was "not in any important sense a Jewish play."[47]

It should therefore come as no surprise that survivors like my father felt silenced, by Jews and non-Jews alike, in the initial postwar period. To be sure, for some survivors this silence was self-imposed—out of guilt for having lived when others had not and shame for being the bearer of bad news and a reminder of a past that they and others wanted to forget.[48] Among potential Jewish listeners, Davidson observed, "the realization that 'this could have happened to me'" led people to close their ears.[49] Among potential non-Jewish listeners, the survivor was a reminder of their impotence or failure to have "actively intervened to help the victims." More generally, the survivor—and Davidson believed this is true of survivors of other calamities as well—is "a disturber of the peace ... [who] represents the possibility of chaos and disintegration of society." Even worse, the survivor arouses "a feeling of contamination, as if being in contact with their confrontation with death could be contagious."

Israeli Jews in particular—who envisioned a society of self-reliant "new men" achieving mastery over their environment by returning to their ancient homeland and fighting for independence and the creation of a Jewish state—at times held rather disdainful attitudes toward survivors.[50] According to Davidson, for a long time many Israelis implicitly urged Holocaust survivors "to forget their past ... and ... emerge from their background of powerlessness, helplessness, and defenselessness into a new Israeli identity" that repudiated what Israelis perceived as the passivity of the European Jews during the war.[51] Thus, Israelis lent a more receptive ear toward those survivors who had fought as Partisans or who had been involved in armed resistance. In fact, they sought out these individuals, treated them as heroes, and urged them to tell *their* stories. Survivors who could not or would not conform to this expectation were dismissed as inconsequential at best.

A key turning point in this disconcerting view of survivors was the 1961 trial of Adolf Eichmann.[52] Eichmann, the Nazi's leading expert on Jewish affairs and a key architect of the Final Solution, had been apprehended by the Israelis in Argentina and taken to Israel for criminal prosecution. In the minds of Israeli officials, however, the purpose of the trial was not simply to punish Eichmann but to impress upon the rest of the world their moral obligation to support the Jewish state. It was an occasion for building national pride and for highlighting not only Jewish suffering but, more importantly, Jewish resistance. As Attorney General Gideon Hausner, the prosecutor in the case, explained, the trial "was an opportunity to bring before the world the hundreds and thousands of heroic deeds that were not generally known."[53]

The Eichmann trial initiated the construction of an alternative narrative or collective memory of the Holocaust, a new period effect that highlighted the distinctiveness and enormity of Jewish victimization. It was the first time that large numbers of survivors began telling their stories in public, including stories of non-heroic suffering. The entire spectacle was, in Raymond Schmitt's terms, an "emotional reminder," an event or experience that called forth "memories and feelings that have been retained in the psychic body."[54] Several years later, the 1967 Six-Day War between Israel and its Arab neighbors renewed fears among Jews that a second Holocaust was possible. However, the decisive Israeli victory in that conflict brought pride and confidence to Jews around the world and legitimized Israel as a capable ally of the United States, "worthy of support on pragmatic as well as moral grounds."[55] Building on the financial security that Jews had achieved in the United States, survivors increasingly felt empowered to become more vocal about their wartime experiences, and by the late 1970s the Holocaust began receiving widespread exposure in print and film, especially through the 1978 *Holocaust* docudrama.

Jewish leaders in the United States soon discovered that the Holocaust drew more people to public events than any other subject and was capable of appealing to Jews who had only marginal Jewish affiliation. They also discovered that the Holocaust could be used as a fund-raising resource for Jewish causes, particularly for support of Israel and for Holocaust-related organizations and activities themselves.[56] Some Jews hoped that "Holocaust consciousness" would become a vehicle for Jews to embrace the religious core of Judaism, but it also became a "civil religion" of sorts—in the United States and Israel alike—a principle source of Jewish identity and cohesion.[57] Nevertheless, the important thing for survivors, who had for years been deprived of "respectful listeners to their stories," was that they now found themselves in high demand, even held in awe and embraced as revered figures.[58] Listeners wanted to get close to them, to feel their pain, and in doing so become witnesses to history themselves.[59] In turn, survivors came to see themselves as responsible for reminding the world that what happened to them must happen "Never Again!"

Along the way, the Bitburg affair in Germany was a painful emotional reminder for many Jews that the memory of the Holocaust remains contested and tenuous.[60] In 1985 President Ronald Reagan accepted an invitation from West German Chancellor Helmut Kohl to attend a commemorative event honoring German veterans of war at a military cemetery in Bitburg, which, it turned out, was not only the burial site of a couple thousand German soldiers but about fifty SS troops as well.[61] The White House accepted the invitation "in a spirit of reconciliation, in a spirit of forty years of peace, in a spirit of economic and military compatibility,"[62] but Jews (and U.S. veterans) were offended by Reagan's remark that the men buried at Bitburg "were victims, just as surely as the victims in the concentration camps," as if the president wished to recall nothing more about the past than "common sacrifices and a shared code of military honor."[63]

The emotional reminder of Bitburg, however, only served to increase interest in the Holocaust and the experience of survivors. And in 1993, two events brought embracement of the Holocaust to an even higher level: the popular success of Steven Spielberg's *Schindler's List*, and the opening of the United States Holocaust Memorial Museum. The film, according to some observers, may have done "more to educate vast numbers of people about the ... Holocaust than all the academic books on the subject combined," [64] while the museum, situated adjacent to the Washington mall in Washington, D.C., the "ceremonial center" of the United States that holds the nation's most cherished national monuments, placed the Holocaust squarely within the official state-sponsored memory of the country.[65] Importantly as well, Spielberg's Survivors of the Shoah Visual History Foundation, established in 1994, joined other videotape archival projects around the country to document the experiences of thousands of Holocaust survivors whose voices are no longer silenced.[66]

SCHOLARLY CHARACTERIZATIONS OF SURVIVAL

"I wake up shivering, thinking that when we die, no one will be able to persuade people that the Holocaust occurred."[67] This, Elie Wiesel has said, is his worst nightmare. In my view, however, the most pressing question is not *whether* the Holocaust will be remembered but *how* it will be remembered. Typically, survivors themselves attribute their survival to luck, chance, or miracles—a matter of being in the right place or the wrong place at the right or wrong time—hence obviating the need for a social analysis of survival.[68] In turn, there are scholars who also believe that sociological generalizations about survival should be resisted because this would deny "the singular humanity of each survivor." Rather, they argue, each account "stands alone ... [and] paints its own picture."[69]

This was the conventional wisdom at the time I began recording my father and uncle's stories. But in the course of my research, the reading I did, and the stories of other survivors I heard, I came to the conclusion that this view is overly simplistic. As a sociologist, I wish to argue that our understanding of Jewish survival can be enhanced by examining the phenomenon through the lens of sociological analysis. In particular, I examine the question of whether agentive action was at all possible under such structural conditions of extremity: Was it possible for Jews to take action that would maximize, though by no means ensure, their chances of survival? In doing so, I hope to move beyond the psychological theorizing about that has dominated the survival literature and avoid dichotomous characterizations of Jews as overly passive or overly heroic.

The apparent erasure of agency during the Nazi period may explain, in part, why initial scholarly characterizations of the Jewish response to the Nazi onslaught mirrored Abba Kovner's wartime complaint that too many Jews were allowing themselves to be "led like sheep to the slaughter."[70] Both Hannah Arendt and Raul Hilberg, for example, criticized the Jewish Councils that were set up by Nazis to carry out their edicts for being overly compliant and for collaborating with their despotic overseers.[71] Bruno Bettelheim, in an influential early appraisal of concentration camp behavior, described prisoners as regressing to a childish dependency on the SS guards, experiencing deindividuation, abandoning previously inculcated norms and values, and eventually identifying completely with their oppressors.[72] Others noted the physical deprivation and psychological degradation that ground down prisoners into a state of profound apathy and lack of affect, as was the case with the *Muselmänner*, those skeleton-like prisoners or "walking corpses" who were on the verge of death but not yet of it, while other prisoners were described as descending into a primal state of selfpreservation, an "all against all" atmosphere that bred corrupt and predatory behavior.[73] In addition, survivors after the war were described disparagingly as guilt-ridden, emotionally withdrawn, "chronically depressed, anxious, and fearful."[74]

Des Pres was one of the first to observe that these formulations were derived from limited observations and were misleading as generalizations.[75] Bettelheim, for instance, developed his thesis on the basis of camp conditions in the 1930s, at a time when prisoners who held positions of power (trustees) were not political prisoners or Jews but those who had been convicted of predatory crimes, including murder. Increasingly analysts adopted a more nuanced view of the variety and complexity of the Jewish response and turned their attention to the constructive, indeed agentive, strategies for survival that emerged during the Nazi period. Individuals who survived conditions of extremity often emerged from an initial period of shock, despair, and disbelief able to realistically appraise their situation and take strategic courses of action through calculated risk-taking and disobedience. Moreover, many were able to do so without completely abandoning prewar norms of human reciprocity and systems of morality. Survivors' accounts regularly include reports of people maintaining hope, holding onto their humanity, and offering and receiving help from others.[76] Anna Pawełzyńska noted that individuals "who made no revisions" in pre-existing humanitarian impulses perished if they "applied them in an absolute way," but there were always those who united "together in the practice of the basic norm, 'Do not harm your neighbor and, if possible, save him.'"[77] Mary Gallant and Jay Cross characterized survivors as individuals who acquired a "challenged identity" after an initial period of disorientation, which gave them the will to go on by observing others' courageous responses to their common ordeal.[78] Shamai Davidson described the group bonding in camps, which provided individuals with mutual aid and helped them maintain hope and preserve "a sense of self despite the dehumanization and amorality."[79]

At the same time, much of the scholarly literature has tended to psychologize survival and view it as a matter that was endogenous to individuals. Des Pres, for example, emphasized survivors' inherent will to live, which he described as an evolutionary pattern or "biological imperative."[80] Others highlighted the role of internal defense mechanisms, which enabled individuals to block out the horror and focus on their survival needs; or they described survivors in terms of their individual capacity for voluntary action, outward adaptation to the environment, sociability, and readiness to offer and receive support.[81] William Helmreich attributed survival to "personality traits" or inner qualities such as assertiveness, tenacity, courage, willingness to take risks, flexibility, optimism, and intelligence.[82]

I do not wish to deny the psychological traits that enhanced Jews' survival capacity. Indeed, they describe the survivors that I know. I also agree with Viktor Frankl that external conditions alone cannot explain survival; an "inner decision" to persevere and be on the look-out for opportunities to ameliorate one's plight was essential.[83] However,

I do wish to build on these insights and place them in broader analytical perspective. The challenge for the analyst, as Langer has suggested, is to enter the survivors' world and "find an orientation that will do justice to their recaptured experience *without* summoning it or them to judgment and evaluation."[84] This must also be done without turning survivors' personal tragedy into triumphant accounts where even passivity and dying with dignity are romanticized as forms of resistance.[85] According to Langer, surviving the Holocaust "was a thoroughly practical matter" that had little do with "a victory of the human spirit."[86]

During the course of my research, I found valuable the analysis of Patricia Benner, Ethel Roskies, and Richard Lazarus, who posit a general model of stress and coping behavior as applied to Holocaust survival.[87] These psychologists characterize stress as a relational concept that reflects "reciprocity between *external* demands, constraints, and resources" and "*internal* resources to manage them." They do not view survivors as helpless victims or passive responders to circumstances but as persons who attempted to manipulate the stress experience to achieve some degree of control over "those small segments of reality that could be managed … [and contained] possibilities for direct action." Coping proceeded through cognitive appraisal of the stress situation and evaluation of available resources and options. Actions were then taken on the basis of this appraisal. "Any cessation of appraisal, as in the case of individuals who withdrew into … [a] state of apathy, … was a signal of impending death."

Although Benner, Roskies, and Lazarus fall short of a distinctly sociological framework for analyzing Holocaust survival, their stress-coping model can be recast more broadly through sociological theory. In doing so, I will address the questions of whether survival was more than a matter of luck, and whether the apparent randomness of events negates the possibility of a sociological explanation; and I offer my father and uncle's life histories as a case study in this effort.

A SOCIAL THEORY OF SURVIVAL

Life course theory, as noted earlier, postulates that human lives are shaped by a person's unique location in historical time and place and that early life experiences have a significant impact on later life outcomes. Although there are broad cohort effects that impose common parameters on human action in particular social settings, there are also *intra-cohort* variations, that is, the same historical event may impact individual cohort members differently depending on their unique backgrounds or predispositions.[88] In this study, I will show how my father and uncle's particular prewar backgrounds enhanced their agentive capacity to survive the Nazi period.

Life course theory characterizes human action as consisting of "agency within structure,"[89] but agency-structure theory conceptualizes this relationship in particular ways. Agency, as noted earlier, entails a person's capacity for self-direction, an ability to make decisions and exercise a degree of control over their life, even transform the social relations in which they are enmeshed. According to William Sewell, Jr., it entails "an ability to coordinate one's actions with others and against others … and to monitor the simultaneous effects of one's own and others' activities."[90] Social psychologists describe this as a matter of self-efficacy, that is, the ability to experience oneself as a causal agent capable of *acting upon* rather than merely *reacting to* external conditions.[91] Social structure, on the other hand, consists of *cultural schemas* and *social resources*. Cultural schemas refer to general frameworks of action, both formal and informal, including values, beliefs, customs, habits of speech, and the like; and social resources refer to the organizational and institutional mechanisms by which individuals acquire, maintain, or generate power in social relationships.[92] Although agency and structure may be analytically distinct, in reality they are interrelated: each presupposes the other as both agentive action and social structure are enacted and reproduced in specific situational contexts.

Both life course and agency-structure theory posit that social structures are not only *constraining* but *enabling*. Individuals are born with only a general "capacity for agency, analogous to their ability to use language," and this capacity is nourished or undernourished, as the case may be, by the "specific range of cultural schemas and resources available in a person's social milieu." In its most efficacious form, it entails individuals' ability to apply or extend "their structurally formed capacities" to new circumstances in "creative and innovative ways."[93]

In the case of the Holocaust, the Nazi regime was systematically structured to accomplish the persecution and eventually elimination of all Jews. But some Jews' agentive capacity under these structural conditions of extremity was enhanced by their prewar exposure to cultural schemas and social resources that they were able to transpose to the war-occupation context. As Hilberg argues, "Survival was not altogether random. … Although the German destruction process was a massive leveler, it did not obliterate" all prewar differences.[94] These differences, however, acquired new meaning during the Nazi period. They were no longer a measure of high or low status but of more or less vulnerability. For example, age was a key factor, for survivors were more likely to be relatively young (between their teens and thirties) and in good health at the start of their ordeal, a characteristic that maximized their ability to endure hardship and withstand disease. Additionally, those with particular occupational skills—physicians, carpenters, shoemakers, tailors (my father and uncle's trade)—also fared better because they remained useful to others who might want to keep them alive. And, indeed, the prewar personality traits that I described earlier, which are influenced significantly by family socialization, increased the likelihood that one would not yield to despair. These were important ingredients that helped constitute the "luck" of the survivor.

At the same time, Jews' ability to exercise agency successfully during the war was in large part an interpersonal accomplishment "laden with collectively produced differences in power."[95] In the concentration camps, for instance, survival required an ability to "organize," to use the camp lexicon, that is, to acquire additional life-sustaining resources through unauthorized means. Successful organizing was a matter of *collective* agency and derived from a person's position in the functional hierarchy of the camp and the network of social relationships among prisoners.[96] Similarly, Jews like my uncle who survived outside the camps by passing as Christians were generally dependent on the support they received from members of the non-Jewish population.[97]

Moreover, as Anthony Giddens notes, it is important to distinguish agency from intentions.[98] Human interaction always contains "an emergent, negotiated, often unpredictable" quality, and thus the consequences of actions may differ from those that are intended.[99] It would be unwise, therefore, to overestimate individuals' ability to overcome conditions of extremity and assign privileged status to agency over structure in social analysis. During the Holocaust, all that individuals could hope to accomplish was to hold on a little longer until external conditions over which they had no control changed, that is, until the Allies defeated the Germans in the war. Otherwise, they would have inevitably been killed.

Nonetheless, throughout all this Holocaust survivors experienced numerous occasions of what Norman Denzin describes as "epiphanies," interactional moments of crisis or transformation that left indelible marks on their lives and through which personal character was manifested.[100] Holocaust epiphanies included "crucial moments" in which difficult choices and quick decisions that were the difference between life and death were made. In Sartre's terms, these epiphanies contained a "coefficient of adversity," where external conditions put up substantial resistance to agency.[101] As such, Holocaust epiphanies illuminate the relationship between agency and structure in instances where the tension between them is heightened and the individual resides in a condition of liminality or "no-man's-land betwixt and between … the past and the … future."[102]

THE LIFE HISTORY STUDY

Life course researchers use a variety of methodological approaches, but the life history method based on interviews and conversations with informants is one that is especially suitable to the study of human lives in historical context.[103] This method is a time-honored tradition in sociology that has "vacillated in acceptance and popularity over the years."[104] It aims to advance C. Wright Mills's vision of a "sociological imagination" that grapples with the intersection of biography and history in society and the ways in which personal troubles are related to public issues.[105] By linking personal stories to collective narratives, the life history method takes the individual as the fundamental reference point for sociological analysis without, at the same time, placing the individual outside of his or her social context.[106]

Denzin characterizes life history research as a form of sociological inquiry that respects "human subjects as individuals who can tell true stories about their lives."[107] In the case of Jewish survivors of the Nazi period, it is also a means of bearing witness or providing "testimonial proof" of the events and experiences that have come to be known as the Holocaust. The life history is based on the experiences of my father, Michael Berger (born in 1921), and my uncle Sol Berger (born in 1919), who, as noted earlier, are the only two members of our extended family who had not emigrated from Poland before the war who survived. They come from Krosno, Poland, a small city of about 18,000 people on the eve of World War II, of which about 2,200–2,500 were Jews.[108]

In conducting the research I adopted a "narrative interview" approach, beginning by asking my father and uncle to reconstruct their experiences to the best of their recollection and "according to [their] own relevancies."[109] As is common with autobiographical memories and Holocaust memories in particular, they found a chronological ordering of their experience to be the most effective means of retrieving their memories.[110] Additionally, as Denzin notes, life histories rely on "conventionalized, narrative expressions … which structure how lives are told and written about."[111] Thus my father and uncle implicitly relied on such conventions and constructed a narrative with a beginning, middle, and end, and that is marked by epiphanies and turning points in which the protagonists (my father and uncle) made critical choices and exercised personal agency in the face of adversity, faltered and nearly perished, but ultimately survived. It was the telling of their stories in this manner that first sensitized me to the role of personal agency in their survival.

In the early part of 1988, my father began tape-recording his narrative alone in the privacy of his home. I then transcribed the recording and gave my uncle the opportunity to read it. Afterward, he recorded a narrative of his own that expanded on my father's account of experiences they held in common and that described the particulars of his situation. In the next stage, I tape-recorded (separate) open-ended interviews and prompted each of them to further develop their narratives and fill in gaps in their reconstruction of the events. Since I lived in Wisconsin and they lived in Los Angeles, California, this process took place over a couple of years, at which point I accumulated about twenty hours of interview material, which I transcribed verbatim, giving them an opportunity to review the written record.

My father and uncle's recall ability was impressive, in spite of the time that had elapsed, but this is not unusual for Holocaust survivors. The Holocaust was a "major epiphany," a life-shattering event that contained elements of uniqueness, consequentiality, unexpectedness, and emotionality that facilitate memory retrieval.[112] As Langer observes, there is often "no need to revise what has never died. … Though slumbering memories may crave reawakening … Holocaust memory is an insomniac faculty whose mental eyes have never slept."[113] Moreover, survivors' memories have been kept alive by the emotional reminders of the postwar period; and in my father's case he had the constant reminder of the concentration camp number on his arm.[114] Importantly, participating in the research itself was an emotional reminder that helped stimulate memory retrieval, although this involved some painful reliving of the events. However, there were so many layers of experience to unfold, and as both my father and uncle remarked, "every day is a story in itself."

In the course of the research I attempted to mitigate potential problems of *internal validity*, that is, to ascertain as much as possible whether the factual components of their account such as dates of particular events, travel distances, and the like were accurate. In my father's case, I was able to compare elements of his Auschwitz account by referring to the writings of other Auschwitz survivors.[115] On a trip to Poland in 1989—the first time my father had returned to his homeland since the war—I also had an opportunity to interview a Polish couple, Taduesz and Maria Duchowski, who had provided my uncle with assistance that helped him pass as a Catholic Pole.[116] Both of them corroborated my uncle's account and even contributed details he had forgotten. They also corroborated my father and uncle's account of the Nazi occupation of Krosno and of the liquidation of the Jewish people who once lived there. In addition, I consulted other published sources that are relevant to their experiences.[117]

External validity is another concern in life history research, in this case the question of whether my father and uncle's account is representative of other survivors' experiences. My father and uncle did not have the literary skills, professional training (e.g., psychiatry), or religious commitments of authors of some of the most well-known survivor accounts.[118] Nor were they among the more elite members of the camps or those who were privy to the inner workings of resistance efforts. Nevertheless, their very survival is *prima facie* evidence of the expertise they acquire about the phenomenon of survival, and their understanding of what transpired is as valid as anyone else's. They are extraordinary only in the sense that they are among a minority of Polish Jewry (10 percent) who managed to survive the war.[119]

Additionally, there is no reason to assume that other accounts written at the time (e.g., diaries or letters) more accurately represent what transpired than those remembered years later. Although the former representations are often perceived as more authoritative than those "shaped through hindsight, … [they] may be less reliable in a 'factual sense' because of their proximity to the events."[120] They may have been written to elicit particular responses to what was occurring (e.g., to move allies or potential victims to action) or to disguise information (e.g., regarding resistance efforts) that the writer feared might fall into the wrong hands. In any case, Geoffrey Hartman suggests that we "not try to turn the survivor into a historian, but to value him [or her] as a witness to a dehumanizing situation."[121]

Ann Goetting argues that biography is "not simply a 'true' representation of an objective 'reality'" but an incomplete reconstruction of a remembered past that is inevitably marked by a degree of distortion due to the fallibility of memory and the subjectivity of perception.[122] Just as "two people telling a story about the same event may tell it differently," any one person may tell his or her story differently at different points in their lives.[123] If a story of a person's life is told honestly, to the best of his or her ability, it may be the closest approximation to the truth he or she can muster, but it is not the invariant "truth" of what happened. My father and uncle, like other survivors, reconstructed their experience "from the context of normality *now*" and at times had difficulty finding the words to describe "the nature of the abnormality *then*."[124] But this makes their account no less authentic, because how they grasped and related "their experiences comprises the actual core of 'their story.'"[125] In spite of their suffering and deep (though often repressed) sense of family loss, they were able to think rationally about what occurred (though at times with sadness and anger) and assimilate their experiences in a way that allowed them to move forward with their lives.[126] Denzin cautions that the "reactive effects of the observer" need to be monitored in life history research.[127] The potential for bias may be of concern in this case because the subjects are relatives. This problem is often present in life history research, where it is not unusual for subjects and observers to become close friends. However, I do not believe that either my father or uncle would have been willing (especially in the pre-*Schindler's List* period) to have focused in as much detail about their experiences if the interviews had been conducted by an "outsider." Although I felt able to maintain the role of the professional interviewer, I took seriously Nora Levin's concern that survivors not be forced to suffer their experiences "once literally and then imaginatively again."[128] I was thus cautious when probing them in ways that elicited the emotional pain of memory. I felt it important to respect the "protective shield" that had helped them restore themselves to the normality of prewar and postwar life and not push them too far to relive their anguish for the purpose of a more nuanced analysis of the subjective experience of trauma.[129] As Denzin reminds us, "our primary obligation is always to the people we study, not to our project … or discipline. … [Their] lives and stories … are given to us under a promise that we protect those who have shared with us."[130]

My father told me that the experience had "hardened" him and that he got "choked up" only when he thought about the loss of his family. My uncle said that "there is no other experience like it. It stays with you for the rest of your life. Years ago I couldn't talk about it without crying. But now I can finally deal with it." Both of them were pleased to finally have the opportunity to tell their story to interested listeners and to know that there would be a permanent record of what happened to them and their family. My father said that the recounting was a welcomed "outlet" that helped him relieve the burden of [his] memory." He started serving as a docent at the Simon Wiesenthal Center's Museum of Tolerance in Los Angeles,[131] and he began speaking to students (from middle school to college) in various educational settings.

My uncle was initially more reluctant to speak in public, in part because he felt that he was not an authentic representative of the survivor experience because he had not been in a concentration camp. But when my father was dying of lung cancer at the end of 1994, he asked my uncle to promise him two things: help my mother take care of her financial affairs; and take his place as our family's representative of the Holocaust. Since that time, and to this very day—my uncle is ninety years old at the time of this writing—he speaks publicly in a variety of venues. He has videotaped his story for both the Spielberg Shoah Foundation and the Jewish Federation of Los Angeles; and he was one of the survivors who was featured in the audio production *Voices of the Shoah: Remembrances of the Holocaust*, which was broadcast on national radio in 2000.[132] He also finally returned to Poland himself in 2008, and he has made additional video-recordings, with the help of his daughter and son, about his experiences both during the war and after arriving in the United States. In addition, my uncle introduced me to Dr. Alexander White, also a survivor and a childhood friend of my father's who was living in Scottsdale, Arizona. We spoke on the phone and communicated by e-mail, and he sent me his self-published memoir and referred me to other Polish sources that provided additional information about what happened in their hometown.[133]

Henry Greenspan observes that the telling of survivors' stories is an ongoing process and a collaborative project for both survivors and listeners.[134] As the history of silence about the Holocaust shows, survivors cannot tell their stories if we're not ready to listen. But if we are ready to listen, our lives will be enriched in the telling. Moreover, as Hartman notes, "Every time we retrieve an oral history … [we create] a line of resistance against" the erasure of memory.[135]

DISCUSSION QUESTIONS

1. How could a life course perspective be applied to another topic of sociological interest? Provide an example.

2. Berger describes people who were unaware of the Holocaust until they learned of the event in college. Have you had a similar experience with any other historical events? Find information about the debate that goes into what information should be included in history textbooks. What do you think about this process of constructing history?

3. How do popular events like the success of Steven Spielberg's *Schindler's List* and the opening of the United States Holocaust memorial Museum shape public perception of the Holocaust? How does this differ from the role of more academic oriented books or documentaries in shaping public perception of the Holocaust?

4. Why are first-hand accounts of events like the Holocaust important? How does this relate to the practice of ethnography and interviewing within sociology and other social science disciplines?

NOTES

1. Quoted in Lanzmann, *Shoah*, pp. 145–146. The Sonderkommando was the special detail of concentration camp prisoners who worked in the gas chambers and crematoria. See also Müller, *Eyewitness Auschwitz*.

2. Although Elie Wiesel was not the first to use the term "Holocaust," he is credited with bringing it into popular discourse when he began using it in print in the late 1950s. It has its etymological roots in Greek and the Greek translation of the Hebrew Bible, where the terms *holokaustos, holokaustuma*, and *holokaustosis* (based on the Hebrew *ólah*) were used to refer to a sacrificial burnt offering made to God. For this reason, some people object to it being used to describe the genocide of the Jews. It is now generally understood to mean total destruction by fire, thus alluding to the open-air pits and crematoria that the Nazis used to dispose of the dead bodies of Jews (see Garber, *Shoah*; Novick, *The Holocaust in American Life*; and Rubenstein and Roth, *Approaches to Auschwitz* [2003]).

3. Gonzales, *Deep Survival*, pp. 13, 24, 27.

4. Sherwood, *The Survivors Club*, pp. 15-16. Readers of this book are also directed to The Survivors Club website at www.thesuvivorsclub.org, where survivors can share their stories, create support groups, and get advice on family, health, and financial matters.

5. Cultural critic Christopher Lasch (*The Minimal Self*) was among the first to make this observation. See also Greenspan, *On Listening to Holocaust Survivors*.

6. Wendy Kaminer makes this observation about adult children of alcoholics (*I'm Dysfunctional, You're Dysfunctional*); and Peter Novick about abortion, AIDS, and animal rights (*The Holocaust in American Life*). Feminists Betty Friedan (*The Feminist Mystique*), Mary Daley (*Gyn/Ecology*), and Andrea Dworkin (*Pornography*) have also used Nazi metaphors to describe women's subordination in society. In her memoir *Life So Far*, Friedan expressed regret for her use of this analogy. Both Israelis and Palestinians have used such metaphors to characterize the threat posed by each other (Anti-Defamation League, *Hitler's Apologists*. Novick, *The Holocaust in American Life*. Roiphe, *A Season for Healing*. Segev, *The Seventh Million*), as have Americans of both the political Left and political Right, most recently, right-wing critics of President Barack Obama (Gerson, "At the Town Halls, Trivializing Evil"). Christian evangelical preacher Pat Robertson has even gone so far as to suggest: "Just what Nazi Germany did to the Jews, so liberal America is now doing to evangelical Christians" (quoted in Rosenfeld, "The Americanization of the Holocaust," p. 135).
7. Bettelheim, *The Informed Heart*. Bloch, "The Personality of Inmates in Concentration Camps." E. Cohen, *Human Behavior in the Concentration Camp*.
8. Levi, *Survival in Auschwitz*. Wiesel, *Night*.
9. Lifton, *Death in Life*.
10. Lifton, "The Concept of the Survivor," pp. 113-114.
11. Ibid., pp. 113, 117, my emphasis.
12. Des Pres, *The Survivor*, p. v, 6-8.
13. Des Pres offers examples from classic fictional literature.
14. Life course theory as a sociological perspective traces its sociological roots to the pioneering study, *The Polish Peasant in Europe and America*, by W. I. Thomas and Florian Znaniecki. Although it is an interdisciplinary field of inquiry, sociologist Glen Elder is arguably its most prominent figure. See Elder, "The Life Course Paradigm"; Elder, Monica, and Crosnoe, "The Emergence and Development of Life Course Theory"; Giele and Elder, "Life Course Research"; and Settersten, "Propositions and Controversies in Life-Course Scholarship."
15. Elder et al., "The Emergence and Development of Life Course Theory," p. 4.
16. Jeffrey Alexander was among the first sociologists to argue for a general theory of this nature, which he framed as a matter of "action" and "order," that could illuminate problems of the most ramifying and empirical characters (*Action and Its Environments*, p. 224, and *Theoretical Logic in Sociology*).
17. Langer, *Holocaust Testimonies*, p. 199.
18. On the concept of cohort and the distinction between cohort and generation, see Alwin and McCammon; "Generations, Cohorts, and Social Change"; Cain, "Age-Related Phenomena"; Elder and Pellerin, "Linking History and Human Lives"; and Settersten, "Propositions and Contoversies in Life-Course Scholarship."
19. J. Alexander et al., *Cultural Trauma and Collective Identity*.
20. A. Berger, *Children of Job*. R. Berger, "To Be or Not to Be." Epstein, *Children of the Holocaust*. Fogelman, "Survivors. Fox, *Inherited Memories*. Hass, *In the Shadow of the Holocaust*. Hoffman, *After Such Knowledge*. Wardi, *Memorial Candles*. Stein, "Trauma and Origins."
21. Elder et al., "The Emergence and Development of Life Course Theory," p. 13.
22. Couch, "Collective Witness."
23. Rosenbloom, "Lessons of the Holocaust for Mental Health Practice," p. 158.
24. Halbwachs, *The Collective Memory*, and *On Collective Memory*.

25. Hass, *The Aftermath*. Novick, *The Holocaust in American Life*.

26. For discussions of this film, which I consider further in Chapter 8, see Cole, *Selling the Holocaust*; Doneson, *The Holocaust in American Film*; Levy and Sznaider, *The Holocaust and Memory in the Global Age*; Novick, *The Holocaust in American Life*; Shandler, "Schindler's Discourse." For a review of the broader corpus of Holocaust films, see Insdorf, *Indelible Shadows*.

27. For discussions of I.G. Farben, see Borkin, *The Crime and Punishment of I.G. Farben*; Hayes, *Industry and Ideology*; Pingel, "I.G. Farben"; and Steinbacher, *Auschwitz*.

28. Epstein, *Children of Survivors*. See also note 20 above.

29. Fogelman, "Survivors." On the more general interest in roots and genealogy, see also Erben "Genealogy and Sociology"; Frerking, "Look Homeward Boomers"; Gans, "Symbolic Ethnicity"; and Stein, "Trauma and Origins."

30. Haley, *Roots*.

31. Settersten, "Propositions and Controversies in Life-Course Scholarship."

32. Anti-Defamation League, *Hitler's Apologists*. Lipstadt, *Denying the Holocaust*. Shermer and Grobman, *Denying History*. Vidal-Naquet, *Assassins of Memory*. Wistrich, "Holocaust Denial."

33. Gans, "Symbolic Ethnicity," p. 9.

34. For discussions of sociology's neglect of the Holocaust, see Baehr, "Identifying the Unprecedented"; Bauman, *Modernity and the Holocaust*; Gerson and Wolf, *Sociology Confronts the Holocaust*; and Halpert, "Early American Sociology and the Holocaust."

35. Freeman, "The Theory and Prevention of Genocide," p. 187.

36. Markle et al., "From Auschwitz to Americana," p. 200.

37. Bauer, "Is the Holocaust Explicable?" Marrus, *The Holocaust in History*.

38. Davidson, *Holding on to Humanity*, p. 24. See also Hoffman, *After Such Knowledge*.

39. J. Alexander, "On the Social Construction of Moral Universals," pp. 197, 199.

40. Hilberg, "Opening Remarks."

41. Novick, *The Holocaust in American Life*.

42. Shirer, *The Rise and Fall of the Third Reich*.

43. J. Alexander, "On the Social Construction of Moral Universals," p. 209.

44. Hilberg, *The Politics of Memory*.

45. Wiesel, *All Rivers Run to the Sea*.

46. E. Alexander, *The Holocaust and the War of Ideas*. Doneson, "The American History of Anne Frank's Diary." Levy and Sznaider, *The Holocaust and Memory in the Global Age*. Novick, *The Holocaust in American Life*. Rosenfeld, "The Americanization of the Holocaust."

47. Quoted in Rosenfeld, "The Americanization of the Holocaust," pp. 254, 257.

48. Davidson, *Holding on to Humanity*. Friedlander, "Trauma, Transference, and 'Working Through' in Writing the History of the Shoah."

49. Davidson, *Holding on to Humanity*, pp. 14–15, 149, 207.

50. Cole, *Selling the Holocaust*. Davidson, *Holding on to Humanity*. Hass, *The Aftermath*. Levy and Sznaider, *The Holocaust and Memory in the Global Age*. Novick, *The Holocaust in American Life*. Segev, *The Seventh Million*. Shapira, "The Holocaust and World War II as Elements of the Yishuv Psyche until 1948." Young, *The Texture of Memory*.

51. Davidson, *Holding on to Humanity*, p. 20.

52. Bach, "Eichmann Trial." Yablonka, "Eichmann Trial."

53. Quoted in Segev, *The Seventh Million*, p. 353.

54. Schmitt, "Sharing the Holocaust, p. 247.

55. Miller, *One by One, by One*, p. 223. I will discuss this further in Chapter 8.

56. R. Berger, *Fathoming the Holocaust*. Cole, *Selling the Holocaust*. Finkelstein, *The Holocaust Industry*. Freedman, *Jew vs. Jew*. Novick, *The Holocaust in American Life*.

57. Novick, *The Holocaust in American Life*. Vital, "After the Catastrophe." Young, *The Texture of Memory*.

58. Miller, *One by One, by One*, p. 231.

59. Weissman, *Fantasies of Witnessing*.

60. Outright Holocaust denial is arguably the greatest source of concern (see note 32 above).

61. R. Berger, *Fathoming the Holocaust*. Hartman, *Bitburg in Moral and Political Perspective*. Marcuse, *Legacies of Dachau*. Markle and McCrea, "Forgetting and Remembering." Schmitt, "Sharing the Holocaust."

62. Quoted in Miller, *One by One, by One*, p. 47.

63. Quoted in Hartman, *Bitburg in Moral and Political Perspective*, pp. xiv, 5.

64. Quoted in Rosenfeld, "The Americanization of the Holocaust, pp. 139-140.

65. Linenthal, *Preserving Memory*, p. 2. See also R. Berger, "It Ain't Necessarily So."

66. The Fortunoff Video Archive, founded in 1979 and housed at Yale University in 1984, preceded the project sponsored by Spielberg.

67. Quoted in Miller, *One by One, by One*, p. 220.

68. Des Pres, *The Survivor*. Hass, *The Aftermath*. Helmreich, *Against All Odds*. Holocaust Educational Foundation Volunteers, "Tellers and Listeners." Kraft, *Memory Perceived*. Langer, *Holocaust Testimonies*. Mack, *The Alchemy of Survival*. Rothschild, *Voices from the Holocaust*.

69. Markle et al., "From Auschwitz to Americana," p. 200.

70. Kovner, a prize-winning poet from Vilna, Lithuania, "led one of the first Jewish resistance organizations in the ghettos of eastern Europe" (Rubenstein and Roth, *Approaches to Auschwitz* ([2003], p. 217). Kovner later regretted the remark for the way it was used as a code for negative stereotyping of Jews.

71. Arendt, *Eichmann in Jerusalem*. Hilberg, *The Destruction of the European Jews*.

72. Bettelheim, *The Informed Heart*. For a discussion of Bettelheim's thesis and the critical response to it, see Bartrop, *Surviving the Camps*.

73. Bloch, "The Personality of Inmates in Concentration Camps." E. Cohen, *Human Behavior in the Concentration Camp*. Des Pres, *The Survivor*. Frankl, *Man's Search for Meaning*. Levi, *Survival in Auschwitz*. Lifton, "The Concept of the Survivor." Marrus, *The Holocaust in History*. Wiesel, *Night*. The

74. Helmreich, *Against All Odds*, p. 14. See Chodoff, "Psychotherapy of the Survivor"; Davidson, *Holding on to Humanity*; Eitinger, "The Concentration Camp Syndrome and Its Late Sequelae"; Lifton, "The Concept of the Survivor"; and Wiesel, *Night*.

75. Des Pres, *The Survivor*.

76. Bartrop, *Surviving the Camps*. Benner et al., "Stress and Coping Under Extreme Conditions." Des Pres, *The Survivor*. Dimsdale, "The Coping Behavior of Nazi Concentration Camp Survivors." Kraft, *Memory Perceived*. Luchterhand, "Prisoner Behavior and Social System in the Nazi Concentration Camp." Pingel, "The Destruction of Human Identity in Concentration Camps." Shostak, "Humanist Sociology and Holocaust Memorialization." Unger, "The Prisoner's First Encounter with Auschwitz."

77. Pawełczyńska, *Values and Violence in Auschwitz*, p. 144.

78. Gallant and Cross, "Surviving Destruction of the Self." See also Gallant, *Coming of Age in the Holocaust*.

79. Davidson, *Holding on to Humanity*, p. 121.

80. Des Pres, *The Survivor*, p. 201.

81. Botz, *I Want to Speak*. Unger, "The Prisoner's First Encounter with Auschwitz."

82. Helmreich, *Against All Odds*, p. 111.

83. Frankl, *Man's Search for Meaning*, p. 87.

84. Langer, *Holocaust Testimonies*, p. 183.

85. Ibid., critiquing Martin Gilbert's *The Holocaust*.

86. Langer, *Holocaust Testimonies*, p. 180.

87. Brenner et al, "Stress and Coping Under Extreme Conditions," pp. 219, 235-236, 238 (emphases mine). See also Dimsdale, "The Coping Behavior of Nazi Concentration Camp Survivors."

88. Settersten, "Propositions and Controversies in Life-Course Scholarship."

89. Ibid., p. 30.

90. Sewell, "A Theory of Structure," p. 21 (see also note 16 above).

91. Bandura, *Self-Efficacy*. Gecas, "Self-Agency and the Life Course," and "The Social Psychology of Self-Efficacy." Maddux, *Self-Efficacy, Adaptation, and Adjustment*.

92. Giddens, *The Constitution of Society*, "Reply to My Critics." Sewell, *"A Theory of Structure."* This conception of social structure is similar to the one found in the literature on social capital (Field, *Social Capital*. Halperin, *Social Capital*).

93. Sewell, "A Theory of Structure," pp. 4, 20.

94. Hilberg, *Perpetrators, Victims, and Bystanders*, pp. 159, 188.

95. Sewell, "A Theory of Structure," p. 21.

96. Des Pres, *The Survivor*. Pawełczyńska, *Values and Violence in Auschwitz*.

97. R. Berger et al. "Altruism Amidst the Holocaust." Oliner and Oliner, *The Altruistic Personality*. Paldiel, *Sheltering the Jews*. Tec, *When Light Pierced the Darkness*.

98. Giddens, *The Constitution of Society*.

99. Denzin, *The Research Act in Sociology* (1989), p. 5.

100. Denzin, *Interpretive Biography*, and *Interpretive Interactionism*.

101. Sartre, *Being and Nothingness*, p. 457

102. Turner, "Dewey, Dilthey, and Drama."

103. Giele and Elder, "Life Course Research."

104. Goetting, "Fictions of the Self," p. 5.

105. Mills, *The Sociological Imagination*.

106. Alexander, *Action and Its Environments*, p. 25.

107. Denzin, *Interpretive Biography*, pp. 48, 82.

108. In addition to my father and uncle's testimony, sources on Krosno used in this book include: Kagan, *Poland's Jewish Heritage*; Leibner, "Jewish Inhabitants of Krosno, Galicia, Poland Prior and During WWII," "Historical and Genealogical Sources for the Krosno Area," "The History of Krosno," and "Krosno, Poland"; and White, *Be a Mensch*.

109. Helling, "The Life History Method," p. 223. The formal properties of the "narrative interview" approach were first outlined by the German sociologist Fritz Schutze. For discussions in English,

see Helling and Flick, *An Introduction to Qualitative Research.* I did not adopt this approach *in toto*, but only as a general methodological orientation.

110. Holocaust Educational Foundation Volunteers, "Tellers and Listeners." Robinson, "Temporal Reference Systems and Autobiographical Memory."

111. Denzin, *Interpretive Biography*, p. 17.

112. Brewer, "What is Autobiographical Memory?" Denzin (*Interpretive Interactionism*) distinguishes four types of epiphanies: major, minor, cumulative, and relived epiphanies.

113. Langer, *Holocaust Testimonies*, p. xv.

114. My father also recalled with anger President John Kennedy's 1962 visit to Germany, where he declared, *"Ich bin ein Berliner."* But I believe the most important emotional reminders in my father and uncle's case were the State of Israel itself and the threat they perceived to its wellbeing, as well as their awareness of those who deny the Holocaust altogether.

115. Frankel, *I Survived Hell.* Levi, *Survival in Auschwitz.* Nahon, *Birkenau.* Wiesel, *Night.*

116. They spoke in Polish, and my father served as the translator.

117. See especially Gutman, *Encyclopedia of the Holocaust.*

118. For example, see Frankl, *Man's Search for Meaning*; Levi, *Survival in Auschwitz*; and Wiesel, *Night.*

119. Gutman and Rozett, "Estimated Jewish Losses in the Holocaust."

120. Young, *Writing and Rewriting the Holocaust*, pp. 25, 33.

121. Hartman, "Learning from Survivors," p. 1714.

122. Goetting, "Fictions of the Self," p. 13.

123. Atkinson, *The Life Story Interview*, p. 60.

124. Langer, *Holocaust Testimonies*, p. 22. Langer distinguishes between *common memory*, the structured narrative as seen through the eyes of the present, and *deep memory*, the emotionally laden unstructured reliving of the event that provides the raw material of common memory. See also Kraft, *Memory Perceived.*

125. Young, *Writing and Rewriting the Holocaust*, p. 39. See also Atkinison, *The Life Story Interview*; Greenspan, *On Listening to Holocaust Survivors*; Goetting, "Fictions of the Self "; and Gusdorf, "Conditions and Limits of Autobiography."

126. Davidson (*Holding on to Humanity*) notes that "in the life cycle of individuals who experienced the Holocaust, the passage of forty years enabled many … to arrive at a degree of emotional distance that allowed a greater recalling of traumatic memories without the agonizing pain that a time close to the events brought" (p. 22). See also Hass, *The Aftermath*; and Helmreich, *Against All Odds.*

127. Denzin, *The Research Act in Sociology* (1970), p. 243.

128. Levin, "Some Reservations about Lanzmann's Shoah," p. 92.

129. Friedlander, "Trauma, Transference, and 'Working Through' in Writing the History of the Shoah," p. 51. This raises the methodological question of reliability, that is, whether another interviewer would have uncovered different elements of the life story. I do believe, nonetheless, that another researcher would have reached the same conclusions regarding the data that was generated by my interviews.

130. Denzin, *Interpretive Biography*, p. 83.

131. The Museum of Tolerance, which opened two months after the Washington, D.C. museum, has a section preceding its Holocaust exhibit that situates the Holocaust in the context of other human rights abuses around the world and details the civil rights struggle of African Americans in the

United States. See R. Berger, *Fathoming the Holocaust*; Rabinbach, "From Explosion to Erosion; and Rosenfeld, "The Americanization of the Holocaust."

132. David Notowitz produced the documentary for Rhino Records (Los Angeles, CA). On February 16, 2009, Sol was also featured in a front-page story called "The Selves He'd Left Behind" written by Tami Abdollah for the *Los Angeles Times*.

133. See note 108 above.

134. Greenspan, *On Listening to Holocaust Survivors*.

135. Hartman, "Public Memory and Modern Experience," p. 245.

Race, Class, and Bachelor's Degree Completion in American Higher Education

Examining the Role of Life Course Transitions

By Josipa Roksa

T he 20th century was the century of access—the massive expansion of higher education facilitated transition to college for ever growing proportions of high school graduates. Policymakers focused on opening doors to college opportunities while scholars studied enrollment patterns, and in particular, how they varied across students from different sociodemographic groups (see Arum, Shavit, and Gamoran chapter in this volume). In the early 21st century, completion has become a pressing issue. President Obama noted in his first speech to a joint session of Congress in February 2009: "In a global economy where the most valuable skill you can sell is your knowledge, a good education is no longer just a pathway to opportunity—it is a pre-requisite." And he made the commitment that: "We will provide the support necessary for you to complete college and meet a new goal: by 2020, America will once again have the highest proportion of college graduates in the world."

Focus on completion comes amid recent reports suggesting that the United States is losing ground in comparison to other nations. Drawing on Organisation for Economic Co-operation and Development (OECD) data, Goldin and Katz (2008) reported that the United States has the highest share of college graduates among those aged 55 to 64 but trails behind 12 nations on 4-year college graduation rates for young people (those under 25). Similarly, considering educational attainment measured by the mean years of schooling completed for individuals 25 to 34 years old, the United States ranks 11th out of 30 countries for males and 10th for females. Although some observers have questioned these international comparisons (e.g., Adelman, 2009), even looking at the trends at home suggests a slowdown in the supply of college graduates over time (see Goldin & Katz, 2008). Between the high school class of 1972 and 1992, the rate of entry into higher education increased from 48% to 71% while the bachelor's degree completion rate decreased: 51% of the class of 1972 and 46% of the class of 1992 graduated with a bachelor's degree within 8 years (Bound, Lovenheim, & Turner, 2009). Similarly, considering educational attainment of different birth cohorts reveals that over the course of the 20th century the proportion of young adults with some college has increased, but the proportion with bachelor's degrees has at best remained stable (Turner, 2004).

The rates of college completion are not only low and stagnating, they are also highly unequal. While the actual percentages vary depending on the specific samples examined (e.g., high school graduates or college entrants; specific age groups or all first-time college entrants; students who enroll in 2-year vs. 4-year institutions), inequalities by race/ethnicity and social class are clearly evident. Among traditional-age students who enter higher education, approximately half of White students complete bachelor's degrees within approximately 8 years of high school graduation (Table 3.1). At the same time,

Table 3.1: Percentage of Students Completing Bachelor's Degrees

DATASET SAMPLE	NELS HIGH SCHOOL SOPHOMORES	NELS POSTSECONDARY ENTRANTS	BPS FIRST-TIME POSTSECONDARY ENTRANTS, 2YR INSTITUTIONS	BPS FIRST-TIME POSTSECONDARY ENTRANTS, 4YR INSTITUTIONS
Race/ethnicity				
African American	16.40	30.80	3.20	43.40
Hispanic	11.60	23.10	5.50	44.00
Asian/Pacific Islander	46.10	52.20	7.40	69.10
White	33.30	48.30	11.40	61.90
Parental education				
High school or less			6.00	43.10
No high school	5.90	16.30		
High school	13.30	25.60		
Some postsecondary	25.70	35.80	8.40	50.90
Bachelor's degree	49.40	58.00	16.20	66.30
Advanced degree			25.20	73.90
Master's	65.40	73.30		
Professional/doctorate	73.30	79.80		

Source: Column 1: Digest of Education Statistics, 2009, Table 326; Column 2: Author's calculations based on NELS; Columns 3 and 4: Digest of Education Statistics, 2009, Table 332.

Notes: NELS refers to the National Education Longitudinal Study of 1988, which began with a nationally representative sample of 8th graders in 1988 and followed through 2000.
BPS refers to the Beginning Postsecondary Students Longitudinal Study, which began with a nationally representative sample of first-time postsecondary entrants in 1995-1996 and followed through 2001.

less than one-third of African American students and less than one-quarter of Hispanic students attain the same level of education. Similarly, while approximately three-quarters of students whose parents hold advanced degrees complete bachelor's degrees, less than a quarter of those whose parents have no college experience complete these credentials.

Scholars have dedicated much more attention to understanding inequalities in access to higher education than in the likelihood of degree completion (Goldrick-Rab & Roksa, 2008). However, as Table 3.1 illustrates, entry into higher education far from guarantees completion, and students from racial/ethnic minority groups and less advantaged family backgrounds are less likely to leave their postsecondary journeys with a degree in hand.[1] Considering these inequalities in degree completion and recent demographic trends, Bowen and his colleagues (Bowen, Chingos, & McPherson, 2009) have argued that increasing the proportion of the U.S. population holding college degrees rests on improving outcomes for students from racial/ethnic minority groups and less advantaged family backgrounds. It is thus crucial to understand what factors contribute to the lower likelihood of degree completion of these disadvantaged groups, even after they pass the hurdle of entry into higher education.

When previous studies have considered inequalities in degree completion, they have often focused on differences with which students enter higher education, particularly academic preparation. Regardless of whether academic preparation is assessed through test scores, high school tracks, or completion of specific courses or curricula, students from disadvantaged family backgrounds and racial/ethnic minority groups fare worse than those from more advantaged groups (Adelman, 1999, 2006; Grodsky, Warren, & Felts, 2008; Kelly, 2007; Lucas, 2001). Academic preparation thus clearly plays an important role in explaining inequalities in degree completion. However, the probability of success is not determined at entry; it is also shaped by what students do after they enroll in postsecondary institutions. In this chapter, I focus on one set of relevant activities that have garnered increasing attention in the higher education discourse: transitions into roles typically associated with adulthood, such as work, marriage, and parenthood. This study addresses two related questions: Do transitions into social roles typically associated with adulthood vary across students from different socioeconomic and racial/ethnic backgrounds? Moreover, do they contribute to the observed racial/ethnic and socioeconomic gaps in degree completion?

LIFE COURSE TRANSITIONS AND DEGREE COMPLETION

By the time students enter higher education, they enter the phase of the life course when they are increasingly likely to make transitions into roles typically associated with adulthood, such as work, marriage, and parenthood. As individuals stay in school longer and as growing proportions of high school graduates, including those from less advantaged groups, enter higher education, schooling is becoming increasingly intertwined with the traditional markers of adulthood (e.g., see reviews in O'Rand, 2000; Shanahan, 2000). Only approximately one quarter of young adults today follow the traditional sequence of transitions to adulthood, characterized by the completion of schooling, followed by finding full-time work, getting married, and having children (Mouw, 2005). Many others alternate or combine schooling with work, marriage, and parenthood (Pallas, 1993). There is thus no single transition from school to work, nor does postsecondary entry preclude transition into family roles. "Transition" by no means implies a final state: students can transition in and out of different social roles as well as pursue them simultaneously or in different sequences.

While this flexibility in life course transitions may be applauded for signaling an absence of rigid norms and allowing individuals to chart their own trajectories, it appears not to be without consequences. Previous research suggests that employment, particularly at high intensities (such as working full-time), is negatively associated with a range of educational outcomes, including degree completion (for reviews, see Pascarella & Terenzini, 2005; Riggert, Boyle, Petrosko, Ash, & Rude-Parkins, 2006). Similarly, students who transition into family roles, and particularly those who have children, have a lower likelihood of degree completion (Bozick & DeLuca, 2005; Jacobs & King, 2002; Roksa & Velez, 2012; Taniguchi & Kaufman, 2005). And indeed, when students who leave higher education are surveyed about their reasons for departure, 50% indicate that they have left for reasons related to family or work (e.g., need to work, conflicts with job/military, change in family status, or conflicts at home) (National Center for Education Statistics [NCES], 2003).

Given the negative association between life course transitions and degree completion, an important question is whether the likelihood of making these transitions varies across racial/ethnic and socioeconomic groups. Previous research is remarkably silent on this point. While many scholars have considered the overall patterns of life course transitions, they have rarely examined variation across sociodemographic groups. The extensiveness of employment in particular has been well documented, with nearly 80% of traditional-age undergraduates working while enrolled in college, and over a quarter of them working full-time (National Center for Education Statistics [NCES], 2002). A much smaller, but substantial, proportion of traditional-age students also transition into marriage or parenthood before or during the pursuit of higher education (Bozick & DeLuca, 2005; Goldrick-Rab & Han, 2011). Only a few studies have considered whether these patterns of transitions into work, marriage, and parenthood vary across sociodemographic groups after students enter higher education, and they have produced contradictory results. For example, some studies have found a relationship between family background and employment patterns (Cooksey & Rindfuss, 2001; NCES, 2002; Roksa & Velez, 2010) while others have not (Bozick, 2007).

Whether transitions into roles typically associated with adulthood vary across sociodemographic groups and whether they contribute to inequalities in degree completion are important questions to address. Students' commitment to the labor market has been on the rise, both in terms of the percentage of students working and the number of hours spent in the labor market (ScottClayton, 2007). Rising tuition, decreasing grant aid, and increasing reliance on loans, have made work an important feature of the higher education landscape. Since students from less advantaged family backgrounds and racial/ethnic minority groups are more reliant on financial aid, employment is likely to play a more prominent role in their journeys through college. Similarly, given the broad patterns of stratification with respect to marriage and parenthood in the society at large, those factors are important to consider when explaining socioeconomic and racial/ethnic gaps in degree completion. Throughout the educational system, students from less advantaged groups follow less favorable pathways, whether researchers examine access to different tracks or institutional types. Does this pattern persist into higher education, leading students from disadvantaged backgrounds to follow less educationally beneficial life course patterns, ones which include transitioning into roles typically associated with adulthood? I address this question and illuminate the contribution of life course transitions to the racial/ethnic and socioeconomic inequalities in degree completion.

DATA AND ANALYTIC STRATEGY

To examine whether life course transitions vary across sociodemographic groups and whether they contribute to the lower likelihood of degree completion among students from less advantaged family backgrounds and racial/ethnic minority groups, I use data from the National Longitudinal Survey of Youth of 1997 (NLSY97; U.S. Department of Labor, 2007), a nationally representative sample of individuals born between 1980 and 1984 (ages 12–16 years as of December 31, 1996). The baseline survey was administered in 1997 to 8,984 individuals in 6,819 households, who were selected using a multistage stratified random sampling design. Respondents have been reinterviewed annually, with the latest available follow-up conducted in 2007. This dataset presents a recent sample of young adults and provides detailed information on schooling and transitions into roles typically associated with adulthood (i.e., work, marriage, and parenthood).

I begin by presenting descriptive results for students' transitions into work, marriage, and parenthood. I consider variation in these transitions for students from different family backgrounds and racial/ethnic groups. Family background is captured by two variables: parental education and income. Parental education is coded as the highest level completed by either resident parent, and is divided into four categories: no college (i.e., high school or less), some college, bachelor's degree, and graduate/professional degree. Income reflects the total household income, and due to the highly skewed distribution is divided into four quartiles. Since the two dimensions of family background reveal similar patterns, the descriptive patterns focus on variation by parental education. Race/ethnicity is represented by four categories: White, African American, Hispanic, and other racial/ethnic groups.

I explore variation in racial/ethnic and socioeconomic patterns of transition into three distinct roles typically associated with adulthood: work, marriage/cohabitation, and parenthood. Once an individual becomes a parent, she or he continues to have this role designation, but the other two roles, particularly employment, are reversible. Students can go frequently in and out of the labor market. Consequently, all variables denoting life course transitions are coded as time-varying for every month that the student is in the dataset. Family transition roles—marriage/cohabitation and parenthood—are coded as dummy variables indicating whether respondents are married/cohabitating and whether they have any children. Marriage and cohabitation are combined due to the age of the respondents. Cohabitation has been on the rise over time, with the majority of young women and men today spending some time in cohabitating relationships (Scommegna, 2002). Individuals in their late teens and early 20s, what Arnett (2004) termed "emerging adults," are particularly likely to engage in more transitional forms of behaviors, such as cohabitation. Thus, in the sample examined, cohabitation was more prevalent than marriage. Among students who entered college, 4% were cohabiting and 2% were married in their first month. Both forms of union formation increased over time: approximately 4 years after college entry, 11% of respondents were married and 13% were cohabitating.

Employment is divided into three categories: low intensity (up to 20 hours per week), moderate intensity (21–35 hours per week), and high intensity (over 35 hours per week), with students who are not working serving as a reference. The high intensity employment category captures students who are working full-time, which is one of the markers of transition to adulthood. Since simply contrasting full-time and non-full-time work would not capture the potential differences in gradations of work hours noted in previous studies, I also include dummy variables for moderate and low intensity employment. Most financial aid programs restrict student work to 20 hours per week, making that the logical choice for the boundary of low intensity work. Moreover, working at high intensity in a given month may not be as consequential as working intensely for an extended period of time. Previous studies have shown that specific *patterns* of employment are related to student success (e.g., Mortimer 2003; Staff & Mortimer, 2007). Instead of considering only whether students are working in a particular month, I examine the cumulative number of months students spend in different employment categories.

Following descriptive results, I estimate a series of discrete time event history models (Allison, 1984; Singer & Willett, 2003) to examine the extent to which different factors, including transition into family and employment roles, are related to degree completion and help to account for racial/ethnic and socioeconomic gaps in completion. A discrete time event history model is preferred to a regular logistic regression due to a large number of right censored cases and the importance of including time-varying covariates in estimation. In order to estimate this model, the data file is organized in a person-month format. The person enters the dataset at the point of entry into higher education, and remains "at risk" until they either experience the event (i.e., they complete a bachelor's degree) or exit the sample. The model is thus estimating the risk of bachelor's degree completion in each month, called the hazard, which is the conditional probability that an individual would obtain a bachelor's degree in the time period j, given that she did not do so in an earlier time period. Background variables remain constant through time while variables capturing transitions to adulthood (marriage/cohabitation, children, and work) take on different values in different time periods. The baseline hazard is estimated using a piecewise constant function (Wu, 2003). This specification provides a better fit than either linear or polynomial (square and cubic) specification.

In addition to the key variables of interest, regression models include other demographic controls, including gender and age at entry into higher education, as well as several measures of academic preparation, including test scores (Armed Services Vocational Aptitude Battery; ASVAB), high school grades, and academic track. I also include an indicator of whether students begin postsecondary education in 2-year or 4-year institutions. Although this is not strictly a measure of academic preparation, the two are related, as students who attend 2-year institutions tend to be on average less academically prepared. Moreover, institutional type is related to both social class and life course transitions (Roksa, 2010), which makes it an important factor to consider in presented analyses. Missing data on family background and control variables was dealt with in two steps. First, if the information was missing for a given year, data from the next year was used, not to exceed students' entry into higher education. That step substantially reduced the number of missing cases. The remaining missing data was dealt with using multiple imputation (Allison, 2002). The imputation procedure was based on creating five distinct datasets with imputed values, each of which was analyzed separately and then combined into the reported parameter estimates using SAS PROC MIANALYZE.

TRANSITIONS INTO WORK, MARRIAGE/COHABITATION, AND PARENTHOOD

Due to the weak link between the educational institutions and the labor market in the United States (Kerckhoff, 2000, 2004), students must construct an "individualized amalgam of school and work" (Mortimer & Kruger, 2000). Students develop complex pathways involving school and work, and those pathways vary across sociodemographic groups. Figure 3.1 reports the proportion of college entrants in selected racial/ethnic and family background groups who are working at high and low intensities. Complete results for all groups, with appropriate statistical tests, are reported in the appendix Table 3.A.

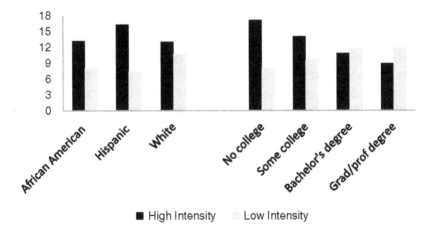

Figure 3.1: Number of months college entrants work at high and low intensities, by selected socio-demographic characteristics. *Source:* Author's calculations based on NLSY97. *Note:* Figure represents cumulative number of months worked at high and low intensities during approximately four years since entr y into higher education.

Although African American students were less likely to report working when they first entered higher education, the gap narrowed over time such that 45 months after entry similar proportions of students from different racial/ethnic backgrounds were employed. However, beneath this similarity of participation in the labor market lies substantial variation in the intensity of employment across groups. White students are more likely to be working at low intensity, and over time spend more time in low-intensity employment (working up to 20 hours per week) than either African American or Hispanic students. Hispanic students spend more time in high-intensity employment, and do so increasingly over time. By 45 months after entry into higher education, only 5% of Hispanic students were working at low intensity and almost 50% of them were working at high intensity. As is evident in Figure 3.1, they thus accumulate the most time in high intensity employment over time.

Differences in employment patterns are even more pronounced among students from different family backgrounds. While employment in the medium intensity category is relatively similar across groups, there is a notable trade-off between the low and high intensity employment that distinguishes students from more and less educated family backgrounds. Only 8% of students whose parents hold graduate/professional degrees work at high intensity one month after entry into higher education, while 22% of students from families without college experience do so. All groups increase their participation in the labor market and intensity of employment over time, but students from less educated families continue to work disproportionately at high intensity. The result of this pattern is an increasing gap between students from different family backgrounds over time. As cumulative measures in Figure 3.1 reveal, students with highly educated parents spend proportionally more time in low intensity employment and less time in high employment than their less advantaged counterparts.

The importance of these patterns is illuminated by considering previous research which has shown that high intensity employment has negative consequences for degree attainment, while low intensity employment is positively associated with educational outcomes, including degree completion (Bozick, 2007; National Center for Education Statistics [NCES], 1998; Staff & Mortimer, 2007). Racial/ethnic minority students and especially students from less advantaged family backgrounds thus spend less time in educationally beneficial types of employment and more time in employment categories that have been associated with negative consequences for educational outcomes. Similarly, previous research has suggested that family transitions, particularly having children, has a negative relationship to degree completion, and as Figure 3.2 shows, family transitions also vary across students from different family backgrounds and racial/ethnic groups. The complete results, including relevant statistical tests, are presented in appendix Table 3.A.

There are pronounced gaps in transitions into marriage/cohabitation and particularly parenthood between students from different family backgrounds, both at entry into higher education, and subsequently. Within 45 months after entry into higher education, very few students (5%) whose parents had graduate/professional degrees had children, while 4 times as many (22%) students whose parents had no college

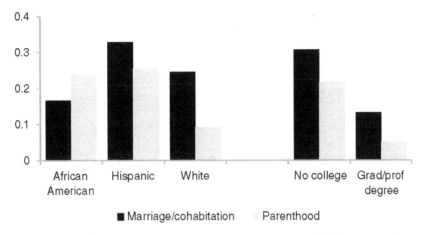

Figure 3.2: Proportion of college entrants transitioning into marriage/cohabitation and parenthood, by selected socio-demographic characteristics. *Source:* Author's calculations based on NLSY97. *Note:* Figure represents family transitions approximately four years since entry into higher education.

experience made this transition to adulthood. Marriage/cohabitation is more prevalent, but still unequally distributed. Approximately 13% of students whose parents completed graduate/professional degrees were married/cohabitating 45 months after entry into higher education. The rate of marriage/cohabitation was twice as high for students whose parents had no college experience, 31% of whom made this transition.

Racial/ethnic differences in family transitions are less pronounced, but still present. Hispanic and especially African American students are more likely to have children at entry into higher education than White students, and although the rate of transition into parenthood becomes more equal over time, the gaps persist. Forty-five months after entry, less than 10% of White students report having children while approximately a quarter of Hispanic and African American students have made the transition into this adult role. Differences in marriage/cohabitation are less pronounced. The same proportion of African American and White students transition into marriage/cohabitation at entry into higher education, but a gap emerges over time, such that a lower proportion of African Americans make this transition. Hispanic students, in contrast, are more likely to make the transition into marriage/cohabitation than White students throughout their educational careers.

UNDERSTANDING INEQUALITY IN DEGREE COMPLETION

Do these differences in life course transitions contribute to racial/ethnic and socioeconomic gaps in degree completion? To answer this question, I begin by estimating the overall gaps in degree completion between students from different sociodemographic groups. The first set of columns in Table 3.2 represents these baseline differences, based on a model that includes both race/ethnicity and family background (parental education

Table 3.2: Estimated Odds Ratios from Event History Models of Bachelor's Degree Completion [selected results for racial/ethnic groups and parental education]

	MODEL 1 BASELINE		MODEL 2 LIFE COURSE		MODEL 3 ACADEMIC		MODEL 4 LIFE COURSE AND ACADEMIC	
	ODDS	DIFFERENCE FROM REFERENCE	ODDS	DIFFERENCE FROM REFERENCE	ODDS	DIFFERENCE FROM REFERENCE	ODDS	DIFFERENCE FROM REFERENCE
Race/Ethnicity [reference: white]								
African American	0.67**	-33%	0.70**	-30%	0.83*	-17%	0.78*	-22%
Hispanic	0.59**	-41%	0.64**	-36%	0.80*	-20%	0.80*	-20%
Other non-white	1.22	22%	0.94	-6%	1.37	37%	1.09	9%
Parental Education [reference: grad/prof degree]								
No college	0.45**	-55%	0.65**	-35%	0.70**	-30%	0.86	-14%
Some college	0.54**	-46%	0.68**	-32%	0.78**	-22%	0.88	-12%
Bachelor's degree	0.85*	-15%	0.91	-9%	1.00	0%	1.00	0%
Controlling for								
Parental income, gender and age at college entry	Yes		Yes		Yes		Yes	
Life course transitions			Yes				Yes	
Academic preparation					Yes		Yes	

*p < 0.05, **p < 0.01

and income). Previous research has shown that students from racial/ethnic minority groups on average come from less advantaged family backgrounds. In a review of the literature Gamoran (2001) concluded that: "the most important reason for educational inequality between blacks and whites is socioeconomic" (p. 137). Indeed, without parental education and income in the model, the gaps in degree completion across racial/ethnic groups are approximately 30% to 40% higher. However, it is notable that even after taking parental education and income into consideration, African American students have 33% lower odds of bachelor's degree completion than White students. The gap is slightly larger for Hispanic students, who have 41% lower odds of attaining this educational credential than their White peers. The gaps in bachelor's degree completion across parental education categories are even more pronounced. Students whose parents had no college experience had 55% lower odds of completing a bachelor's degree than those whose parents held graduate/professional degrees. These findings indicate that even among students who enter higher education there are stark gaps in degree completion among students from different racial/ethnic and family background groups.

The second model considers the extent to which these differences could be accounted for by differential patterns of life course transitions, including work, marriage, and parenthood. While Table 3.2 presents only selected results, it is important to note that life course transitions are related to the likelihood of degree completion. Getting married/cohabitating, and especially having children, has a negative relationship to the likelihood of degree completion. Moreover, the more months students spend in high intensity employment (working over 35 hours per week), the less likely they are to earn bachelor's degrees. Conversely, the more months students spend in low intensity employment (20 hours or less), the more likely they are to complete their degrees. There is no relationship between moderate intensity employment and degree completion. These results indicate that simply being employed is not necessarily a culprit for low degree attainment. Instead, it is high intensity employment (i.e., transitioning into the adult role of full-time employment), that is negatively associated with degree completion (see also Bozick, 2007; NCES, 1998; Staff & Mortimer, 2007).

Descriptive statistics have revealed some differences in life course transitions across students from different racial/ethnic groups and marked differences across students from different family backgrounds. Given the negative association between life course transitions and degree attainment, it would be expected that these patterns account for some of the inequalities in degree completion. As Model 2 shows, including life course transitions in the model changes gaps across racial/ethnic groups only slightly, but it substantially reduces the gaps across students from different family backgrounds.[2] After adjusting for family and employment transitions, the gaps in degree completion between African American and Hispanic students on the one hand and White students on the other hand remain of similar magnitudes as in the previous model—both racial/ethnic minority groups have approximately one-third lower odds of degree completion than their White peers. The gaps between students from more or less educated families remain pronounced as well, but are of much smaller magnitude than in the previous model. After adjusting for transitions to adulthood, including work, marriage/

cohabitation, and parenthood, students whose parents had no college experience had 35% lower odds of degree completion than students whose parents completed professional/graduate degrees—a notable gap, but substantially smaller than in the previous model.

Results suggest that life course transitions play an important role in explaining inequality in degree completion, particularly among students from different family backgrounds. However, they may overestimate the role of life course transitions in explaining inequalities in degree completion because they do not control for other factors that are related to family background as well as the likelihood of degree completion. One factor that is particularly relevant for a discussion of postsecondary educational success is academic preparation. Students from racial/ethnic minority groups and less advantaged family backgrounds score lower on standardized tests (see a review in Grodsky, Warren, & Felts, 2008) and have lower levels of academic preparation measured by other indicators such as coursework completed (Adelman, 1999, 2006), which contribute to their lower likelihood of degree completion. I thus consider the role of academic preparation in Model 3. As would be expected, academic preparation is an important predictor of students' likelihood of degree completion: students who had higher test scores, who were in academic tracks in high school, and who had higher high school GPAs had a substantially higher likelihood of degree completion. At the same time, beginning postsecondary education in 2-year institutions had a negative relationship to bachelor's degree completion.

Do socioeconomic and racial/ethnic gaps persist after controlling for academic preparation? The third model indicates that controlling for academic preparation reduces the racial/ethnic gaps in degree completion by approximately one half in comparison to the baseline model. After controlling for academic preparation, African American students have only 17% lower odds of bachelor's degree completion than their White counterparts. A similar pattern is revealed for Hispanic students. Academic preparation also plays an important role in understanding gaps in degree completion among students from different family backgrounds. After adjusting for academic preparation, students whose parents had no college experience had 30% lower odds of completing bachelor's degrees than those whose parents completed graduate/professional degrees—this is approximately half of the gap that existed in the baseline model.

There are two additional notable findings in Model 3. First, although academic preparation is an important predictor of degree completion, and although there are notable differences in academic preparation across sociodemographic groups, the gaps in degree completion persist. Even after controlling for academic preparation, African American and Hispanic students are less likely to complete bachelor's degrees than White students, and students from less educated families are less likely to attain these educational credentials than students from highly educated families. Another important finding emerges from a comparison of Models 2 and 3. What seems apparent is that academic preparation plays a much more pronounced role in explaining racial/ethnic gaps in degree completion than life course transitions. At the same time, both sets of factors, academic preparation and life course transitions, are consequential for the gaps in degree completion across students from different family backgrounds. Thus, while higher education is stratified by both social class and race/ethnicity, specific factors seem to make unique contributions to the observed inequalities in degree completion.

Since both academic preparation and life course transitions are related to degree completion, and since they both vary across students from different sociodemographic groups, could they jointly explain the gaps in degree completion? This is the question addressed by the final model which includes measures of academic preparation and life course transitions. The first notable finding is that gaps in degree completion across racial/ethnic groups persist. Even after controlling for indicators of academic preparation and life course transitions, African American and Hispanic students have approximately 20% lower odds of degree completion than their White peers. Patterns for parental education are notably different. After controlling for academic preparation and life course transitions, students from different family backgrounds have similar likelihoods of degree completion. Small gaps persist, but those gaps are no longer statistically significant. Neither academic preparation nor life course transitions alone could account for socioeconomic gaps in degree completion; however, considered together, they can help to explain gaps in degree completion between students from more and less educated families.

While this chapter has focused on inequalities in degree completion by race/ethnicity and family background, it is important to mention the issue of gender. Gender has received increasing attention in recent years as women today are more likely than men to complete college (Buchmann & DiPrete, 2006; DiPrete & Buchmann, 2006). Analyses performed for this chapter confirm those patterns, showing that women are substantially more likely than men to complete a bachelor's degree. One relevant question would be whether the relationships between race/ethnicity and socioeconomic status on the one hand, and bachelor's degree completion on the other vary by gender. In the sample examined by Bowen and his colleagues (2009), racial/ethnic minority women had a greater advantage in degree completion than did White women. That, however, does not hold for the sample examined in this chapter. There were no statistically significant interactions between gender and race/ethnicity (or between gender and family background). The issue of gender is thus not explored further in this chapter. However, it is possible that this pattern of a lack of interaction between race/ethnicity and gender is unique to NLSY97 and thus deserves careful attention in future research.

CONCLUSION

Racial/ethnic and socioeconomic inequalities in American higher education are well documented. While previous research has often focused on studying inequalities in entry into higher education, findings presented here indicate pronounced inequalities in degree completion, even among students who enter postsecondary institutions. These inequalities contribute to the low rates of bachelor's degree completion and require careful consideration if we as a nation are to reach the newly set goals for degree attainment.

It is thus crucial to understand what factors contribute to racial/ethnic and socioeconomic gaps in bachelor's degree completion.

When previous studies have considered this question, they have often focused on academic preparation. Since academic preparation is strongly related to degree completion and since students from less advantaged family backgrounds and racial/ethnic minority groups on average tend to have lower levels of academic preparation, academic preparation helps to explain some of the inequalities in degree completion. However, even after controlling for academic preparation, students from racial/ethnic minority groups and less advantaged family backgrounds are less likely to complete bachelor's degrees. What students bring to higher education is important, but it is not sufficient for explaining observed inequalities.

The present study thus focused on what happens after students enter higher education, and in particular, whether they transition into roles typically associated with adulthood, including work, marriage/cohabitation, and parenthood. These analyses illuminate the complexity of higher education trajectories, revealing that young adults today rarely focus exclusively on their studies. Instead, many of them juggle schooling with and against other considerations, including work, marriage/cohabitation, and parenthood. Notably, transitions into adult roles are not randomly distributed: students from racial/ethnic minority groups and especially students from less advantaged family backgrounds are more likely to make these life course transitions. Moreover, transitions into full-time work, marriage/cohabitation, and parenthood are associated with a lower likelihood of degree completion. Additionally, findings reveal that transitions into roles typically associated with adulthood explain a substantial portion of the inequality in degree completion between students from more and less educated families. These transitions play a less prominent direct role in explaining racial/ethnic gaps in degree completion. However, they play an indirect role in the production of racial/ethnic inequality through the association between race/ethnicity and family background. Family background accounts for approximately 30% to 40% of the racial/ethnic gaps in degree completion, meaning that transitions to adulthood are also indirectly relevant for understanding racial/ethnic gaps in completion.

Analyses presented in this chapter illuminate the extent to which different factors, namely academic preparation and life course transitions, contribute to racial/ethnic and socioeconomic gaps in degree completion. Academic preparation is a relatively more important factor than life course transitions for understanding racial/ethnic gaps in degree completion, although both sets of factors contribute to understanding inequalities among students from different family backgrounds. The final set of models present another remarkable set of findings: after controlling for both academic preparation and life course transitions, there are no gaps in the likelihood of bachelor's degree completion among students from different family backgrounds. At the same time, the racial/ethnic gaps, although substantially reduced, continue to persist (see also Lavin & Crook, 1990; Milesi, 2010).[3] These persisting racial/ethnic differences require more attention in future research.

One possible avenue for exploring racial/ethnic gaps in the future is to examine more closely the types of institutions students attend. Several recent studies have highlighted the issue of "undermatching" or students attending less selective institutions than they are academically prepared for. The undermatch seems to be more prevalent among students from less advantaged family backgrounds and racial/ethnic minority groups (Bowen, Chingos, & McPherson, 2009; Roderick, 2008). This can be consequential for racial/ethnic and socioeconomic gaps in degree completion since students who attend more selective institutions have a higher likelihood of degree completion, even net of their own individual characteristics. Moreover, as recent institutional-level studies have shown, colleges and universities vary notably in their racial/ethnic gaps in completion (Carey, 2004). Thus studying the role institutions may play in narrowing the racial/ethnic gaps in degree completion deserves careful attention in future research.

Notes

1. The term *racial/ethnic minority* students used throughout this chapter refers to African American and Hispanic students. Asian/Pacific Islander students have higher degree completion rates than White students and are thus not discussed at length.

2. Although comparing logistic coefficients across models can lead to erroneous conclusions (e.g., Mood, 2010; Winship & Mare, 1984), *y*-standardized coefficients confirm the reported patterns.

3. Bowen et al. (2009) also show gaps in degree completion net of controls, although that seems to be the case only for men: African American and Hispanic males have lower completion rates than White males, but African American and Hispanic women, along with White women, have slightly higher graduation rates than White men. Also, some studies seem to show no racial/ethnic gaps in degree completion (Adelman, 2006).

REFERENCES

Adelman, C. (1999). *Answers in the tool box: Academic intensity, attendance patterns, and bachelor's degree attainment*. Washington, DC: U.S. Department of Education.

Adelman, C. (2006). *The toolbox revisited: Paths to degree completion from high school through college*. Washington, DC: U.S. Department of Education.

Adelman, C. (2009). *The spaces between numbers: Getting international data on higher education straight*. Washington, DC: Institutue for Higher Education Policy.

Allison, P. (1984). *Event history analysis: Regression for longitudinal event data*. Thousand Oaks, CA: Sage.

Allison, P. (2002). *Missing data*. Thousand Oaks, CA: Sage.

Arnett, J. J. (2004). *Emerging adulthood: The winding road from the late teens through the twenties*. Oxford, England: Oxford University Press.

Bound, J., Lovenheim, M., & Turner, S. E. (2009). *Why have college completion rates declined? An analysis of changing student preparation and collegiate resources* (NBER Working Paper 15566). Cambridge, MA: National Bureau of Economic Research.

Bowen, W. G., Chingos, M. M., & McPherson, M. S. (2009). *Crossing the finish line: completing college at America's public universities*. Princeton, NJ: Princeton University Press.

Bozick, R. (2007). Making it through the first year of college: The role of students' economic resources, employment, and living arrangements. *Sociology of Education, 80,* 261–285.

Bozick, R., & DeLuca, S. (2005). Better late than never? Delayed enrollment in the high school to college transition. *Social Forces, 84*(1), 531–554.

Buchmann, C., & DiPrete, T. A. (2006). The growing female advantage in college completion: The role of family background and academic achievement. *American Sociological Review, 71,* 515–541.

Carey, K. (2004). *A matter of degrees: improving graduation rates in four-year colleges and universities.* Washington, DC: Education Trust.

Cooksey, E. C., & Rindfuss, R. R. (2001). Patterns of work and schooling in young adulthood. *Sociological Forum, 16,* 731–755.

DiPrete, T. A., & Buchmann, C. (2006). Gender-specific trends in the value of education and the emerging gender gap in college completion. *Demography, 43*(1), 1–24.

Gamoran, A. (2001). American schooling and educational inequality: A forecast for the 21st century [Special issue]. *Sociology of Education, 75,* 135–153.

Goldin, C., & Katz, L. F. (2008). *The race between education and technology.* Cambridge, MA: Belknap Press of Harvard University Press.

Goldrick-Rab, S., & Han, S. W. (2011). Accounting for socioeconomic differences in delaying the transition to college. *Review of Higher Education, 34,* 423–445.

Goldrick-Rab, S., & Roksa, J. (2008). *A federal agenda for promoting student success and degree completion.* Washington, DC: Center for American Progress.

Grodsky, E., Warren, J. R., & Felts, E. (2008). Testing and social stratification in American education. *Annual Review of Sociology, 34,* 385–404.

Jacobs, J. A., & King, R. B. (2002). Age and college completion: A life-history analysis of women aged 15–44. *Sociology of Education, 75*(3), 211–230.

Kelly, S. (2007). Social class and tracking within schools. In L. Weis (Ed.), *The way class works* (pp. 210–224). New York: Routledge.

Kerckhoff, A. C. (2000). Building conceptual and empirical bridges between studies of educational and labor force careers. In A. C. Kerckhoff (Ed.), *Generating social stratification: Toward a new research agenda* (pp. 37–58). Boulder, CO: Westview Press.

Kerckhoff, A. C. (2004). From student to worker. In J. T. Mortimer & M. J. Shanahan (Eds.), *Handbook of the life course* (pp. 251–268). New York: Springer.

Lavin, D. E., & Crook, D. B. (1990). Open admission and its outcomes: Ethnic differences in long-term educational attainment. *American Journal of Education, 98,* 389–425.

Lucas, S. (2001). Effectively maintained inequality: Education transitions, track mobility, and social background effects. *American Journal of Sociology, 106,* 1642–1690.

Milesi, C. (2010). Do all road lead to Rome? Effect of educational trajecotries on educational transitions. *Research in Social Stratification and Mobility, 28,* 23–44.

Mood, C. (2010). Logistic regression: Why we cannot do what we think we can do, and what we can do about it. *European Sociological Review, 26,* 67–82.

Mortimer, J. T. (2003). *Working and growing up in America.* Cambridge, MA: Harvard University Press.

Mortimer, J. T., & Kruger, H. (2000). Transition from school to work in the United States and Germany: Formal pathways matter. In M. Hallinan (Ed.), *Handbook of the sociology of education* (pp. 475–497). New York: Plenum.

Appendix Table 3.A: Patterns of Work, Marriage/Cohabitation, and Parenthood of College Entrants, by Family Background and Race/Ethnicity

	PARENTAL EDUCATION				RACE/ETHNICITY		
	NO COLLEGE	SOME COLLEGE	BACHELOR'S DEGREE	GRAD/PROF DEGREE	AFRICAN AMERICAN	HISPANIC	WHITE
Married/cohabitating (%)							
Month 1	0.103	0.076*	0.057**	0.025**	0.055	0.104*	0.067
Month 45	0.307	0.272	0.210**	0.132**	0.167**	0.328**	0.246
Children (%)							
Month 1	0.099	0.063**	0.036**	0.022**	0.157**	0.091**	0.038
Month 45	0.216	0.148**	0.085**	0.051**	0.283**	0.254**	0.093
Employment (%)							
Month 1							
Not employed	0.385	0.395	0.472**	0.580*	0.545**	0.385^	0.427
Low intensity	0.193	0.236*	0.254**	0.204	0.156**	0.191*	0.237
Medium intensity	0.205	0.186	0.142**	0.134**	0.152	0.191	0.177
High intensity	0.217	0.182*	0.133**	0.082**	0.147	0.233**	0.158
Month 45							
Not employed	0.179	0.218*	0.239**	0.271**	0.245	0.211	0.218
Low intensity	0.138	0.163	0.251**	0.239**	0.169^	0.106**	0.203
Medium intensity	0.175	0.205	0.189	0.175	0.158^	0.193	0.188
High intensity	0.507	0.414**	0.320**	0.315**	0.429	0.490**	0.391
Employment (months) Cumulative by Month 45							
Low intensity	7.987	9.510**	11.681**	11.820**	8.089**	7.345**	10.588
Medium intensity	8.811	9.004	8.638	7.627**	7.590**	9.179	8.758
High intensity	17.047	14.013**	10.822**	8.942**	13.193	16.291**	13.028

^p<0.10, *p<0.05, **p<0.01 (Reference categories are "No college" for parental education and "White" for race/ethnicity.) All estimates are weighted and significance tests are adjusted for clustering of individuals within families.

Mouw, T. (2005). Sequences of early adult transition: A look at variability and consequences. In F. F. J. Furstenberg, R. G. Rumbaut, & J. Settersten (Eds.), *On the frontier of adulthood: Theory, research, and public policy* (pp. 256–291). Chicago, IL: University of Chicago Press.

National Center for Education Statistics [NCES]. (1998). *Profile of undergraduates in U.S. post-secondary education institutions: 1995–1996, with an essay on undergraduates who work* (NCES 1998-084). Washington, DC: U.S. Department of Education.

National Center for Education Statistics [NCES]. (2002). *Profile of undergraduates in U.S. post-secondary institutions: 1999-2000* (NCES 2002-268). Washington, DC: U.S. Department of Education.

National Center for Education Statistics [NCES]. (2003). *Short-term enrollment in postsecond-ary education: Student background and institutional differences in reasons for early departure, 1996–1998* (NCES 2003-153). Washington, DC: U.S. Department of Education.

Obama, B. (2009, Feburar y 24). *Remarks prepared for the joint session of Congress.* Washington, DC: White House Press Office.

O'Rand, A. M. (2000). Structuration and individualization: The life course as a continuous, multilevel process. In A. C. Kerckhoff (Ed.), *Generating social stratification: Toward a new research agenda* (pp. 3–16). Boulder, CO: Westview Press.

Pallas, A. M. (1993). Schooling in the course of human lives: The social context of education and the transition to adulthood in industrial society. *Review of Educational Research, 63*(4), 409–447.

Pascarella, E., & Terenzini, P. T. (2005). *How college affects students: A third decade of research.* San Francisco, CA: Jossey-Bass.

Riggert, S. C., Boyle, M., Petrosko, J. M., Ash, D., & Rude-Parkins, C. (2006). Student employ-ment and higher education: Empiricism and contradiction. *Review of Educational Research, 76*, 63–92.

Roderick, M. E. A. (2008). *From high school to the future: Potholes on the road to college.* Chicago, IL: Consortium on Chicago School Research.

Roksa, J. (2010). Differentiation and work: Employment patterns and class inequality at two-year and four-year institutions. *Higher Education, 61*, 293–308.

Roksa, J., & Velez, M. (2010). When studying schooling is not enough: incorporating employ-ment in models of educational transitions. *Research in Social Stratification and Mobility, 28*, 5–21.

Roksa, J., & Velez, M. (2012). A late start: Life course transitions and delayed entry into higher education. *Social Forces, 90,* TBD.

Scommegna, P. (2002). *Increased cohabitation changing children's family settings.* Washington, DC: National Institute of Child Health and Human Development (NICHD), National Institutes of Health.

Scott-Clayton, J. (2007). *What explains rising labor supply among U.S. undergraduates, 1970–2003?* Unpublished manuscript, John F. Kennedy School of Government, Harvard University, Cambridge, MA.

Shanahan, M. J. (2000). Pathways to adulthood in changing societies: Variability and mecha-nisms in life course perspective. *Annual Review of Sociology, 26*, 667– 692.

Singer, J. D., & Willett, J. B. (2003). *Applied longitudinal data analysis: Modeling change and event occurrence.* New York: Oxford University Press.

Staff, J., & Mortimer, J. T. (2007). Education and work strategies from adolescence to early adulthood: Consequences for educational attainment. *Social Forces, 85,* 1169–1194.

Taniguchi, H., & Kaufman, G. (2005). Degree completion among nontraditional college students. *Social Science Quarterly, 86*(4), 912–927.

Turner, S. E. (2004). Going to college and finishing college. In C. Hoxby (Ed.), *College choices: The economics of where to go, when to go, and how to pay for it.* Chicago, IL: University of Chicago Press for NBER.

U.S. Department of Labor. (2007). *NLSY97 user guide.* Columbus, OH: Center for Human Resource Research.

Winship, C., & Mare, R. D. (1984). Regression models with ordinal variables. *American Sociological Review, 49,* 512–525.

Wu, L. L. (2003). Event history models for life course analysis. In J. T. Mortimer & M. J. Shanahan (Eds.), *Handbook of the life course* (pp. 477–502). New York: Springer.

Section Three

Understanding Family and Work Roles Over Time

I n this section, readers will gain a deeper understanding of family and employment patterns and expectations during the adulthood part of the life course. The life course perspective makes it possible to conceptualize both continuity and change in family and career development over time, and to recognize and acknowledge divergent pathways. Showcased here are three studies on variability in family and career pathways that can easily go unnoticed.

First, Olsen and Clarke's (2003) qualitative study gives insights into major challenges faced by disabled individuals transitioning to parenthood, as well as parents with traumatic injuries or the sudden onset of a condition. Noteworthy is that the experience of disability is related to that of parenting, and to changes in parenting demands. Interviews with parents who had impairments before parenthood reveal that negative, disapproving attitudes from professionals sometimes led to decisions to terminate a pregnancy. This study underscores the changing nature of what disabled parents and their families go through. Starting with decisions to have more children, disabled parents may also deal with single parenthood and other consequences of ending relationships, emotional or physical threats from former partners, the loss of a child, in some cases for adoption, and parenting children who grow up over time. They thought it important to achieve some sort of stability in their impaired condition, but some of them were also concerned about staying employed or returning to work. Olsen and Clarke (2003) conclude that, without proper support, disabled people experience added difficulties with parenting and, in turn, with fulfilling what is typically considered important adult roles.

Second, a quantitative study by Biggart and O'Brien (2010) investigates issues of work and family for fathers in the United Kingdom, to assess the notion that working longer hours is associated with their role as an economic provider and working fewer hours with their caring role. Given the gender disparity in full-time employment rates, fathers continue to work significantly more hours than mothers. However, gender norms with regard to work and family have been shifting, in that fathers are increasingly expected to contribute more to child care, while mothers' contributions to family income have been rising at a fast rate. Biggart and O'Brien (2010) cite the recent findings that report greater involvement in child-care activities among some fathers who reduced their work hours. Results of Biggart and O'Brien's (2010) research suggest a tentative and complex pattern, where workers who are fathers and those who work as managers or professionals tend to spend more weekly hours for work, compared to those who are not fathers or do not work as managers or professionals.

Third and last, Benson's (2013) work delves into the careers of white-collar criminals from the life course perspective, challenging the commonly held view that white-collar offenders do not commit crimes repeatedly. The author starts out by describing and comparing the social locations occupied by white-collar criminals against other common offenders, in terms of sex, race, age, educational attainment, and employment status. Comparisons are also made between these two groups of offenders with regard to the extent of their social integration measured by marital status, home ownership, financial assets, and community participation such as involvement in community groups, church, and criminal friends. Benson (2013) refers to two studies to identify patterns in previous arrests and convictions and the age of the first offense for the two groups. Furthermore, he compares their family environment, academic performance, and social adjustment. He finds a typical white-collar offender to have a middle-class background rather than an upper-class background, disconfirming the stereotype, but he warns of the possibility that an upper-class offender may avoid conviction more easily. Worth noting is the discovery that white-collar criminals do not fit the life-course trajectories of other criminals that have been identified in the research literature. More research is needed to generate and address life course–related questions surrounding work and family strains that may be linked to white-collar offenses.

Disabled parents are largely unknown and therefore invisible. In addition, it is not clear why fatherhood status increases work hours in this day and age when more mothers work outside the home. Much less is known about white-collar offenders compared to common offenders. Therefore, these three studies add to the literature on work and family, the two important domains thought to define adulthood, by portraying the diversity and complexities of the middle stage of life course trajectories.

REFERENCES

Benson, Michael L. 2013. "Appendix: The Life Course Perspective and White-Collar Crime," pp. 195–214. In *Crime and the Life Course: An Introduction*. M. L. Benson, Ed. New York: Routledge.

Biggart, Laura, and Margaret O'Brien. 2010. "UK Fathers' Long Work Hours: Career Stage or Fatherhood?" *Fathering* 8(3):341–361.

Olsen, Richard, and Harriet Clarke. 2003. "The Life Course: Dimensions of Change in Parenting and Disability," pp. 103–126. In *Parenting and Disability: Disabled Parents' Experiences of Raising Children*, by R. Olsen and H. Clarke. UK: Policy Press.

The Life Course: Dimensions of Change in Parenting and Disability

By Richard Olsen, Harriet Clarke, and Rebekah Widdowfield

INTRODUCTION

This chapter examines the importance of change in the experiences of disabled parents and their families. This involves focusing on hopes and experiences of becoming and being parents, within a life-course perspective. By this we mean exploring choices and expectations around parenting, from childhood through adolescence and into adulthood. Parenting is often perceived as a 'normal' feature of independent adult life. And yet attitudes towards disabled people do not always reflect this. We argue, therefore, that a life-course perspective is vital to the debate of parenting and disability, and the policy shaped to deal with it[1].

The relative invisibility of disabled parents, particularly when compared to the exposure of children who have been defined as 'young carers', is related to the concentration of social policy on the beginning and the end of the life course. This is also reflected in approaches to the support of family life; that is, research on family transitions is largely concerned with the transition to parenthood (and the early parenting years), and transitions into adulthood. The concept of the life course is more flexible than the previous conception of the lifecycle, which presented a normative description of key stages through which each individual passed. However, the experiences of disabled people can be defined and restr icted by a policy framework that continues to individualise the life course.

> For those disabled people who do seek to operate as independent 'adults' two issues seem central—work and parenting. Idealised constructions of adulthood emphasise parenting and partnering as a signifier of adult status. (Priestley, 2000, p 430)

Our findings are intended to comment on the significance of change, both in terms of the experiences of disabled parents and their families, and in terms of the ability of formal and informal supports to respond. We have been concerned to present our examination of change in the broadest possible terms. Therefore, we have looked not only at the implications for parents of the changing needs of children as they grow up, but also at the changes that take place in family composition, and in the nature of disability impairments. Our analysis, then, highlights the importance of understanding that the experience of disability is closely linked to the changing experience of parenting, and the changing demands of the parenting role. This broader context of change also requires inclusive definitions of parenting to be as important as inclusive definitions of disability.

IMPAIRMENT, DISABILITY AND THE LIFE COURSE

In Stages One and Two, we included parents whose impairments predated parenthood as well as those who were already parents at their onset. For half of the Stage One sample, the impact (though not necessarily the initial onset) of their impairments began after having become a parent. Therefore, the parents in our sample, irrespective of impairment group, reported various 'starting points' in their life as a disabled person. This allowed us to examine the experiences of those who were disabled people before becoming parents, and those who had already had children beforehand.

We can state in broad terms that, in most families where disability long predated having children, we found parents were less likely to see their impairment as central to their experience of parenting. However, we are unwilling to make overgeneralisations on the basis of such a classification of different experiences. Not only did some respondents find that a pre-existing impairment was significantly altered having become a parent (for women, this was often as a result of pregnancy), families also experienced other significant changes that altered family life (such as changes in the employment status of parents).

Clearly, it can be difficult for some people to pinpoint a particular period in their lives when they felt that they had become a disabled person (indeed if they felt that way at all). The point of diagnosis often bore no relation to the parent's experience of onset, especially for those parents who felt that their mental health and/or physical impairments should have been identified and recognised at a much earlier stage by medical professionals.

Reference to the diagnosis of a condition or pinpointing the 'onset' very much represents a medical approach to what may have been a gradual process. Furthermore, this process may have been a reflection of increasingly inaccessible environments (in the broadest sense) rather than deteriorating impairments. Although receipt of a medical diagnosis can provide a key to support (such as disability benefit), the diagnoses themselves were not always considered to encapsulate either the personal experience or the history of impairment. Some parents reeled off numerous diagnoses that they had received over the years, variously accepting and rejecting the labels applied to them. This was most often the case in relation to mental health impairments.

It became quite natural, then, for some parents to link adulthood experience of impairment to childhood experiences. For example, we interviewed a number of women who discussed their mental health impairments and their experience of parenting specifically alongside experiences of abuse or difficult family relationships in childhood. We also spoke to parents with physical impairments who stressed that while no 'diagnosis' occurred prior to their becoming a parent, they felt that the deterioration of their physical functioning had begun during childhood. For example, one man described how he began to find walking difficult as a young teenager, yet was in his 30s before he was eventually diagnosed with multiple sclerosis (MS). Some of those with gradually developing impairments felt that not much could have been done to speed up a diagnosis. Others spoke, however, of how there had been reluctance on the part of professionals to take their symptoms seriously. In short, then, our research sample included a group of people who felt that they had become parents after the onset of impair ment but before they received a diagnosis, medical intervention and/or support.

Let us now turn our attention to some specific difficulties faced by those parents who, having had their impairment identified, had felt unsupported—and effectively disabled—in their desire to become parents in the first place.

Disabled people's experience of the transition to parenthood[2]

Some of those who had experience of disability before becoming a parent spoke about their own and other people's (including professionals') attitudes. Consequently, it was possible to gain detailed insights into key barriers faced by some disabled people as potential parents, such as professionals who had been either supportive or unsupportive when they expressed their wish to have children. (Of course, our sample's parents had successfully gone on to become parents, despite the barriers they had faced[3].)

One single parent with four children provided us with a stark reminder of the lack of encouragement in employment and parenting she had experienced as a result of her segregated education as a disabled child. Not only had she received little or no support in terms of taking qualifications, low expectations were also expressed about her potential for having a partner and for having children.

> A teacher told me I would never have kids—I was 14. She said "You'll never have children, no one will have you".
>
> *Mother, (PI), single-parent family*

When we interviewed this parent, we found that she had a stable and adequate income (largely through compensation payments), a well-adapted home, her own transport and a strong sense of her own ability as a mother. Indeed, her feeling of 'if they could see me now' was expressed by other parents who felt that others had not expected them to make a success of parenting. Expressing one's enjoyment of parenting also proves to oneself, as well as to others, that you can have and bring up children. For these parents, the problems—rather than the possibilities—associated with parenting had been stressed.

> I suppose it's nice to know I could carry a child … . I've proved to people, I've done it, as I didn't know I'd be able to have children.
>
> *Mother (PI), dual-parent family*

Respondents indicated how professionals in their adult life had sometimes reinforced this disapproval. Some mothers described how they had been dissuaded on health grounds rather than any (overt) prejudice. In these situations, it was often stressed how access to supportive healthcare workers had been very important in deciding to get pregnant, and in managing any difficulties experienced during pregnancy and labour. One woman, now a single parent, had been warned by doctors of the potential physical stress of pregnancy. She stated specifically that, since her husband was a health professional, she "knew what was available and what my chances were". Another mother with physical impairments said that her GP had expressed the view that she could not look after herself, let alone a child. The difficult relationship that developed from his attitude meant that her support in pregnancy came instead from her hospital consultant and a gynaecologist.

Social care and other professionals were also reported as having occasionally expressed disapproving attitudes. One mother said that a social worker had told her that "disabled people shouldn't have children if they cannot look after them". Another single mother, who had experienced long-term mental health impairments, said "I've had social workers tell me not to have them [children]". This message—that to be a parent with 'mental illness' or 'disability' is irresponsible—is bound up with beliefs that disabled parents are unable to provide security for children, as well as concerns about the child's own 'mental health', be that the result of a genetic, social or behavioural risk. Beresford and Wilson argue that this dissuasion from parenthood continues to be experienced by mental health service users. The current message is that they:

> have a moral responsibility not to have children in the interests of preventing further unnecessary suffering. (Beresford and Wilson, 2002, p 547)

This was the message given to many of the parents in our sample. Even among those who had not received such explicit 'advice', often the feeling was that it was broadly considered inappropriate for disabled people, who themselves required support, to have children. This attitude could be read into experiences of conflict with services. For example, one mother said that she and other disabled people could feel guilt about having disabled children in the first place. Although she did not overtly link this to her difficult relationship with social services, these feelings of guilt are likely, at least in part, to reflect the way in which she had felt defined by services as a *problem* to her family, rather than more positively as a *parent*.

It is clear, then, that negative attitudes towards disabled women in particular led to anxiety in childhood and early adulthood about their future prospects for relationships and children[4].

The immediate advantage of an increased visibility of disabled mothers and fathers is that it challenges the attitudes of non-disabled adults. It may also broaden the parental aspirations for (and of) younger disabled people in relation to the transition to adulthood. The experiences of women can be particularly pertinent, since some may require specific medical care during pregnancy to protect themselves and/or the child.

Pregnancy and postnatal care

For some women in our sample, pregnancy had implications for their physical and/ or emotional health. In many cases, a successful pregnancy was emotionally satisfying for those who had not previously been encouraged to become a parent. Other positive personal experiences reported were relief from physical pain, to a more positive attitude among disabled parents than might be experienced by non-disabled parents to the potential of impairment in a child. In addition, some women received increased support from formal services with regular access to a general practitioner, consultant or nurse, which was often immensely reassuring.

For some women, pregnancy posed a threat to their own wellbeing, such as those who had to change, or temporarily stop taking, medication that could potentially harm the foetus. For them, medical advice and other support had been very important and reassuring. However, these women often reported that professionals were unsympathetic to their specific needs during this time. Most often, it was parents with mental health impairments who spoke about these issues, although they are clearly relevant to parents with other health concerns (such as epilepsy). For example, one mother who had manic depression said that she did not take her medication during pregnancy, because of the risk to her child. She did not return to medication after her son was born, and had no outpatient care until she was admitted to hospital with her baby a few months later. She believed that her consultant was "obviously one of those people that didn't think I should have children". Indeed, during her pregnancy her husband, who also had a mental health diagnosis, had spent some time in hospital on a psychiatric ward. During a visit to her husband, and therefore outside of a formal consultation, a professional thought it appropriate to comment negatively on her pregnancy. What, then, of the importance attached to the individual consultation and confidentiality, at least within psychiatrists' public accounts of their relationships with patients?

> I got pregnant and he [husband] got ill [laughs] but I was fine throughout …. Even visiting you in the ward when the consultant said to me, "I believe you suffer with manic depression?". I said, "Yes". He said, "You do realise you will

be ill soon?". Because, there was me with my bump. I said, "Thank you very much". [Laughs]. You know, that's *really* helpful.

Mother (MHI), dual-parent family (Family E, Interview One)

This mother's experience illustrates how, in addition to the day-to-day difficulties inherent in parenting (such as a lack of appropriate support), parents could be faced with such negative and demeaning responses from professionals to news of a pregnancy. Needless to say, such pressures and attitudes could lead to pregnancy itself being a traumatic experience. In a small number of families, we heard how termination of the pregnancy had been chosen or considered, sometimes at the suggestion of a medical practitioner. We did not specifically ask about this, but parents would describe their own decision processes. For example, one couple told us how they had only decided against a termination because the trauma of an abortion was more likely to be detrimental to the mother's mental health than having another child to look after. On the other hand, however, continuing with unplanned pregnancies could also be traumatic. One woman told us that she had previously had a ter mination after contraception had failed, at a time when she was already planning a sterilisation. The subsequent sterilisation failed, owing to medical negligence, and she became pregnant again. She then had a second termination as she felt she could not continue with that pregnancy having previously terminated one. In addition to the stress felt given these experiences this mother suffered physical ill health resulting from poor medical care, and she felt the combined stresses were linked to her later development of a neurological impairment.

Women who had exper ienced problematic, or previously unsuccessful, pregnancies reported how this could make the transition to parenthood and ongoing parenting more difficult. For some, increased levels of distress were experienced, and pregnancy or the postnatal period marked the first time in which a diagnosis (sometimes of postnatal depression) and/or psychiatric care had been received. For example, one woman told us that she first started taking antidepressants after miscarrying. Although she had experienced some mental health impairments before this, they were not recognised by a professional until after the miscarriage.

As we have already seen, mothers with physical impairments were sometimes advised not to have children because of the physical demands of (and risks to) pregnancy and childbirth. Before successfully giving birth to her daughter, one woman in our sample had experienced miscarriages. These had the effect of planting seeds of doubt about whether or not she would be able to carry a child for long enough for it to survive. Consequently, when she did have her baby, she felt that her previous lack of confidence in the pregnancy prevented her from bonding well with the child.

We had a number of mothers in our Stage One sample who reported that MS, depression or back problems developed or worsened just before or after the birth of their child. For parents with a physical impairment, the emotional consequences of an increased severity in impairment following pregnancy were often stressed more so than the impairment itself. We look at this further later in this chapter when considering the experience of parenting young children.

CHANGES IN FAMILY COMPOSITION

In Chapter Six, we focus specifically on parents' experiences of their ongoing relationships with partners and children. Here, we want to deal with the important way in which the experience of parenting can change over time through alterations in family shape. We do this by looking specifically at parents' reports of their decisions to have (or not have) more children, the ending of relationships with partners, and the experience of losing a child.

Decisions to have further children

In Stage One, we asked the disabled parent to say whether or not they had considered having more children in the future (Table 5.1). The vast majority of parents felt that their families were complete, with only five parents seeing future children as certain or likely.

While one child was a positive choice for some parents, others spoke of how they had hoped for further children. Although this is an experience shared by other families, parents did sometimes talk about the consequences of this in the context of parental impairments:

> Some days I thought it would be nice for my daughter. For instance, if I was ill, she would have a playmate.
>
> *Mother (PI), dual-parent family*

Several parents gave a similar reason for wanting another child. Therefore, decisions to add to the family were made *despite* any concerns about impairments and health problems. One father, for example, described how his wife's MS worsened considerably after the birth of their third child; yet they were determined that this daughter should have another sibling due to the large age gap between her and her elder sisters.

Table 5.1: "Do you think you will have more children in the future?"

	NUMBER
Currently expecting	2
Yes	1
Probably yes	2
Probably not	5
No	53
Don't know	2
Not answered	2
Total	67

Earlier in this chapter, we saw that professionals could have an important part to play in enabling disabled people to become parents in the first place. Often decisions to have further children were made in negotiation with health professionals—20 parents had been advised at some time by professionals not to have any—or any more—children. None of these parents felt that they would be likely to have any more children, with 17 certain that they would not. However, professional responses to potential or actual pregnancies ranged from specific advice in the context of a consultation, to casual remarks. Sometimes it was simply the manner in which the professional responded to a parent that conveyed their (sometimes influential) disapproval. One single mother diagnosed with manic depression, who had two children living with her as well as an older child living with her ex-husband, said that she would not have any more children. In fact, her psychologist made a 'funny face' at her when she said she wanted another baby. Similarly, people received input from others in inappropriate circumstances. For example, a paediatrician whom a mother visited with her son made a comment aside from her son's health problems:

> He wanted to give me counselling so I wouldn't have more kids—he kept saying, "Are you pregnant?".
>
> *Mother (PI), dual-parent family*

Parents whose family life was already operating under considerable pressure often internalised the feeling that it was something wrong with their parenting that had lead to difficulties. Earlier in this chapter we referred to a mother who said that social workers had told her not to have children. She was a single mother, whose sons' had emotional and behavioural difficulties, and she felt that both she and her sons had been unsupported over a number of years. While she did not talk specifically about her own childhood, she did volunteer information about her difficult years before becoming a mother, including having had a custodial sentence as a young woman. She thought that she would probably not have another child, despite having also said that she would quite like another one. While recognising that her sons had difficulties with which they required more support than they received, she also expressed her own feelings of failure. She stated that if she were to have another child:

> I might get it right this time.
>
> *Mother (MHI), single-parent family*

A father's impairment could also influence a couple's decision about whether or not to consider having another child. Not one of the disabled fathers in the Stage One sample thought that they would have any more children. It may be less likely for professionals to offer 'advice' to families in the case of a disabled father, and perhaps this is in part due to assumptions concerning men's role in parenting. A father with MS told us that no professional had ever talked to him about whether or not he wanted more children, but that it had been an important issue to himself and his wife:

> MS is very important. We do talk about it—my wife would like to [have another child]. I know it would be a struggle and now I'm not working.
>
> *Father (PI), dual-parent family*

It would be wrong to suggest that many of the parents in our sample were unhappy about their decision to have no more children, or that their impairment was always a central factor in this. Rather, just as some parents had mainstream considerations at the fore when deciding to go ahead with more children (such as wanting a sibling for a previous child), many felt that their families were complete, and/or had concerns about money and employment issues—sometimes linked to disability—which led them to decide against further pregnancies.

Others were pragmatic about their decision not to have more children on health grounds. However, mental distress (linked to either a mental ill health diagnosis or painful experiences during pregnancy) also featured. Two such parents were among a small group who stated that soon after their last pregnancy they or their partner had been sterilised:

> I sent him [partner] to the doctors after our son was born as I didn't want more. If I'd had any more, I'd be gone—I wouldn't be living.
> *Mother (MHI), dual-parent family*

> I said I didn't want no more. They [professionals] said don't get sterilised until Sally is one—how horrible that pregnancy was. When Sally was one I was sterilised. I don't think my spine would take another pregnancy anyway.
> *Mother (PI, MHI), dual-parent family*

The responses of the parents in our sample therefore suggest that very few had in-depth advice from professionals concerning their decisions to have more children. Anyhow, many felt that this was a decision they could make on their own. Fathers particularly seemed to be least likely to receive information from medical professionals (for instance, on potential support available). While some mothers felt they had received good care and information, others felt that there was often limited information and *directive*—rather than *supportive*—input. Some felt that professionals were trying to police decisions that they felt capable of making on their own in the light of information provided. This highlights a need for parents to have access to good-quality information and advice, and in appropriate settings. Our data also show that decisions about whether or not to have children are closely interwoven with concerns about disability (public and professional attitudes, the anticipated extra difficulties, and so on) and impairments (for example, the effect of pregnancy on existing impairments, and the effect of taking or not taking medication during and after pregnancy, among other things).

Relationships: endings and their consequences

Single parenthood, rather than impairment itself, was often put forward by some parents in our sample as the main source of strain in parenting. Significantly, the earlier chapters of this book indicated the additional barriers faced by single parents in accessing support, as well as the additional socioeconomic disadvantage faced by disabled parents, and the likelihood that the children of single parents would take greater responsibility for domestic and 'caring' work.

As part of our research, we did not pursue details about separations, or the death of a child's other parent. However, parents were often open about their past relationships, and why they had ended, and the extent to which children maintained contact with a non-resident parent. As one would expect, where impairment had been present before a relationship began and had remained relatively stable, the impairment was not usually seen to be a factor in a separation. A small number of parents, however, and particularly those with mental health impairments, identified destructive or abusive relationships that had exacerbated and/or focused upon their distress. One woman told us that, although her last partner found her manic depression 'hard' to cope with, she differentiated this relationship (from which she continued to derive support) from her previous marriage:

My ex-husband used to say "You're a psycho"—he was verbally abusive.

Mother, (MHI), single-parent family

While a high level of input from the child's other parent could be a great support, for others it impacted on their own relationship with their child, and particularly the extent to which they felt a child should provide them with support. The only single father in our sample, who was also interviewed at Stage Two, continued to care for his son in close negotiation with his son's mother. So much so, in fact, that the mother called in during the first interview and the father felt it improper to consent to his son's taking part in the research without asking her permission. Their separation had occurred at the same time that his health difficulties began and he was unsure about whether or not these were related. He was concerned not only about protecting his son from involvement in care tasks, but also about criticisms from his ex-partner:

I mean there are occasions, you see, when I fall down at home .... I can't pick myself up. I know that he wants to help me then, but I can't ask him to do that ... . He's not quite old [enough?]. ... And apart from that, his mother would give me a hard time if she thought I was using him as a carer.

Father (PI), single-parent family (Family J, Interview Two)

Parents also raised concerns about how much to inform an ex-partner about their impairments. Another father in our sample, who had shared caring tasks with his daughter's mother (and who had re-partnered), felt unable to explain his impairment to his daughter. He was held back by the worry that his expartner would rush the child to the doctors to 'have her checked out'[5].

The extent to which non-resident parents continued to have contact both with the disabled parent and their children was clearly an important factor for most single parents and 'reconstituted' families. Single parents identified perceived threats to their children's wellbeing, which reduced the capacity of the child's other parent to sustain their involvement in parenting. These factors ranged from the other parent living abroad, to their coping abilities, and to alcoholism. For such single-parent families, accessing the support of a child's other parent was not always an option. Families who had experienced domestic violence faced particular difficulties. Where an ex-partner was perceived to be a continued (physical or emotional) threat, and where the parent felt undersupported, the consequences were often isolation and fear. One mother told us how she and her children had to change their family name and sever all ties that could link them to her children's father. After some time at a women's refuge, they had a protracted period when they were moved to various 'safe houses' before finally settling in a village. Here, however, the family (and the mother in particular) felt extremely isolated. Another single mother, the victim of her ex-partner's violence from when their child was just six months old, expressed fear. She had been unable to isolate herself from him completely, and her ex-partner had at times tried to abduct the child, despite an out-of-court access agreement. At the time of our interview, the father had recently been seen waiting close to her son's school, causing her to be concerned that he might again try to take the child.

These experiences can be contrasted with a small number of families where an ex-partner maintained very strong links with the day-to-day lives of the family. For example, a mother talked about the important part played by her son's father, who not only maintained regular contact with their child, but was also heavily involved in supporting her domestically (with household chores that she found very difficult to carry out during periods of mental distress). As with other single parents, therefore, the long-term impact of a separation on parenting responsibilities was very varied.

Loss of a child

Within our interviews, there were three ways in which parents had experienced loss in a parenting relationship:

- the death of their child;
- their child(ren) being taken into local authority care;
- their child(ren) moving to live with another parent.

One family highlighted how the loss of a child prior to the mother's disability had in fact strengthened family coping resources. A Stage Two family (Family C) had lost their youngest son when he was five years old, before the onset of his mother's MS. The parents felt that this loss had significantly affected how they and their two other children had subsequently coped with both the mother's diagnosis, and the progression of the condition. The father viewed his two remaining sons as having always been there to provide support, and felt that the family's earlier loss had equipped them to deal with their upset at their mother's diagnosis.

Unfortunately, we found one clear example of how formal services exacerbated the difficulties of a family who experienced the death of their disabled child. This was one of our families interviewed at Stage One and Stage Two (Family H), who, between interviews, had been bereaved when their teenage daughter died suddenly. Preceding this, there had been a long battle with local services for support for both their daughter and the mother, in which they had eventually succeeded in obtaining home adaptations and direct payments. The grief experienced by this family was exacerbated by a social work report prior to their daughter's death that had expressed the view that the mother was not an appropriate model for the daughter to 'emulate' as a disabled person, since this did not aid her development. This was in contrast to the feelings of the mother, who felt that their different impairments had actually provided them with a special relationship of camaraderie. Since the child's death, the swift approach of the benefit agency for information, and subsequently slow processing of the family's benefits, at a time when they were looking to meet funeral costs, had created further hurt. Their grief was further impinged on by a plan by local services to have the family convert the daughter's bedroom into a bathroom in their plans for adapting the family home. The primary sources of support for the family had been their local church and their daughter's school. Both groups had expressed sadness at the girl's death, and showed concern for the family's loss. These basic human responses were sadly lacking in the actions of the formal agencies.

We also heard of social services expressing disapproval towards a young man's decision to return to live with his mother, after having been in local authority care. For a long time, his mother had been living on her own as her children were living in various local authority placements. Her husband had died after a long illness when their children were very young. She described each of her sons as having had 'behavioural special needs', and she had often been unhappy about the inadequate support they had received. She saw the estate where she lived as a threatening place for her children to live, and felt she could do little to protect them. She and two of her children had experienced violence from neighbours—she saw this as the cause of her children being looked after by the local authority. At the time of our interview, her eldest son had returned to live with her, after living with his girlfriend's family for a short time, and he had regular contact with his grandparents (although his younger siblings did not). His mother told us that his plan to return home was not treated positively by a social services team leader. In fact, he had been warned that, if he did live with his mother, he would feel guilty "because your mum's disabled".

Both of these cases highlight long-term difficulties that can be faced by parents who struggle to receive supports that are relevant to their family's needs as a whole. Of particular concern is the way in which disabled parents in both families appear to have been considered as 'problems' in themselves.

Three disabled parents did inform us that a child of theirs had been adopted into another family. One woman, who spoke briefly about a baby she had given up for adoption, said that, in retrospect, she felt that she should have accepted the emotional support that had been offered to her to help her come to terms with this loss, which in any event was considered to have been her only possible course of action. Another family, however, who had lost custody of one of their children some years ago when she was only a baby, talked about the effect that inadequate support had had on their confidence in their abilities as new parents. In particular, the requirement that the mother prove her ability to look after an infant—while on an adult psychiatric ward and barred from using the staff kitchen to ster ilise bottles or make feeds—was seen as overwhelming and unfair. Her hand impairments also made using old-fashioned nappy pins difficult; yet her difficulty in using them was interpreted as a deficit on her part, rather than the environment in which she was expected to parent. Subsequently, her lack of confidence came to be used against her and her husband as evidence of inadequate skills, which was used to justify placing their child for adoption.

For single parents, there was sometimes the option of a child living primarily at the other parent's home. One mother, interviewed in Stage One and Stage Two (Family G), had three sons, one of whom had moved to live with his father, over 100 miles away. This was a result of his emotional and behavioural problems, which had been present in the years following his parents' separation: he had 'dissolved' his mum to tears, and failed to keep to work plans with the child psychologist and the social worker. In the Stage One interview, the mother said that her son had decided that he wanted to go to his father, although she was not sure whether her son now felt that he had made the right decision. However, just over a year later at the Stage Two interview, it became clear that there had indeed been significant difficulties. Her son (now aged 16) had left his father and his stepmother (who were apparently treating him poorly) and was living at a friend's house:

> In the end it got really bad and he ran away to his friend's house and they've kept him there ever since and that was about 18 months ago.
>
> *Mother, (MHI), single-parent family (Family G, Interview Two)*

Her son, then, remained resident *near* to his father, but still a long way from his mother and younger brothers. While this seemed to be a difficult situation for his mother, because of her concern for her son, it was a situation she could at least accept, especially since having seen for herself the situation her son was now in. She felt that his friend's family had "turned him around" and that he was now looking forward to living with a group of other boys while taking his A levels. It was also important to her that they were now very close emotionally, and that he visited her and his brothers regularly, for holidays and weekends[6]. However, at the second interview, she also talked about how it was difficult for him to slot back in on these visits, and referred specifically to her mental health impairments:

> It is hard because … he knows I'm not so well, I don't do things. I don't do the washing up and I've got a thing, what people laugh at: … even though I don't do the washing up I don't like germs, and if I don't do it for four days all I do is just go squirt, squirt with the germ spray and walk away and leave it. But, they're all so efficient and they want to do the washing up, "Come on [middle child], let's do the washing up". He doesn't wanna do it, you know, and I say "Oh leave it, don't worry about it", you know. It's just because he lives in a different household.
>
> *Mother, (MHI), single-parent family (Family G, Interview Two)*

PARENTING OVER TIME

As we specifically sought families with older children (who might be willing to be interviewed) in our recruitment strategy, our research includes more information about parenting those children of school age. However, a small number of families included young babies or toddlers, and many more parents we interviewed also discussed issues relating to parenting younger children in depth. Here, then, our focus is on parenting children of pre-school age and on parents' changing experience of their children's education.

Parenting young children

Of course, when parents discussed difficulties in parenting younger children, what featured prominently were the issues of time limitations and tiredness faced by all families. Some parents, though, felt that they faced specific physical, emotional and social problems. One mother we spoke to in Stage Two compared her experience of having a baby prior to her ill health with her current experience of having a young daughter while suffering from ME. She herself had concerns that she was unable to provide her daughter with the range of experiences that her son had encountered. When she was first interviewed, her daughter was six months old. Her ME had made it physically very difficult for her to get out of the house, and she was unable to drive. On the rare occasions when she met other mothers with small children, she could still feel isolated as a disabled parent:

> I mean, I think one of the things that I've learnt over the last year … as a disabled parent, disabled parents are not part of mainstream society at all. I mean, even when I go to an NCT [National Childbirth Trust] coffee morning, even though that's quite rare, you are the only person, I mean, you're there with your walking stick, and you know, you're sort of, sometimes you have to ask other people to change a nappy, or lift the baby into the car.
>
> *Mother (PI, MHI), dual-parent family (Family L, Interview Two)*

Although she felt there had been an improvement in some aspects of her wellbeing, at the Stage Two interview the mother explained how, now her daughter was older and heavier, childcare tasks could threaten her health, particularly by intensifying her fatigue. Since her son was now older, she had the option of involving him in caring for his sister, and she and her son would both be involved in bathing her, and would split other tasks between them. She felt that, although they were adapting to circumstances, this was far from satisfactory. This family had been unable to gain access to any formal support, and their informal support consisted of a friend of the parents taking their young daughter out for fresh air every day. The husband explained how he saw the situation:

> There is no provision for the children of disabled parents, especially young children. You know, the children's team won't fund it 'cos the child isn't disabled, the disabled team won't fund it because the child the parent wants support with helping isn't disabled, you know? … But to improve the quality of life for both, somebody should say, "Right, well, this needs doing", you know, it's a need that's not identified. But hopefully with more and more people who are disabled having children, pressure will come to bear, but at the moment people write rules and they like to put people in boxes and if you don't fit the box there's nothing there.

Father, dual-parent family (mother, PI/MHI) (Family L, Interview Two)

The potential long-term impact of those particular stresses faced when caring for young children and lack of support for parents provide a good example of the importance of looking at disabled parents' experiences over time. For example, in one of our Stage Two families, the mother's depression did seem to be specifically postnatal, and later linked to demands associated to parenting a child with autism. The father described his wife's mental health history as follows.

> Well we were married about two years when [our first son] was born and after he was born [my wife] had … what they said was postnatal depression and was ill for about four years. And sort of got over it a bit and had [our second son] and then she had it again for a couple of years and then we had [our third son] and we had it again for a couple of years. And then she got better after that and then we found out about [our second son's] disability and we had a lot of problems with the school he was at. So [my wife] was ill again after that and has been ill for about three years now. So she's been ill on and off for … about 16 years now.

Father, dual-parent family (mother MHI) (Family D, Interview One)

For others, postnatal depression was linked to physical impairment rather than to a response to childbearing. For example, one mother found her impairments had deteriorated following her final pregnancy and subsequently experienced severe depression. It was only after this last pregnancy that her spina bifidarelated impairments began to impact on her day-to-day life. She felt that, had she and her family been better supported during the early days, when she was coping with small twins and her own impairments, her emotional problems would not have been so debilitating. There were broader social and economic consequences for the family. It was this profound depression, rather than her physical support needs, that had led her husband to give up work to become a full-time carer.

Parenting school-age children: maintaining contact with schools

In Chapter Four of this book, we discussed the balance that parents tried to strike between allowing young children to be involved in household activities (due to their desire to lend a helping hand) and ensuring that they would not become overinvolved. In particular, parents expressed the view that, as children grew older, the importance of them being able to concentrate on schoolwork and exams increased. However, while parents often felt that they were able to organise their parenting within the home in a way that was satisfactory to them, greater difficulties often emerged when they discussed the extent to which they could gain positive working relationships with schools.

While many parents in our sample had no contact with social services, health services (other than general practitioners), the benefits system, or local authority housing departments (and so on), each one had direct experience of sending children to school and of trying to maintain what they saw as satisfactory levels of involvement with the education system.

Two thirds (44) of the disabled parents that we interviewed had been able to attend a parents' evening in the past 12 months. The majority of parents were fairly satisfied with the level of contact they had with schools: 23 felt contact was 'good', 25 felt that it was 'adequate', and 15 that it was 'less than adequate'. However, interesting findings emerged from our data regarding the importance of change in influencing the way in which parents were involved in school life. In particular, several factors often conspired to make it increasingly difficult for parents to maintain the level of involvement desired as their children progressed through the education system.

The number of parents who commented on the difference in terms of accessibility between primary and secondary schools was striking. The relative inaccessibility of secondary schools was partially a straightforward issue of the physical environment of the school. For example, several parents talked about difficulties they had encountered when attending open days at their children's new secondary school, given the older architecture, the separation of schools into various sites on a single campus, and the reliance on stairs both inside and outside the school. One parent commented:

> His secondary school has been much more difficult to access, although they are trying to address it. Basically, it is a school built for non-disabled students and that affects us as parents.
>
> *Father, dual-parent family (mother, PI, MHI)*

Other parents talked about the assumptions that lay behind access problems they had encountered at secondary schools. One non-disabled father commented on the fact that in recent years only he, and not his wife, had been attending parents' evenings:

> In the last few years it has only been me really that's been going to parents' evenings. The primary schools were much better, I think, because they have a kind of pushchair mentality which obviously people using wheelchairs can benefit from.
>
> *Father, dual-parent family (mother, PI)*

That primary schools are likely to take access issues relatively more seriously because of the likelihood of parents also having pushchairs lends weight to broader arguments concerning the willingness of schools to respond to the access needs of children much more positively than to the access needs of their parents, despite the apparent overlap of interests between the two groups. It could be argued that more recent initiatives that have looked at disability, access and education have been rigorous in their examination of the needs of disabled pupils, but less so with regard to the educational needs of the children of disabled parents (DfEE, 1999). Indeed, this reinforces our argument concerning the invisibility of disability as a parenting issue (since research into disability and family life is dominated by a focus on childhood disability). Here, then, is a clear example of how disabled adults can be excluded from a key element of their parenting role.

However, the factors inhibiting involvement in secondary school education were not limited to issues of access; rather, they were compounded by other interrelated factors. For instance, one mother talked about a particularly difficult period when social services had contemplated placing her son on the 'at risk' register. The strong relationship the family had established with their son's form teacher at primary school was seen as extremely supportive, and the input of the teacher, being a person who appreciated the problems faced by the family, was seen as very important. The mother contrasted this strong relationship with a single form teacher at primary school with the absence of relationships with teachers at secondary school.

Distance is another factor exacerbating the difficulties of disabled parents' involvement in secondary schools. Primary schools are typically much closer to where children live than large secondary schools, since secondary schools' intake comes from a much wider catchment area (particularly in rural or semirural areas). This can often compound any transport and mobility barriers that disabled parents already face.

Closely related to this is the central role of parental choice in their children's schooling, especially in the secondary sector, where children are increasingly likely to attend schools other than the one closest to their home. One father described the different ways in which the practicalities of family life had changed as his two children went from attending a local village school, which was within walking distance of their home, to attending a secondary school in the nearest large town, 20 miles away. This led to the loss of informal networks for parents and children alike, as other children from that year group went to a wide variety of schools. While this happens in many families, the difficulties were compounded by the fact that his wife was recovering from a period of severe depression, which had precipitated hospitalisation. Taking medication meant that she was unable to drive, forcing the family to confront the problems that the daily use of public transport often entails, especially as she did not have the confidence to accompany her children to school. The family did receive support from the father's employer, who allowed him to leave the office earlier and catch up on work later in the evening, and by the willingness of a family friend to 'baby-sit' the children at his office until their father was able to drive them home from school.

This case illustrates how the changes that ordinarily occur as part of family life, such as the progression of children through different parts of the education system, can be experienced very differently by disabled parents. Our interviews strongly suggest that, when children move from primary to secondary school, it can be much more difficult, for a variety of reasons, for disabled parents to maintain the kind of ongoing contact that they would like. This is particularly significant given the importance of the shift from primary to secondary school at a moment when parents might be successfully engaged and support offered (Henricson et al, 2001). Difficulties in maintaining contact with schools may be particularly acute for parents experiencing dramatic change in other areas of their lives, and especially for those with progressive and deteriorating conditions. One single mother talked about the very rapid 'death' of her informal network. Not only had her son moved from primary to secondary school, but her impairments had worsened and she had lost her only form of assistance with transport when her own father had suffered a stroke.

RECENT CHANGES IN PARENTAL IMPAIRMENT: ONSET AND VARIABILITY

We now consider the extent to which parents felt as though their parenting responsibilities were adequately understood by professionals. Often, with retrospect, parents felt that there had been a lack of awareness of the potential consequences of impairment and disability for people's family lives. For instance, one father described his wife's consultant delivering her diagnosis thus:

> He said "You've got MS—some people change from butter to margarine. You've just got to get on with it".

Father, dual-parent family (mother, PI)

While for some parents impairments developed gradually over time, others experienced either a sudden (and often physical) development of impairment, or great variability (often mental health impairments). This group was our prime concern throughout Stage Two of our research.

Sudden onset

Many of the respondents we spoke to in Stage Two had recently experienced either the onset of a condition or a traumatic injury. Parents often highlighted the impact that this had had on their children, which could in turn lead to greater demands on them as parents. In two families, a parent had experienced a traumatic injury, as a result of a road traffic accident. In each case, the injuries sustained were reported as having had a particularly strong impact on the family's daughter, who wanted to be close to the disabled parent. One father described the situation as follows:

> Our daughter has found it quite difficult to cope with mummy not being quite as she was and … possibly she's been traumatised by it because she wakes up at night at the moment, not every night but some nights, and she wants to come in and sleep with us. So we've sort of erected a sort of makeshift bed, which we put up every night, next to our bed. But, and she's fine, you know, she'll sleep there, but then mum can't sleep, so she ends up going off to our daughter's bed.

Father, dual-parent family (mother PI), (Family A, Interview One)

Similar responses were reported from a mother who had recently started having epileptic seizures. Her daughter had witnessed her first seizure and had seen her mother taken to hospital in an ambulance.

> To be honest with you, when it first happened our daughter used to be a bit, she used to sometimes get a bit upset, because she used to think, you know,

say she'd had a bit of a bad day at school, she'd sort of, like, come home, she'd think, she'd be worried about me, a lot, at first, when she'd go to school. She'd, like, rush home from school to make sure that I was all right. And that I had come home from work.

Mother, dual-parent family (PI), (Family B, Interview One)

Professional advice and support in relation to parenting seemed to be most likely to be forthcoming when impairments were seen as more stable and predictable. A rare example of a father feeling that his doctor was more than aware of his need to be involved in family life was given during our Stage Two interviews. He had recently had his leg amputated, and there was concern on the part of his consultant to organise operations in a way that would ensure that he and his wife had a holiday with their children. His wife told us his story:

So right from day one when, when he was first in hospital and I said, "We've got a holiday booked in July, do you think I ought to cancel it?". And he said, "No." He said, "You want to try and go on that holiday, whatever happens, you're going to need it by then". So I mean, all along we've been asking every time we've sort of, every month we've gone, "Are we still all right for the holiday?". "Yes, yes, you're still going on that holiday." Then when the problems started with the knee, we said, "Does this mean that the holiday's going to be … [cancelled]?". He said, "No way, we'll work, we will work round that, you give me your holiday dates and I will make sure we work round it".

Mother, dual-parent family (father, PI), (Family F, Interview Two)

While the mother was positive about the consultant's family awareness, the father did feel surprised at the extent to which the early input focused on his medical needs when emotionally the family as a whole had other needs, such as counselling support. He also felt his own emotional needs were overlooked, since while he was on the ward the hospital staff had seen him as a 'coper' and even suggested that he try to cheer up another man who was not considered to be dealing with his injuries so well. Therefore, even when health professionals were family-aware, there could be a lack of psychological support for both disabled parents and their families.

Variability

When parents spoke about whether or not their impairments had an impact on their parenting, or talked about the support they required, a key feature was the extent to which their condition was viewed as stable. Related to this was the extent to which people felt future changes could be foreseen, and whether parents felt that they could hope to maintain or achieve their desired level of independence (or interdependence). Concerns about ongoing deterioration, relapse, or more rapid variability could make thinking about the future difficult, especially when the family did not feel positive about the extent of support experienced, be that currently or in the past.

Many of the parents we talked to spoke about the importance of achieving a period of stability. For those parents who felt that they were currently more stable in their condition, it was clearly hoped that this would be something that could be maintained in the long term. For one family taking part in Stage One of our research, the father's variable mental health impairments highlighted the way in which families have to keep on adjusting, and how concerns and difficulties can remain even where a previously 'ill' parent is currently perceived as 'well'. The father had needed extensive periods of sick leave from his job, since his severe anxiety and depression made it difficult for him to leave the house. At the time of our interview, he was pleased with his progress and with the medication he was taking, and was back at work. His wife and daughter were both keen to state that his problems were behind him, although his wife maintained that she continued to be concerned about his future health.

Parents also talked about how they had learned more about their condition over time, so that variability could eventually become more manageable. However, apparent improvements could also come at a cost for parents. For instance, a mother with ME (Family L) told us on our first visit that her level of fatigue meant that she was unable to drive. On our second visit, she reported that she was able to drive now, but that it would have significant costs for her after a trip out:

> The fact that I'm driving now means that the fatigue is worse afterwards. So, I mean, I'm wiped out today because we took the cat to the vet yesterday …. Although it is a good thing that I can actually drive a little bit, it, it tends to backfire on me because I'll do something and then I'm, you know, sort of completely wrecked for two or three days afterwards.
>
> *Mother (PI, MHI), dual-parent family (Family L, Interview Two)*

This need for self-care might be particularly difficult to express to services or through benefits assessments. This mother spoke of how it could be very difficult for people with ME to access benefits, partly because of its variability and also because of the lack of recognition of it as a condition. Her concern was widely expressed by those with variable conditions, and particularly those who had mental health impairments:

> But certainly it's something that is a cause of concern for anybody with disabilities, the fact that they can just take your benefits off you like that, and it's very worrying.
>
> *Mother (PI, MHI), dual-parent family (Family L, Interview Two)*

Likewise, variability in condition could also mean insecurity about access to support, and about future income.

LOOKING TO THE FUTURE

Planning for the future, then, is greatly affected by variability in impairments, and uncertainty about future services and benefits. Parents themselves spoke of concern (and sometimes fear) about their future, and that of their family, including financial wellbeing and the potential physical and emotional costs of 'caring' on family members. We referred earlier in this book to Family C who felt their personal resources to respond to the mother's MS had been strengthened by their shared experience of the terminal illness of one of their children. However, the father did indicate that it was the 'not knowing what might be round the corner', both in terms of the MS and of support, which made planning for the future difficult. Concerns about impairment and personal, family and social resources were often discussed alongside economic concerns.

Finances

For some parents, the opportunity to stay in—or return to—work was a key issue. Work could be seen as important for both financial security and social contact. For each of the Stage Two parents who had experienced traumatic injuries, the question of whether or not they would be able to return to work was of central importance. One parent received support, both from her employers and a psychologist, enabling her to return to her professional job. The other was a father who had worked in a factory—he, on the other hand, experienced greater insecurity about a possible return to work. His employer had said that they would keep his job open for two years, but he had already received letters that offered him voluntary redundancy.

> Never been on the dole in me life, I've always found something to do. I've never been out of work and I don't want to, I don't want to sit and go to an office and sign on ... . If I have to I will do but I, I'll strive to get a job somewhere ... . I'll feel like I'm just dragging everything out of the system and I don't want to do that I want to—I still want to put into it if I can, but if I can't in the end, well, I'll have to accept that, but then that's going to be a bit more of my self-respect gone.

> *Father, dual-parent family (PI), (Family F, Interview Two)*

Concern about future employment among parents who had a longer experience of impairment, and who had remained in work, was greater when variability was a feature of the condition. There were cases of extremely supportive employers, but it was often unclear whether this support would be maintained in the long term. Only 12 of our parents had any regular paid employment; therefore, in dual-parent families where a partner had continued to work, the ability of the partner to stay in employment was often a key concern:

> As I say, you know, the pressure's on me, well, to carry on working. I mean, ... there's two ... pensions or, you know, I've got to provide a retirement for two of us. There's not many people know that, once you finish work, you cannot have a private pension. That's one of the first things that happened, when my wife finished work. Before we got any benefit, or anything, there was a letter through from the ... pension company to say, "The pension's on hold".

> *Father, dual-parent family (mother PI), (Family C, Interview Two)*

Similar pressures were felt in families where neither parent was employed. A father discussed how he and his partner might use a future inheritance, given the lack of access they had to financial services, particularly mortgages and pensions:

So then we've got to think right, well, we've got to put all that money into a house, we won't get a mortgage 'cos we're not working. I mean, it's the same, same thing as, like, you can't get a pension if you're not working. I mean a lot, a lot of these things you find out over the course of time.

Father, dual-parent family (mother, PI), (Family L, Interview Two)

Parents therefore did discuss the impact of disability on current and future plans, and often felt that information to support this was gradually accrued rather than readily available.

CONCLUSIONS

Our study has focused primarily on current support needs, but we have also been able to sketch out some of the key issues involved in parents' experiences of family life over time. It is important to include what might be viewed as 'mainstream' experiences (such as contact with schools and financial security) alongside other factors specific to the experience of disability and impairment. Our research highlights that experience of disability and parenting over the life course must be grounded in the changing social and economic framework within which parenting and family life takes place.

Our focus has been disability, time of onset and variability in impairment with reference to the life course. Some of the parents we interviewed discussed the impact of negative attitudes towards disabled people becoming parents: we argue that this reflects their relative invisibility (in contrast to 'young carers') in public and policy discourses. It is clear that, for some of our respondents, having a family was achieved despite a lack of support or approval from others, including both family or professionals. Indeed, within our sample we found clear evidence of how disabled people were actively discouraged from expecting access to Priestley's (2000) two cultural signifiers of independent adult life—employment and parenting. Negative attitudes could continue to be expressed by professionals from the beginning of pregnancy through to parenthood. While parents would often welcome infor mation concerning parenting with an impairment, some clearly felt that they were being given little room to make, and little respect for, their own decisions (for instance, about having more than one child), given the explicit disapproval of others.

What our research has also highlighted is the potential long-term impact of the demands of parenting young children alongside little or no support. For example, physical or mental health impairments—even where they predated having children—could be exacerbated by (and experienced as) creating dayto-day difficulties for the first time having become a parent. Our brief review of changes in family shape and the later onset or impact of impairment (a family life course) highlights the importance of understanding the experiences of impairment and of disability in the context of relationships. This is the focus of Chapter Six.

Notes

1. Normative concepts of the life course are extremely influential in shaping social policy, and the invisibility of disabled parents reflects the way in which disabled people are often excluded from such expectations of adulthood.

2. Each of the parents in our sample had children aged at least four years. Consequently, our research did not focus on the experience of becoming a first-time parent.

3. Since our sample does not include disabled people who did not become parents, we have been unable to consider what factors are important for those who decide not to have children, or feel that they were dissuaded from becoming parents.

4. Unfortunately our sample did not include a sufficient number of fathers to measure whether or not disabled men had felt similarly limited in their expectations, and how these expectations had impacted on their experience of becoming parents.

5. Despite having only two fathers in single-parent or reconstituted families on which to draw, their experiences suggest to us that fathers feel more limited than mothers do in their ability to make decisions about how to involve their children in disability-related family issues. This is likely to be due to the higher level of involvement of mothers in these cases than we found of fathers in the other single parent or reconstructed families.

6. Research has not yet paid sufficient attention to the difficulties faced by children when returning to live for brief periods with their disabled parent. Instead, it has concentrated on the experiences of resident children. This situation is perhaps more often relevant to disabled fathers, and merits further attention.

UK Fathers' Long Work Hours: Career Stage or Fatherhood?

By Laura Biggart and Margaret O'Brien

O ver the last thirty years, fathers' roles have been changing, from that of primary breadwinner, with economic provision as a focus, to a more caring role, where fathers are expected to be more involved in the care of children. In terms of role attitudes and expectations, there is a legacy of traditional gendered views about work and family responsibilities, with fathers constructed as the economic "provider" (Hood, 1986) and mothers as responsible for childcare and domestic matters. These attitudes still exist today, although they are no longer the dominant view (Crompton, Brockmann, & Wiggins, 2003). In the same time frame, a combination of economic need, the cultural impact of feminism, and improvements in the work opportunities available to women, has resulted in a large increase in the numbers of women now in the workplace in the UK; rising from 56.4 percent of women in the workforce in 1971 (Self & Zealey, 2007) to 69 percent by 2008 (Office for National Statistics, 2009). As a consequence there is less time for working mothers to carry out childcare and domestic work. This time shortage has been partly addressed, individually, by greater use of public childcare and, organisationally, with greater provision of flexible working options. The time dilemma has also been met, in part, by fathers who have shown small increases in the care of children (Gershuny, 2001; Smith, 2007). The associated increase in UK dual earner families means that fathers are now under more time pressure from home responsibilities.

The UK governmental policy framework of the last decade has aimed to facilitate greater work-life balance, particularly for parents, through the Employment Act 2002 and the Work and Families Act 2006. Although the main policy attention has been on mothers, there has been an increasing focus on fathers, with the objective to extend work-family choice for both parents to earn and spend time with and children (Supporting Families, 1999). In particular, there has been strong policy steer to increase flexible working options for mothers and fathers. Of course informal voluntary flexible working arrangements had been in place before new legislation but not promoted or part of a formal "right to request." UK governmental emphasis continues to focus on extending choice of flexible working options rather than impose working hour reductions (DTI, 2003; Walsh, 2008), and although the British government have accepted the EU Working Time Directive 1998, it has retained the opt out clause allowing employees to volunteer to work more than the 48 hour annualised limit.

FATHERS' AND MOTHERS' EMPLOYMENT PATTERNS

Fathers' roles have been changing, over the last thirty years, from that of primary breadwinner, with economic provision as a focus, to a more caring role, where fathers are expected to be more involved in aspects of childcare (Thompson, Vinter, & Young, 2005; Warin, Solomon, Lewis, & Langford, 1999). The male breadwinner identity stems from the era of industrialisation and development of the capital economy (Bernard, 1981). The breadwinner ideal stipulates that men provide for the family economically whilst women undertake the household chores and caring responsibilities (Hood, 1986). The male breadwinner role, in real income terms, has rarely met the criteria of sole male economic provider for the family. These circumstances were briefly achievable for families between 1940–1970 (Hood, 1986) but have been less economically possible for most families since then. In recent times, women's contribution to household income has been increasing at a higher rate than that of men. In Britain there has been a 31 percent increase in contribution to household income for women compared to 13 percent for men between 1996/97 and 2003/04 (Department for Work and Pensions, 2005). Nonetheless the psychological impact of the breadwinner concept has been longer lasting for the construction of male identity (Warin et al.). In this qualitative study men still show strong connections to the breadwinner role as illustrated by one of the respondent fathers:

> Providing for them is absolutely critical because it justifies-it justifies to a certain extent my existence, that 'why am I doing this? (Warin et al., 1999, p. 17)

Whilst achievement of the single earner "ideal" status appears untenable in current economic circumstances, adherence to the breadwinner identity still seems strong for many men (Burghes, Clarke, & Cronin, 1997; Dex, 2003). In contrast, societal attitudes towards family roles have changed with decreasing proportions of men and women agreeing with the statement: "A man's job is to earn money; a woman's job is to look after the home": 28 percent agreed with this statement in 1989, decreasing to 17 percent by 2002 (Crompton et al., 2003). In studies of men's attitudes towards men's work time, high proportions of fathers wish to reduce their work hours to spend more time with the family (Kodz et al., 2003). Fatherhood scholars have outlined increases in fathers' involvement in family life (Lamb & Lewis, 2004; Pleck & Masciadrelli, 2004) and surveys have revealed the dilemmas that fathers face in managing work and family (Thompson et al., 2005). Although there is evidence of the caring fatherhood model, when looking at the work hours and patterns of flexible working for fathers, compared to mothers, the gap is still large. Moreover, when comparisons between fathers and non-fathers are made for work hours, fathers have been found to work more hours than non-fathers (Kodz et al., 2003; O' Brien & Shemilt, 2003). However, recent evidence indicates that this effect of fatherhood status does not hold when other variables such as age and occupation are controlled (Dermott, 2006; Natti, Anttila, & Vaisanen, 2006). Further evidence on fathers' employment activity rate and work hours outlined below provide a background context from which the current issues have emerged.

In spite of a perceived transition of the father role, the structure of British fathers' employment remains significantly different to that of mothers', both in terms of working hours and patterns. Nonetheless, employment rate trends by gender from the Office of National Statistics (2001) show a convergence of men's and women's employment rates, with a steady increase in the rate of participation in employment by women of 47 percent in 1959 to 70 percent in 1999 and a parallel decrease in participation by men from 94 percent in 1959 to 79 percent in 1999 (Mill et al., 2001). Latest figures indicate that while employment rates have remained at this level proportionally for men and women, there are still more men within the workforce than women, 79 percent of men, 70 percent of women (Office for National Statistics, 2008). By 2009, figures indicated that while employment rates had remained at this level proportionally for men and women, there were still more men within the workforce than women, 75 percent of men, 69 percent of women (Office for National Statistics, 2009). In spite of the large increase of women entering the workforce over the last thirty years, the distribution of men and women within the workforce is still very different, with more men working full-time compared to women and differing gender composition across occupations. This gender disparity is largely due to the changes in work patterns of parents. The differences between mothers' and fathers' working patterns are greater than that for gender differences. Since 2001, figures showed that fathers with preschool children have higher employment rates than mothers, 90 percent compared to 57 percent for mothers in 2008 (Office for National Statistics, 2008). In addition, with regard to full-time employment rates, the proportion of fathers employed full-time in the workforce by 2001 stood at 86 percent, a much higher rate than mothers at 31 percent (O'Brien & Shemilt, 2003).

Although UK working patterns are becoming more diverse, with more flexibility on offer, the majority of men still work full-time, 93 percent in 2008. Numbers of men working part-time have increased in recent years, from 3 percent in 2001 to

7 percent in 2007 (Office for National Statistics, 2008). Although, one reason for this increase in male part-time working could be due to more fathers increasing their caring role, employment figures examining men's employment patterns show that: only 4 percent of fathers worked part-time compared to 7 percent of men without children in 2007 (Office for National Statistics, 2008) suggesting that fathers are more likely to work fulltime compared to men without children. Furthermore socio-demographic data shows that amongst couples with children, the UK has the highest proportion (40 percent) of full-time/part-time households in Europe (Crompton, 2006; Franco & Winqvist, 2002), which primarily consist of male full-time earners and female part-time earners. International attitudinal survey evidence indicates a strong preference for the full-time breadwinner plus part-time carer model in the UK (Connolly & Gregory, 2008; Crompton & Le Feuvre, 2000) providing additional explanation for stability in fathers' long work hours in the UK.

Work Hours over the Life Course

These differences in gender ratios for full-time working, particularly those for fathers, suggest that mothers still take on the primary responsibility for childcare. Other figures also support this interpretation, for example in employment activity rates for parents at different ages across the life course. Differences in employment activity rates for fathers and mothers show a gap of 24 percent at age 30–34 years, the prime years for birth of first child. Mothers' employment activity rate drops to 68 percent at this time, but fathers' employment activity rate remains high at 92 percent (Mill et al., 2001). Furthermore, the age of the child also has a negative impact upon mothers' employment rates, with the largest gap of 56 percent between fathers and mothers' employment rates when the age of the youngest dependent child is between 0 and under four years (Paull, 2008). This impact of child age upon mothers' work patterns can also be seen in mothers' employment rates and work hours' reduction (Office for National Statistics, 2008) and goes some way to explaining the high prevalence of mothers' part-time work in Britain. In summary, the high employment activity rate for British fathers supports assumptions embedded in the father as breadwinner model.

Fathers' Work Time

In analyses of fathers' work time from UK datasets spanning the last 24 years, fathers have been found to work longer weekly hours than men without children (Brannen, Moss, Owen, & Wale, 1997; Kodz et al., 2003; O'Brien & Shemilt, 2003). Fathers' work time in the UK reached prominent status when it was reported in 1996 that UK fathers worked the longest hours in the EU, 46.9 hours per week (Deven, Inglis, Moss, & Petrie, 1998). Information from the Labour Force Survey show that, although no longer the highest hours in Europe, UK fathers' mean hours per week were still 47 hours per week in 2001 (O'Brien & Shemilt). More recent data from the Labour Force Survey show decreased working hours per week for fathers from 47 hours in 1998 to 45 hours by 2007 (O'Brien, 2008). In the First Work Life Balance Survey in

2000 fathers showed a high tolerance for working long hours with 60 percent of fathers satisfied with work-life balance at 48 hours per week and 50 percent at 60 hours per week (O'Brien & Shemilt).

An international comparison of fathers' work hours in 2002 by Medalia and Jacobs (2008) shows that Japan, the UK and USA stand out as unusual for developed countries for fathers' weekly work hours because they show similar high weekly work hours (51, 50 and 48 hours, respectively) as poorer countries of Chile and Mexico (52 and 51 hours respectively), whilst the majority of other developed countries show lower than average (46 hours) weekly work hours for fathers (see Figure 1). The UK has consistently shown long weekly working hours, particularly for fathers (O'Brien & Shemilt, 2003). It is argued that closer evaluation of differences in work hours between fathers and men without children is particularly worthwhile in the context of the gender gap in both work hours and pay.

Whilst fathers mean work hours are considered high, comparisons with non-fathers assess the significance of fatherhood status. In multivariate analyses, Brannen et al. (1997) found that fathers worked longer hours than non-fathers when controlling for age and Kodz et al. (2003) found that fathers were more likely to work more hours than nonfathers when controlling for age, occupation and qualifications. This evidence supports the proposition that the breadwinner role for fathers is still predominant. More recent work by Dermott (2006) re-tested the disparity between fathers and non-fathers' work hours controlling for age, earnings, occupation, education and partner's work status and found no significant difference between fathers and non-fathers work hours once age was introduced into the regression analysis. Dermott suggested that fatherhood status had been conflated with career stage, as both life stages coincide. Natti et al. (2006) also found no effect for fatherhood status in their regression analyses on men in Finland, which included the same variables. Given that age had been included in earlier analyses finding fatherhood status to be a significant predictor of work hours, it raises a question about the breadwinner model: Has the fatherhood role as breadwinner become less salient so that fathers are now adopting a working hour regime more typical of men without children? Or are significant numbers of fathers adopting the caring role and reducing their hours to the extent that they now cancel out the effect of traditional fathers? A U.S. study by Kaufman and Uhlenberg (2000) suggests that treating fathers as a homogeneous group will mask differences between groups of fathers undertaking changing roles. They found that fathers who saw their role as breadwinners worked longer hours compared to fathers who undertook the caring more involved role.

Kaufman and Uhlenberg's (2000) findings with regard to fathers' changing behaviour are supported by Reynolds et al. (2003) study, which report that some fathers have been found to make sacrifices in their career prospects to spend more time with their children (Reynolds, Callendar, & Edwards, 2003). In the same manner recent evidence from the Millennium Cohort Survey (Tanaka & Waldfogel, 2007) found that fathers who worked less hours when their child was under one year spent more time in childcare activities such as changing nappies, feeding the baby and getting up in the night. Another study (Yeung et al., 2001) found that fathers' time with the child in play

Figure 1: Fathers' Weekly Work Hours by Country Using Data from the International Social Survey Programme 2002

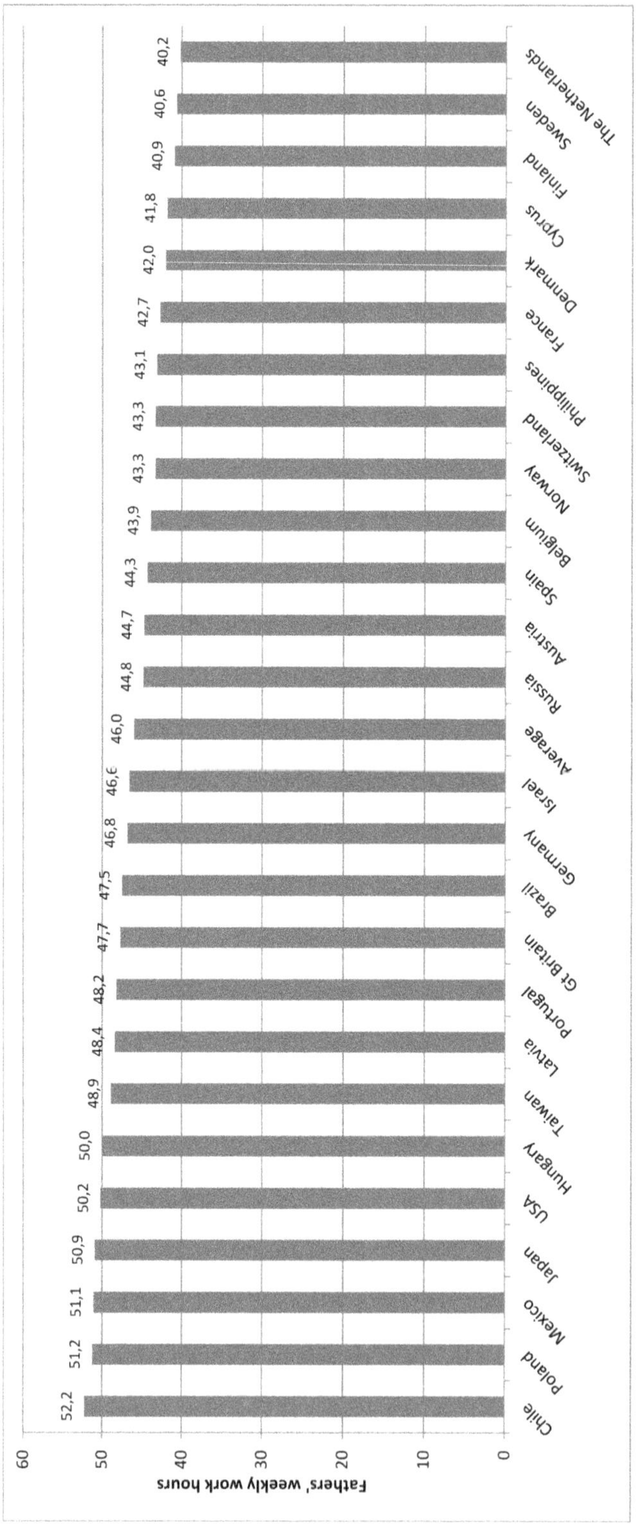

Adapted from Medalia and Jacobs (2008, p. 151).

and care giving activities decreases as their child's age increases. Fathers in Yeung et al.'s study spent more childcare time in the week with children aged 0-5 years.[1] It is also clear from a number of attitudinal studies (Fagan, 2003; Kodz et al., 2003) that fathers state that they would prefer to work reduced hours.

Clearly these findings run counter to the breadwinner hypothesis and empirical findings which show that fathers work more hours than non-fathers. However, in times of role transition it would be likely that contradictory behaviours are observed as fathers endeavour to find ways to accommodate new roles within existing social and economic constraints. Recent changes in UK legislation for paternity leave and the right to request flexible working have enabled UK fathers to change their work patterns whilst their children are still under six years old.

The caring father model and evidence cited above suggests that fathers with young children under 6 years old may be more likely to work fewer hours than fathers with older children and non-fathers, whilst the breadwinner model suggests that fathers with young children will work more hours than fathers with older children and non-fathers. The effect of child age will be included in the analyses here to test previous UK research which did not include child age in their models.

The first research questions consider fathers' work hours compared to non-fathers and assess whether fatherhood status is a significant predictor of the number of hours worked. Recent evidence with different employment datasets (Dermott, 2006, Natti et al., 2006) shows that when age is taken into account, fatherhood status as a predictor of work hours, no longer has an effect. It has been suggested that the stage of fatherhood within the lifecycle, between 25–45 years, coincides with a key development stage for career, between 30–50 years, and that it is the career stage that has an impact on working hours rather than fatherhood (Dermott).

This analysis proposes to add the age of child as a predictor of working hours, as the early child years make fatherhood status particularly salient (Flouri & Buchanan, 2003) and might therefore be a better predictor of fathers' behaviour. Age of child is considered a useful indicator of the level of caring responsibilities for parents as younger children require more caring time (Fisher, McCulloch, & Gershuny, 1999). Findings indicating a negative correlation between mothers' employment activity status and age of child, but not for fathers (e.g., Paull, 2008) suggest that the breadwinner father model is still dominant.

There are a number of factors that have been found to influence working hours that cut across individual, job, organisational culture and economic levels of analysis. Factors under consideration here are: parental status, partnership status, age of child, occupation, pay, education and age. These factors have been chosen from previous research to test the hypothesis that fatherhood status is one factor which increases working hours in line with the theoretical breadwinner model and empirical evidence showing that

---

1 Note: this effect is not solely due to fathers' availability, young children are, by the nature of their dependency on parents, also more available at a young age than when they are older and more independent.

fathers work longer hours than men without children (Feldman, 2002; Kodz et al., 2003; O'Brien & Shemilt, 2003).

The following variables were chosen as controls for the analysis which are described below. Income has been shown to be strongly positively associated with working hours (Weston, Gray, Qu, & Stanton, 2004) and for those occupations (manual/semi-skilled), where hours relate directly to income this is no surprise, however the relationship of working hours with income for professional occupations is less overt. Long hours worked by those in professional occupations do not immediately translate into income, but contribute to an impression of work commitment, which is then rewarded in terms of promotion at a later date (Kalleberg & Epstein, 2001). Income is nonetheless an important co-variate as income has been shown to be strongly positively associated with working hours (Weston, Gray, Qu, & Stanton).

Occupation is an important variable to consider in relation to work hours as long working hours are more common amongst men, managers, professionals, and operative and assembly workers. Manual workers usually get paid for overtime, while managerial and professional employees generally do not. Manual workers see the main benefit of long hours working in terms of increased earnings, while managerial and professional workers see it in terms of improved promotion prospects and greater job security (La Valle, Arthur, Millward, Scott, & Clayden, 2002). Education has been found to be related to working hours via its links to occupation, but also directly for those with higher levels of education who work fewer hours than those with lower levels of education (Anxo, Boulin, & Fagan, 2006) and was therefore included as a variable for the analysis.

Men's age was included in the analysis to act as a proxy for career stage which could confound findings that fathers' work longer hours than men without children. Dermott (2006) found that age controls removed the significance of the relationship between fatherhood and working hours. Previous findings indicate that fatherhood tends to coincide with the most productive times for career stage between the ages of 30–49 years (Kodz et al., 2003) and therefore fathers' working hours are likely to be highest during this life stage.

Child age has strong effects upon mothers' working hours with mothers of children under the age of 4 years working fewer hours per week than mothers with older children or women without children (Paull, 2008). Child age also appears to be negatively related to fathers' employment rates which decrease after a child age of 16 years (Walling, 2005). Child age was therefore also considered to be a factor which could influence fathers' work hours.

The breadwinner model would suggest that the employment status of a man's partner would influence his work hours, however, evidence on the impact of partner employment status on fathers' working hours is mixed (Pleck & Masciadrelli, 2004; Weston et al. 2004). The UK has a high proportion of households with one full-time and one part-time breadwinner (Weston et al., 2004) which could operate to increase fathers' working hours, but neither Weston et al. nor Deven et al. (1998) found any significant relationship with partner employment status and fathers' working hours.

The regression analyses on the Third Work Life Balance 2006 dataset aims to test Dermott's (2006) findings using the British Household Panel Survey and the National Child Development Survey showing that, contrary to other studies (O'Brien & Shemilt, 2003; Smith, 2007), fatherhood status is not a sufficient predictor of working hours, and that working hours are more associated with career stage.

If the breadwinner model holds true we would expect fathers to work more hours than non-fathers even when controlling for other factors known to also affect working hours, such as income, education and occupation. In addition, we speculate that fathers with very young children, under 6 years old, will work more hours than fathers with children 6 years and over and non-fathers in order to make up for an expected loss of income, as British mothers often return to work part-time after maternity leave (Burchell, Dale, & Joshi, 1997; Connolly & Gregory, 2008). In contrast, under the 'caring father' model we would expect fathers with children under 6 years old to work less hours than fathers with children aged 6 years and over and non-fathers.

Therefore, if there are differences between men's working hours on the basis of fatherhood status, we might expect that:

1. Fathers will work longer hours per week than non-fathers when directly compared.
2. Fathers with children under 6 years will work more hours per week than fathers with children 6 years and over and non-fathers.
3. Fatherhood status is predictive of working hours per week for men with children controlling for: age, occupation, earnings, partner employment status, employment status, and educational level.
4. Fatherhood status is predictive of working hours per week for men with children under 6 years controlling for: age, occupation, earnings, partner employment status, employment status, and educational level.

METHODS

Dataset

This paper presents findings from analysis of fathers' and non-fathers' employment behaviour from the *Third Work-Life Balance Employee Survey (2006)*. The *Third WorkLife Balance Employee Survey* is a cross-sectional survey conducted in February and March 2006 of adults of working age (16 to 64 for men and 16 to 59 for women) living in Great Britain, working as employees in organisations employing five or more employees at the time of the survey. The final number of interviews completed was 2,081. Further detail about the sampling methodology can be found in the main report (Hooker, Neathy, Casebourne, & Munro, 2007) and related technical report (Latreiile & Latreille, 2008).

Sampling

To achieve a representative sample, interlocking quotas were used at the sampling stage based upon sex, age and whether employee was employed in the public or private sector.

After data screening a post-stratification weight based on SIC (Standard Industry Classification) was applied to the data. For further details on response rates and sampling methodology see the technical report (Latreille & Latreille, 2008).

The sample comprised 2081 employees working as employees in organisations employing five or more employees at the time of the survey, no self-employed people were included. There were 55 percent male employees (n = 1096) and 45 percent female (n = 985). Fathers in the survey were defined as male with dependent child in household who was under 16 or under 19 and a full-time student. Of the total sample, 12 percent were fathers (n = 244) and 13 percent were mothers (n = 263).

As a proportion of just male employees, 27 percent were fathers and, of the female employees, 39 percent were mothers. When compared to the Labour Force Survey (2007) sample, the Work Life Balance (2006) parents are proportionately under represented, particularly fathers. Of the total Labour Force Survey (2007) sample 22 percent were mothers and 22 percent were fathers and as a proportion of all males in the Labour Force Survey (2007), 43 percent were fathers and of all females 46 percent were mothers. In the Work Life Balance Survey (2006) the mean age of fathers was 41 years compared to the mean age of all men of 40 years, and non-fathers 39 years.

Design and Analysis

OLS regression, t-test and chi-square were used to address the research questions. Post-hoc power calculations confirmed statistical power of 1 for regression analyses of this sample size (n = 948) to detect small effects at an alpha level of .05, with nine predictor variables.

Variables Used in the Analyses

Dependent variable. The dependent variable is working hours using the question (B05) asking about the usual number of hours the respondent worked in the week (Brannen, et al., 1997). Hours worked per week is the respondents' reported total usual hours worked per week in their main job,[2] including overtime.

Predictor variables. Predictor variables for the regressions were chosen on the basis of previous findings and theoretical importance. Variables were entered using hierarchical entry with hourly pay, education, occupation, age and partner's work status entered in block 1 and fatherhood status entered in block 2.

Fatherhood status. Fathers are defined for this analysis as males with a dependent child co-resident in the household (where the child is under 16 or under 19 and a fulltime student). For this paper analysis is focused on couple[3] fathers in full-time[4] employment, the majority pattern. Fathers are not a homogeneous group and other notable sub-

2   Although Dermott (2006) included second job as a predictor variable, data about fathers' other jobs was not available from WLB3 for this study.
3   Couple defined as living with partner, constructed using question Z01.
4   Full-time is defined as working over 30 hours per week and the variable constructed using question B05 (usual work hours) in order to boost fathers' sample size.

groups are lone fathers and part-time employed fathers with different circumstances for managing their work and family time. A focus on partnered fathers in full-time employment avoids data from other distinct sub-groups of fathers confounding the results. Fathers are compared to full-time male employees with no resident dependent children (titled "non-fathers"). There were 195 (10 percent of total sample) couple full-time employed fathers and 740 (37 percent of total sample) full-time employed non-fathers in this dataset. For the analysis which assesses the influence of child age for fathers' work hours, a dummy variable was created as follows:

0—men without children (constant);

1—fathers with children under 6 years;

2—fathers with children 6 years and over.

Control Variables

Income. Income was included in the analysis as a continuous variable representing weekly income.

Occupation. Occupation was coded as a dichotomous variable with managerial and professional occupations compared to non-managerial and non-professional occupations using UK SOC 2000 occupational codes.

Education. Education was coded into two categories: No quals/ gcse/ other vs. Voc/ A level/ degree/ higher degree.

Men's age. Men's age was categorised into three bands: 16–30 years, 31–49 years and 50+ years.

Child's age. Due to the low number of fathers with young pre-school children in the WLB3 dataset, a dichotomous variable was created to compare the numbers of fathers with young children under 6 years with fathers with children 6 years and older.

Partner working/not working. The WLB3 survey does not allow the part-time/ fulltime partner work status to be examined as it only includes a dichotomous partner working/ not working question. Therefore a dummy variable was created for the analysis to assess whether a partner was in paid employment or not and coded as follows: 0—men with no partner (constant); 1—men with partners who are employed; 2—men with partners who are not employed.

RESULTS

Descriptives

Parental working hours. Comparisons of full-time employed couple fathers with equivalent non-fathers' working hours show that fathers work significantly more hours per week, mean 45.7 hours, *SD* 8.67 than non-fathers' weekly work hours mean

Table 1: Mean and Median Full-Time Fathers and Non-Fathers Weekly Working Hours

	MEAN WORK HOURS PER WEEK	SD	MEDIAN WORK HOURS PER WEEK	N UNWEIGHTED BASE
Full-time couple fathers	45.7	8.67	44	195
Full-time non-fathers	43.5	8.10	40	740

Table 2: Long Weekly Working Hours Proportions by Fatherhood Status

Usual work hours per week (Banded)	30or less		>30–35		>35–40		>40–48		48 and more		Total	
(Unweighted Base)	N	%	N	%	N	%	N	%	N	%	N	%
FT Couple fathers	3	2	7	3	76	38	46	22	63	35	195	100
FT NON-fathers	14	2	53	7	308	43	204	27	161	22	740	101*

*Over 100% due to rounding

43.5 hours, SD 8.1 t (295) = -3.298, p < .001 (Table 1). Similar differences in median work hours across full-time parental groups are significant (X^2(5, n = 1569) = 125.25, p = .001)[5] and support Hypothesis 1 and confirm previous findings showing differences between fathers' and non-fathers' work hours in a direct comparison (O'Brien & Shemilt 2003; Kodz et al., 2003).

Fathers' working hours. Working long hours, defined as over 48 hours per week for this study, is of policy concern and previous research has indicated that fathers as a group work particularly long hours (Hayward, Fong, & Thornton, 2008; Hooker et al., 2007). In this sample it was also found that a substantial proportion of fathers worked long hours. As shown in Table 2 the proportion of fathers working over 48 hours per week (35%), using banded hours, is significantly more than non-fathers (22%), X^2 (4,968) = 15.62, p < .01. However, within the long hour category of over 48 hours there is no significant difference between the mean work hours per week for fathers (56 hours) and non-fathers (55 hours).

Multivariate analyses[6]—*Factors predicting fathers' work hours.* In spite of evidence from fathers' and non-fathers' work hour comparisons other studies adopting a multivariate approach have found that fatherhood status per se is not a significant predictor

---

5   Krusal Wallis test (uneven sample sizes).
6   Zero order correlations can be found in Table 4.

Table 3: Descriptive Distributions for All Variables

		FULL-TIME COUPLE FATHERS		FULL-TIME NON-FATHERS	
		%	N	%	N
Age	16–30yrs	8	13	29	206
	31–49yrs	80	154	40	306
	50+ yrs	12	26	31	222
	Total	100	193	100	734
Occupation	Professional/				
	Managerial	57	113	46	346
	Non-professional	43	69	54	350
	Total	100	182	100	696
Partner employment					
	Partner works	66	131	71	293
	Partner does not work	34	64	29	118
	Total	100	195	100	411
Child Age	Under 6yrs	30	53		
	6yrs and over	70	123		
	Total	100	176		

of work hours for men once other variables are controlled, particularly that of men's age (Dermott 2006; Natti et al., 2006). In this study regression models are also developed in line with Dermott's procedure, using non-fathers working hours as the reference category. The control variables are: age, income (weekly earnings), education, occupation and partner's work status (working or not working). A final model explored the effect of age of child on fathers' working hours.

Age. Fathers' age distribution across the three age bands shows a significantly high concentration of fathers in the age band 31-49 years (80%) compared to non-fathers (40%) who are more evenly spread across the age bands, $X^2(2, 961) = 102.98, p < .001$, as shown in Table 3.

Occupation. As can be seen in Table 3, there are significantly more fathers in managerial occupations than non-fathers, $X^2(1, 908) = 7.44$ (with Yates continuity correction), $p < .01$.

Partner's work status. Although slightly higher proportions of fathers (34%) have partners who do not work to non-fathers (29%), this is not statistically significant.

Child's age. There are more fathers with the youngest dependent child being 6 years and over ($n = 123$) in this sample than fathers with children under 6 years ($n = 53$).

For the first regression model (see Table 5), testing hypothesis three, earnings, education, managerial status, partner work status and age, were entered as controls in block 1 and fatherhood status in block 2. The variables entered in block 1 explained

Table 4: Zero Order Correlations Between All Variables

VARIABLE	M	SD	1	2	3	4	5	6	7	8	9	10	11
1 Male weekly work hours	41.33	11.40	1.000	.013	.301***	.086	-.035	.095***	.091***	.000	.110***	.043	.098**
2 Male hourly pay	11.45	27.90		1.000	.121***	.062**	-.022	.001	-.020	.089***	-.004	-.008	.003
3 Occupation					1.000	.263***	.089***	.027	.121***	-.036	.091**	.054	.076*
4 Education						1.000	.018	.019	.011	-.096***	-.005	-.022	.003
5 Partner works							1.000	-.360***	.107***	-.003	.227***	.047	.258***
6 Partner does not work								1.000	.044*	.080***	.184***	.176***	.044
7 Age—31–49 yrs									1.000	-.553***	.328***	.195***	.250***
8 Age—50+ yrs										1.000	-.173***	-.152***	-.079**
9 Father											1.000	.510***	.807***
10 Father with dependent child under 6 years												1.000	-.096**
11 Father with dependent child 6 years and over													1.000

*p< .05, **p< .01, ***p < .001

Table 5: OLS Regression—Model 1. Fatherhood Status as a Predictor of Weekly Work Hours

VARIABLE	STANDARDIZED BETA	UNSTANDARDIZED BETA	STANDARD ERROR
Hourly pay	−.029	−.008	.011
Education	.018	.476	.985
Occupation	.291***	7.730	.993
Partner works	−.074	−1.951	1.065
Partner does not work	.037	1.431	1.567
Age—31–49 years	.070	1.840	1.176
Age—50+ years	.064	1.941	1.321
Father	.081*	2.629	1.292
Constant	32.426		
R^2	.11		
$R^{2\,adj}$	.10		

Constant:
Education: No quals/ gcse/ other vs. Voc/ A level/ degree/ higher degree
Occupation: non-professional vs. professional
Partner: No partner
Age: 16-30 years
Fatherhood: Men without children vs father
*p< .05, *** p< .001

9.6 percent of the variance in work hours R^2 adj = .096, F (7,711) = 11.91, p < .001. Only one significant predictor from block 1 emerges, that of occupation; specifically being in a managerial or professional job. Adding fatherhood status in block 2 explained 10 percent of the variance in work hours, R^2 adj = .10, $F(8,710)$ = 10.99, p < .001. Occupation remained a predictor of increased work hours, but fatherhood status explained an additional 0.5 percent of the variance in work hours, R^2 change = .005, $F(1, 710)$ = 4.14, p < 0.05. However, the standardised beta values indicate that occupation explains more of the variance in work hours (beta = .291, p < .001) than fatherhood status (beta = .081, p < .05). This analysis supports hypothesis three and suggests that fatherhood status is a small but significant predictor of working more weekly hours alongside being in a managerial or professional occupation, after controlling for age, earnings, education and partner's work status.

The next regression model (see Table 6) includes further fatherhood variables which distinguish between child age, 0–5 years, and 6 years and over, testing hypothesis 4; that fathers with very young children, 0–5 years, will work longer hours per week than nonfathers and fathers with children 6 years and over. In this model, fathers with older children (6 years and over) significantly predict work hours R^{2adj} = .10, F (9,691) = 9.60, p = .000, contradicting hypothesis four that fathers with younger children would work more hours. Occupation remains significant predictor of work hours in this model.

Table 6: OLS Regression—Model 2. Fatherhood and Child Age as Predictors of Weekly Work Hours

VARIABLE	STANDARDIZED BETA	UNSTANDARDIZED BETA	STANDARD ERROR
Hourly pay	−.028	−.008	.011
Education	.017	.462	.999
Occupation	.291***	7.725	1.006
Partner works	−.077	−2.009	1.080
Partner does not work	.043	1.669	1.577
Age—31–49 years	.067	1.763	1.196
Age—50+ years	.059	1.780	1.343
Father with dependent child Under 6 years	.028	1.572	2.153
Father with dependent child Over 6 years	.085*	3.283	1.519

Constant:
Education: No quals/ gcse/ other vs. Voc/ A level/ degree/ higher degree
Occupation: non-professional vs. professional
Partner: No partner
Age: 16-30 years
Father and child age: men without children
*$p < .05$, *** $p < .001$

DISCUSSION

This paper has explored whether long working hours, typically noted for fathers, compared to similar men without children, is best explained by career stage or parental status. The extent to which being a parent promotes greater economic activity during a time in life when a career is particularly time hungry has been debated in academic circles (e.g., Dermott, 2006). Assumptions underlying traditional role theory would suggest that the presence of children enhances the salience of a breadwinner role for men activating the elevation of working hours. The results of the UK WLB3 analysis reported here does indeed confirm that fatherhood status (being a father rather than not being a father) is a small but significant predictor of working more weekly hours, alongside being in a managerial or professional occupation, after controlling for age, earnings, education and partner's work status. These results showing that fatherhood status predicts work hours, albeit to a small degree, align with Kodz et al.'s (2003) early analysis of the UK Work Employment Relations (WERS) 1998 data set, but not with other studies (Dermott; Natti et al., 2006) suggesting an uncertain pattern and so a need for more research triangulating different data sets.

Although this finding may be interpreted as a forced or chosen work ethic connected to fatherhood in the British context, it may also reflect cohort and selectivity effects, particularly in such a small sample of fathers found in the WLB3 dataset. For example, the findings here do not include self-employed fathers, who are known to work longer hours than employees. We would expect the inclusion of self-employed fathers into this analysis to strengthen the breadwinner hypothesis; however, Dermott (2006) included self-employed fathers in her analysis and found no effect of fatherhood status. At the other extreme, this analysis does not include part-time employed fathers who could cancel out small effects of fathers working longer hours, although the proportions of part-time fathers in the WLB3 dataset suggest otherwise (only three fathers worked less than 30 hours per week). Nonetheless, running a series of analyses to account for the heterogeneity in both working hours, contract type and fatherhood circumstance would be warranted. For example, a similar study by Dommermuth and Kitterød (2009) on Norwegian fathers separated fathers into groups according to child number and child age, but omitted to include step-fathers in the analysis. Maintaining definition and variable consistency across analyses of different datasets remains a challenge, but would be most achievable through the use of LFS datasets, which are most likely to be similarly designed for international comparison. The interplay of working hours, parental status and life stage is complex and cannot be fully understood through cross-sectional investigation. These issues would benefit from further analysis especially through longitudinal cohorts and more detailed psychological studies (e.g., Kaufman & Uhlenberg, 2000). The emerging picture is limited by the inherently narrow scope of quantitative employment activity data but, nevertheless, suggestive of issues worth pursuing in further studies.

These findings also show that fathers who have older children (six years and over) are more likely to work longer hours, contradicting hypothesis four that fathers with younger children would work more hours. This finding supports Dommermuth and Kitterød (2009) who also found that fathers with older children (six years and over) work longer hours than men without children. They argue that this may be due to the fact that it is possible for fathers to maintain contact with their older children later into the evening than is possible with younger children. Their findings from analysis of the Norwegian LFS show that fathers are reducing their hours for young children, but increasing them once they reach school age. From the findings on child age in our study, a replicated analysis of the UK LFS would be interesting to test this pattern.

Whilst the definition of fathers for this paper is tightly defined, the definition of non-fathers rests solely on two characteristics: no dependent children and full-time employment. Clearly there may be some men in the non-father sample who may have non-dependent children residing elsewhere, but this is difficult to assess from the WLB3 dataset. Nonetheless, further comparisons between fathers and different groups of men classified in other life course terms, for example—co-habiting relationship status, single men or couple full-time men without dependent children, may help isolate the specific contribution of fatherhood to working hours further.

The other significant factor predicting work hours for men, regardless of fatherhood status, was occupation. Those in managerial and professional occupations were more likely to work longer hours than those not in these occupations. This pattern has been found to be the case in other studies and has been suggested to occur as a result of managers and professional jobs being subject to increases in work intensity (Green, 2001; Kodz et al., 2003) and having greater autonomy and control over the job (Hayward et al., 2008). Lyonette, Crompton, and Wall (2007) have found a similar effect for professional mothers in the UK, who worked more weekly hours than either intermediate profession mothers or manual occupation mothers. Their work-family conflict levels were also higher. In the same study, a similar comparison of men showed higher work hours for professional men compared to intermediate occupations, but not for manual occupations, who had the highest work hours, contrary to other findings. Nonetheless, such findings support an interpretation that occupation is a more important predictor of working hours than parenthood, for men and women, but that further differentiation of parental occupational group will be helpful in future exploration of this interrelationship.

In spite of the stronger effect of occupation on working hours in this study, the variance explained by the model was low (10 percent). Dermott's (2006) analysis from two larger national datasets with the same predictors in the model (apart from second job) explained 24 percent and 29 percent from her regression models using data from the National Child Development Study and the British Household Panel datasets respectively. It is possible that the WLB3 dataset, with the relatively low number of fathers (22 percent) compared to Labour Force Survey proportions (43 percent) contributed to this pattern, coupled with the inability to include the variable of second job within the model may all go some way to explaining the lack of explanatory power in the overall model.

The interplay of working hours, parental status and life stage is complex and cannot be fully understood through cross-sectional investigation. It clearly requires further analysis especially through longitudinal cohorts and more detailed studies (e.g., Kaufman & Uhlenberg, 2000). The emerging picture is limited by the inherently narrow scope of quantitative employment activity data but nevertheless suggestive of issues worth pursuing in further studies.

REFERENCES

Anxo, D., Boulin, J., & Fagan, C. (2006). Decent working time in a life course perspective. In J. Boulin, M. Lallement, J.C. Messenger, & F. Michon (Eds.), *Decent working time: New trends, new issues* (pp. 93-122). Geneva: International Labour Organisation.

Bernard, J. (1981). The good-provider role: Its rise and fall. *American Psychologist, 36*(1), 1-12.

Brannen, J., Moss, P., Owen, C., & Wale, C. (1997). *Mothers, fathers and employment: Parents and the labour market in Britain 1984–1994.* London: Department for Education & Employment.

Burchell, B., Dale, A., & Joshi, H. (1997). Part-time work among British women. In H.P. Blossfield & C. Hakim (Eds.), *Between equalization and marginalization: Women working parttime in Europe and the United States of America* (pp. 210–243). Oxford: Oxford University Press.

Burghes, L., Clarke, L., & Cronin, N. (1997). *Fathers and fatherhood in Britain.* London: Family Policy Studies Centre.

Connolly, S., & Gregory, M. (2008). Moving down: Women's part-time work and occupational change in Britain 1991-2001. *The Economic Journal, 118*(526), F52–F76.

Crompton, R. (2006). *Employment and the family: The reconfiguration of work and family life in contemporary societies*. Cambridge: Cambridge University Press.

Crompton, R., & Le Feuvre, N. (2000). Gender, family and employment in comparative perspective: The realities and representations of equal opportunities in Britain and France. *Journal of European Social Policy, 10*(4), 334–348.

Crompton, R., Brockmann, M., & Wiggins, R.D. (2003). A woman's place.... Employment and family life for men and women. In A. Park, J. Curtice, K. Thomson, L. Jarvis & C. Bromley (Eds.), *British social attitudes: The 20th report* (pp. 161–187). London: Sage.

Department of Trade and Industry (DTI). (2003). *Balancing work and family life: Enhancing choice and support for parents*. London: HMSO.

Department for Work and Pensions. (2005). Individual incomes of men and women 1996/97 to 2003/04: Women and Equality Unit, London.

Dermott, E. (2006). What's parenthood got to do with men's hours of paid work. *The British Journal of Sociology, 57*(4), 620-634.

Deven, F., Inglis, S., Moss, P., & Petrie, P. (1998). State of the art review on the reconciliation of work and family life for men and women and the quality of care Services. In *Department for Education and Employment and European Commission* (Ed.). London: HMSO.

Dex, S. (2003). *Families and work in the twenty-first century*. York: Joseph Rowntree Foundation.

Dommermuth, L., & Kitterød, R.H. (2009). Fathers' employment in a father-friendly welfare state: does fatherhood affect men's working hours? *Community, Work & Family, 12*(4), 417–436.

Fagan, C. (2003). *Working-time preferences and work–life balance in the EU: some policy considerations for enhancing the quality of life*. Dublin: European Foundation for the Improvement of Living and Working Conditions.

Feldman, D.C. (2002). Managers' propensity to work longer hours: A multilevel analysis. *Human Resource Management Review, 12*(3), 339–357.

Fisher, K., McCulloch, A., & Gershuny, J. (1999). *British fathers and children*. Colchester: University of Essex, Institute for Social and Economic Research.

Flouri, E., & Buchanan, A. (2003). What predicts fathers' involvement with their children? A prospective study of intact families. *British Journal of Developmental Psychology, 21*, 81–98. Franco, A., & Winqvist, K. (2002). *Women and men reconciling work and family life*. Luxembourg: Eurostat.

Gershuny, J. (2001). *Changing times*. New York: Oxford University Press.

Green, F. (2001). It's been a hard day's night: The concentration and intensification of work in late twentieth-century Britain. *British Journal of Industrial Relations, 39*(1), 53–80.

Hayward, B., Fong, B., & Thornton, A. (2008). *The third work-life balance employer survey*. BERR Employment relations research (Vol. Series No. 86). London: HMSO.

Hood, J.C. (1986). The provider role: Its meaning and measurement. *Journal of Marriage and the Family, 48*(2), 349–359.

Hooker, H., Neathy, F., Casebourne, J., & Munro, M. (2007). *The third work-life balance employee survey: Main findings*. London: Institute for Employment Studies.

Kalleberg, A., & Epstein, C.F. (2001). Temporal dimensions of employment relations. *American Behavioral Scientist, 44*(7), 1064–1075.

Kaufman, G., & Uhlenberg, P. (2000). The influence of parenthood on the work effort of married men and women. *Social Forces, 78*(3), 931–949.

Kodz, J., Davis, S., Lain, D., Strebler, M., Rick. J., Bates, P., et al. (2003). *Working long hours: A review of the evidence. Volume 1—Main report*. London: DTI.

La Valle, I., Arthur, S., Millward, C., Scott, J., & Clayden, M. (2002). *Happy families? Atypical work and its influence on family life*. Bristol: The Policy Press.

Lamb, M.E., & Lewis, C. (2004). The development and significance of father-child relationships in two-parent families. In M.E. Lamb (Ed.), *The role of the father in child development* (4th ed., pp. 272–306). New York: Wiley.

Latreille, P.L., & Latreille, J.A. (2008). The third work life balance survey: Technical report. prepared for Department for Business Enterprise and Regulatory Reform. London: HMSO.

Lyonette, C., Crompton, R., & Wall, K. (2007). Gender, occupational class and work-life conflict. *Community, Work & Family, 10*(3), 283–308.

Medalia, C., & Jacobs, J.A. (2008) *Working time for married couples in 28 countries*. In R.J. Burke & C.L. Cooper (Eds.), *The long working hours culture: Causes, consequences and choices* (pp. 137–158). Bingley: Emerald Group publishing.

Mill, N., Busuttil, V., Harper, R., King, N., Lillistone, C., Manners, A., et al. (2001). *Social focus on men*. London: Office for National Statistics.

Natti, J., Anttila, T., & Vaisanen, M. (2006). Managers and working time in Finland. In J. Boulin, M. Lallement, J.C. Messenger, & F. Michon (Eds.), *Decent working time: New trends, new issues* (pp. 289–313). Geneva: International Labour Office.

O'Brien, M. (2008). *Fathers' working hours and work-family policies: The UK experience*. Paper presented at the International Sociological Association Family Research Conference: Family Diversity and Gender, Lisbon.

O'Brien, M., & Shemilt, I. (2003). *Working fathers: Earning and caring*. Manchester: Equal Opportunities Commission.

Office for National Statistics. (2008). *Focus on gender*. London: Office for National Statistics.

Office for National Statistics. (2009). *Labour market statistics: October 2009*. London: Office for National Statistics.

Paull, G. (2008). Children and women's hours of work. *The Economic Journal, 118*(526), F8–F27.

Pleck, J.H., & Masciadrelli, B.P. (2004). Paternal involvement by U.S. residential fathers: Levels, sources and consequences. In M.E. Lamb (Ed.), *The role of the father in child development* (pp. 222–271). New Jersey: John Wiley & Sons.

Reynolds, T., Callendar, C., & Edwards, R. (2003). *Caring and counting: The impact of mothers' employment on family relationships*. Bristol: Joseph Rowntree Foundation.

Self, A., & Zealey, L. (2007). *Social trends 37*. London: Office for National Statistics.

Smith, A.J. (2007). *Working fathers in Europe: Earning and caring?* Edinburgh: Centre for Research on Families and Relationships.

Supporting Families. (1999). *Supporting families*. London: The Home Office.

Tanaka, S., & Waldfogel, J. (2007). Effects of parental leave and work hours on fathers' involvement with their babies. *Community, Work & Family, 10*(4), 409–426.

Thompson, M., Vinter, L., & Young, V. (2005). *Dads and their babies: Leave arrangements in the first year*. London: NOP Social and Political.

Walling, A. (2005). Families and work. *Labour Market Trends, 113*(7), 275–283 [London: Office for National Statistics].

Walsh, I. (2008). A review of how to extend the right to request flexible working to parents of older children. Prepared for The Department for Business Enterprise and Regulatory Reform. London.

Warin, J., Solomon, Y., Lewis, C., & Langford, W. (1999). *Fathers, work and family life*. London: Family Policy Studies Centre.

Weston, R., Gray, M., Qu, L., & Stanton, D. (2004). *Long work hours and the wellbeing of fathers and their families*. Australian Institute of Family Studies.

The Life Course Perspective and White-Collar Crime

By Michael L. Benson

APPLYING THE LIFE COURSE APPROACH TO WHITE-COLLAR OFFENDERS

Applying the life course perspective to white-collar crime is difficult because of the paucity of longitudinal data on white-collar offenders. There are no prospective longitudinal studies that include information on white-collar type offenses. Until recently, most of what was known about the social characteristics and social backgrounds of the people who commit white-collar offenses came from case studies of individuals or corporations that were selected primarily because of their high social status or because they had committed particularly egregious offenses. Following Sutherland's (1940) original definition of white-collar crime, as a crime committed by respectable people in the course of their occupations, many researchers have investigated cases involving high-status individuals, such as corporate executives, professionals, and high-ranking public officials (Hochstedler 1984; Hills 1987; Ermann and Lundman 1992; Cullen et al. 2006). These individuals, of course, look nothing like traditional street criminals. They occupy positions of power and influence. They have families and are financially stable. Some are active in civic affairs and known as "pillars of the community." Indeed, part of the reason the offenses appear so shocking and interesting is that the perpetrators do not come from disadvantaged backgrounds and do not have histories of run-ins with the law.

At first glance, their offenses seem completely out of character and not part of a pattern of deviant behavior. This image of white-collar offenders is widespread among the general public and law-enforcement officials (Benson 1985b; Wheeler, Mann, and Sarat 1988). It suggests that the life course trajectories of whitecollar criminals differ from those of common criminals along almost all relevant dimensions, such as occupation, education, family background, and, of course, criminality.

That there are such high-status offenders cannot be denied. There is no shortage of case studies that document their existence. Nevertheless, it is important to keep in mind that these cases were selected for study precisely because they were unusual and precisely because they fit preexisting conceptions about the high social status of white-collar offenders. Do they present a misleading picture of the average white-collar offender? Evidence that not all those who commit business-related offenses occupy positions of high social status has been around for some time (Cressey 1953; Spencer 1965). For example, some of the subjects in Cressey's (1953) classic study of embezzlement were low-level clerks or cash register attendants and not corporate executives. More recent evidence suggests that contemporary white-collar criminals are often not economic elites.

Beginning in the late 1980s, several studies called into question the classic stereotype of the white-collar offender (Croall 1989; Daly 1989; Weisburd et al. 1991). These studies were based on relatively large samples of individuals convicted in U.S. federal courts of presumptively white-collar offenses (Weisburd et al. 1991; Benson and Moore 1992; Benson and Kerley 2000). A very important study, Crimes of the Middle Classes, by David Weisburd, Stanton Wheeler, Elin Waring, and Nancy Bode, was based on a sample of 1,094 persons convicted between 1976 and 1978 in U.S. federal courts of eight selected offenses: bank embezzlement, tax fraud, credit fraud, mail fraud, securities fraud, false claims, bribery, and antitrust activity (Weisburd et al. 1991). These offenses were called the criterion offenses. For comparative purposes, the researchers also collected data on a sample of 204 persons convicted of non-white-collar criterion offenses.

This data set is one of very few that include a large random sample of offenders and that contain information on the social-class backgrounds of offenders as well as information on their criminal histories. David Weisburd and Elin Waring have recently extended the original study by gathering data on the original sample's criminal activities for over ten years following their convictions in federal courts (Weisburd et al. 2001).

At about the same time, Brian Forst and William Rhodes put together another data set similar to the one collected by Wheeler et al. (1988). The Forst and Rhodes study sampled persons convicted of ten offenses tried in U.S. federal courts between 1973 and 1978. Of the ten criterion offenses, six were white-collar crimes: bank embezzlement, bribery, false claims and statements, income-tax violations, mail fraud, and postal embezzlement. The four remaining offenses, which represent common crimes, include bank robbery, homicide, narcotics offenses, and postal forgery. The sample included 2,643 individuals sentenced for the six white-collar crimes and 2,512 individuals sentenced for the four common crimes.

Both Wheeler and colleagues and Forst and Rhodes gathered data primarily from the Pre-Sentence Investigation Report (PSI). PSIs are prepared by federal probation officers for judges. They describe the offense of conviction and provide detailed information on the defendant's educational, medical, employment, family, and criminal history (Weisburd et al. 1991, 14). In a sense, the PSI is like a retrospective life history, with the probation officer serving as the interviewer. In preparing PSIs, probation officers attempt to give judges a sense of who offenders are, where they came from, and what brought them before the court. Because judges regard evidence of prior criminal activity as an extremely important factor in sentencing, information on the nature and timing of prior arrests and convictions is usually quite detailed in the PSI. Although PSIs contain a wealth of social information, they are administrative documents produced to satisfy administrative needs. As Weisburd and colleagues (1991, 15) note, PSIs are "filtered through the eyes of probation officers and may be subject to whatever biases they may bring to their work."

THE SOCIAL LOCATIONS OF WHITE-COLLAR AND COMMON OFFENDERS

Table A.1 presents information on the demographic characteristics, employment history, and educational attainment of the individuals in the Wheeler et al. and Forst and Rhodes data sets. For comparative purposes, information is also included on sample members who were convicted of common crimes.

Beginning with demographic characteristics, in both data sets the whitecollar offenders are overwhelmingly males. They constitute 85.5 percent of the Wheeler et al. white-collar sample and 77.6 percent of the Forst and Rhodes sample. The common offenders are also disproportionately male. In both samples, dramatic differences are observed between white-collar and common offenders in race and age. Over 80 percent of Wheeler et al.'s whitecollar offenders are white, compared to only 34.3 percent of common offenders. In the Forst and Rhodes sample, the comparable figures are 73.9 and 49 percent white for the white-collar and common criminals, respectively. The age differentials between white-collar and common criminals are nearly identical in both samples. On average, the white-collar criminals are ten years older than the common criminals. If you invited the more than 3,500 white-collar criminals represented in both studies to a party, the middle-aged white males would be the least likely to feel out of place.

The standard image of the white-collar offender pictures him as a "him" and as a person of power and accomplishment, a member of the upper social classes. The data on education presented in Table A.1 suggest that this image is misleading. Just over one-quarter of the Wheeler et al. white-collar sample and less than one-fifth of the Forst and Rhodes sample are college graduates. Thus, in these two samples a sizable majority of the white-collar criminals were not college graduates. Although they are much better educated than common criminals, most of the white-collar criminal samples lack one of the standard markers of high social status that Sutherland and other white collar

Table A.1: Demographic, Employment, and Education Characteristics of White-Collar and Common Criminals

	WHEELER ET AL.[1]		FORST AND RHODES[2]	
	COMMON CRIMINALS	WHITE COLLAR CRIMINALS	COMMON CRIMINALS	WHITE COLLAR CRIMINALS
Demographic Characteristics				
Sex (Male)	68.6%	85.5%	84.2%	77.6%
Race (White)	34.3%	81.7%	49.0%	73.9%
Age (Mean Age)	30	40	30	41
Education				
High-School Graduates	45.5%	79.3%	45.7%	71.2%
College Graduates	3.9%	27.1%	3.3%	17.0%
Employment				
Unemployed	56.7%	5.7%	59.1%	30.2%
Steadily Employed[3]	12.7%	58.4%	24.1%	65.8%

1 Adapted with permission from Tables III and IV from Wheeler, Stanton, David Weisburd, Elin Waring, and Nancy Bode, 1988, "White Collar Crime and Criminals," *American Criminal Law Review*, 25:331–57.
2 The data utilized in this publication were made available by the Interuniversity Consortium for Political and Social Research. The data for *Sentencing in Eight United States District Courts, 1973–1978* were originally collected by Brian Forst and William Rhodes. Neither the collectors of the original data nor the consortium bear any responsibility for the analyses or interpretations presented here.
3 In the Wheeler et al. study the reference period for steady employment is five years. In the Forst and Rhodes study, the reference period is two years.

scholars often refer to as distinguishing white-collar criminals (Wheeler, Weisburd, Waring, and Bode 1988, 360).

Not surprisingly, the white-collar offenders were much more likely to be employed at the time that they committed the criterion offense than the common offenders. Yet, the data on employment also suggest that many white-collar offenders are not entrenched in the occupational mainstream. At the time of the criterion offense, over 90 percent of the Wheeler et al. whitecollar criminals were employed. In the Forst and Rhodes sample, about 70 percent were employed. The high rate of employment results in part from having to hold an occupational position in order to commit certain types of white-collar crimes. In stark contrast, a majority of common criminals in both data sets were unemployed at the time of their offense, and most had not been steadily employed prior to conviction. These results clearly indicate differences in employment between common and white-collar offenders. However, these dramatic differences should not blind us to the fact that steady employment does not characterize the employment history of a substantial proportion of white-collar offenders. In the Wheeler et al. data set, over 40 percent of the white-collar offenders did not have uninterrupted employment during the five years preceding their conviction. In the Forst and Rhodes study, a twoyear reference period was used, but the results are very similar. Nearly 35 percent of the white-collar offenders were not steadily employed for two years prior to their conviction. These results suggest that a notable proportion of the white-collar offender population "cannot depend on steady and stable employment at the time of their crimes" (Wheeler et al. 1988, 340).

Besides education and employment, there are other markers indicating where an individual stands in the structure of American society. For adults, marital status, homeownership, and the accumulation of financial assets can be thought of as indicators of whether an adult is conforming to society's age-graded expectations. Adults are supposed to settle down, get married, buy homes, and begin to accumulate a nest egg of financial savings. Whitecollar criminals are much more likely to conform to these expectations than common criminals (see Table A.2). In the Forst and Rhodes data set, over 60 percent of the white-collar criminals were married at the time of their conviction, versus less than 30 percent of the common offenders. A similar rate of marriage is observed in the Wheeler et al. white-collar sample (58 percent). About half (50.3 percent) of the Forst and Rhodes white-collar criminals owned homes, and so did 45.3 percent of the Wheeler et al. sample, but only 11.8 and 6.6 percent of the common criminals in the two samples owned homes. Finally, at the time of conviction, just over one-third of the Forst and Rhodes white-collar criminals had financial assets in excess of $10,000. Less than 5 percent of the common offenders were similarly welloff financially (Benson and Kerley 2000). The Wheeler et al. white-collar criminals were also much better off financially than the common criminals. The median for financial assets for white-collar criminals is $11,000 versus $180 for common criminals.

When a white-collar criminal appears at sentencing, it is not unusual for his or her lawyer to ask for a reduced sentence because the client is supposedly an upstanding citizen who has made a substantial contribution to the community (Mann, Wheeler, and Sarat 1980). A defense attorney, of course, has a professional obligation to put his or her client in the best possible light. But is it really true that the average white-collar

Table A.2: Adult Integration Into Society for Common and White-Collar Criminals

	WHEELER ET AL.[1]		FORST AND RHODES[2]	
	COMMON CRIMINALS	WHITE-COLLAR CRIMINALS	COMMON CRIMINALS	WHITE-COLLAR CRIMINALS
Married	—	58%	28.2%	61.9%
Own Home	6.6%	45.3%	11.8%	50.3%
Financial Assets Greater Than $10,000	—	—	4.5%	35.3%
Median Assets	$180	$11,000	—	—

1 Adapted with permission from Table 3.3 in Weisburd, David, Stanton Wheeler, Elin Waring, and Nancy Bode, 1991, *Crimes of the Middle Classes: White-Collar Offenders in the Federal Courts*, p. 63. New Haven, CT: Yale University Press.

Table A.3: Community Activities and Criminal Friends for Common and White-Collar Criminals

	COMMON CRIMINALS	WHITE-COLLAR CRIMINALS
Involved in Community Groups	4.7%	18.7%
Involved in Church	3.3%	11.8%
Attend Church Regularly	15.8%	31.3%
Criminal Friends	36.2%	8.4%

Note: Data are from the Forst and Rhodes sample.

criminal is a pillar of the community? The data presented in Table A.3 suggest that defense attorneys may be stretching the truth in many cases. In the Forst and Rhodes white-collar sample, the PSIs indicated that under 20 percent of the white-collar criminals were involved in social or other community groups and just over 10 percent were involved in church or other religious activities. White-collar criminals are twice as likely to attend church regularly as common criminals, 31.3 to 15.8 percent respectively. Yet, nearly seven out of ten white-collar criminals apparently have other things to do on Sunday mornings. At least they are not hanging out with other criminals. Only 8.4 percent of the whitecollar criminals were judged to have criminal friends, compared to 36.2 percent of the common criminals.

Although white-collar offenders lead more conventional lives than common offenders, it is misleading to describe them as highly integrated into community life. Over 80 percent of white-collar offenders are *not* involved in community groups. Nearly 90 percent are *not* involved in church-related activities, and about 70 percent do not attend church regularly. Nor can it be safely assumed that all white-collar criminals have high social status. Most are not college educated, and well over a third lack steady employment. Taken together, these results indicate that many of the people who violate what are often thought of as white-collar statutes are not pillars of the community. Rather, they appear to be quite ordinary people leading middle-class lives.

Although the evidence reviewed above modifies our image of the typical white-collar offender, it certainly does not indicate that white-collar and common criminals are the same. White-collar offenders may not always come from the privileged sectors of society, but neither do they share social space with common criminals. White-collar offenders occupy distinctly different places in the American social structure than common offenders. Based on their analyses, Weisburd et al. concluded that

> ... [W]hatever else may be true of the distinction between white-collar and common criminals, the two are definitely drawn from distinctively different sectors of the American population. While there is substantial diversity in the types of people that are found in white-collar crime, even the lowest end of our offender hierarchy is easily distinguished from offenders in common-crime

categories … [White-collar offenders] appear to represent the very broad middle of society.

(1991, 73)

The life course perspective prompts us to ask how they arrived at these different locations. What social and criminal trajectories did they follow? We turn to these questions now, beginning with trajectories in crime.

WHITE-COLLAR CRIMINAL CAREERS

The term "white-collar criminal career" seems like an oxymoron. The white-collar criminal is generally thought to be a "one-shot" offender, whose first encounter with the criminal justice system is his or her last (Weisburd et al. 1990). To make a career out of crime involves a commitment to deviance and nonconformity that is assumed to be the antithesis of the white-collar criminal's lifestyle.

Contrary to the popular image of the white-collar criminal as a person who has never done anything wrong, a substantial proportion of the white-collar criminals in the Wheeler et al. and Forst and Rhodes data sets have prior criminal records. As Table A.4 shows, in both samples approximately four out of ten offenders have a prior arrest. One-third of the sample members have prior convictions. Nevertheless, as a group the white-collar offenders appear to be much less involved in crime than common criminals. Over 80 percent of the common criminals in both samples have prior arrests.

Deciding what it takes to qualify as a "career criminal" is a matter of judgment. Different cutoff points can be used. The passage of "three strikes and you're out" laws suggests that for society in general the threshold number is three. Lawmakers apparently assume that individuals with three convictions have demonstrated that they are not just fooling around when it comes to crime, but rather are seriously committed

Table A.4: Prior Arrests and Convictions for Common and White-Collar Criminals

	WHEELER ET AL.[1]		FORST AND RHODES	
	COMMON CRIMINALS	WHITE-COLLAR CRIMINALS	COMMON CRIMINALS	WHITE-COLLAR CRIMINALS
Prior Arrests	89.5%	43.4%	81.8%	39.3%
Four or More Prior Arrests	—	12.0%	51.0%	15.4%
Prior Convictions	81.4%	35.4%	73.9%	31.3%

1 Adapted with permission from Table 3.3 in Weisburd, David, Stanton Wheeler, Elin Waring, and Nancy Bode, 1991, *Crimes of the Middle Classes: White-Collar Offenders in the Federal Courts*, New Haven, CT: Yale University Press; adapted from Table 2 in Weisburd, David, Ellen F. Chayet, and Elin Waring, *Crime and Delinquency*, 36(3):342–55. Copyright © 1990 by Sage Publications. Reprinted by permission of Sage Publications.

to troublemaking. Several studies on persistence in criminal careers indicate that a reasonable cutoff point to use to identify serious offenders is four arrests or convictions. Analyses of the Philadelphia cohort data, West and Farrington's Cambridge data, and Shannon's Racine cohort data indicate that the probability that a first offender will be rearrested or reconvicted ranges from 0.5 to 0.6. This probability increases after each subsequent event. Up to a point, the more arrests or convictions a person has, the more likely he or she is to persist in crime and to be rearrested or reconvicted again. This "persistence probability" reaches a plateau of between 0.7 and 0.9 following the fourth event (Blumstein, Cohen, Roth, and Visher 1986, 89). So, the chance that someone who has been arrested four times will be rearrested for a fifth time is high. If we use four arrests as the cutoff point, 12 percent of the white-collar criminals in the Wheeler et al. sample and 15.4 percent in the Forst and Rhodes sample qualify as career criminals.

As we learned earlier, many white-collar offenders are not persons of high social status. This finding raises an important question about the repeat offenders in our white-collar crime samples, and it illustrates how definitions may change results. Would our results on prior criminal activity have been different if we had defined white-collar crimes in Sutherland's terms as crimes committed by persons of high social status? Perhaps recidivism occurs only among low-status white-collar criminals.

David Weisburd and his colleagues (1990) explored this question in the Wheeler et al. data. They analyzed the criminal histories of a "selected group of offenders who held elite positions or owned significant assets, and who committed their crimes in the course of a legitimate occupation" (Weisburd, Chayet, and Waring 1990, 347). (Unfortunately, the Forst and Rhodes data set does not contain information that would permit similar analyses.) Using this definition, they were left with only about one-third of their original sample. With this more restrictive definition of white-collar crime, a smaller proportion of offenders had prior criminal records. It would not be correct, however, to say that all of these high-status offenders had led saintly lives. Over one-quarter of the high-status offenders had criminal records. Ten percent of the restricted sample of offenders had prior felony convictions. Thus, even elite white-collar offenders may have criminal careers.

Having established that many white-collar criminals are repeat offenders, it becomes important to determine how their criminal careers resemble or differ from those of common criminals. The important dimensions of career offending are age of onset, desistance, and specialization (Blumstein et al. 1986). Recall that in earlier chapters we learned that most offenders are arrested for the first time in their mid-teenage years and have desisted by their mid-twenties, and most offenders do not specialize in any one type of crime. Are these patterns evident among white-collar offenders?

With respect to age of onset of offending, white-collar offenders do not follow the standard pattern. In the Wheeler et al. data, the mean age of onset for the entire sample of white-collar criminals is 35 (see Table A.5). In the Forst and Rhodes data set, the mean age for the white-collar sample is 41, and it is 30 for the common criminals. If we consider only criminals with prior arrests, the mean age of onset declines to 27 for the Forst and Rhodes white-collar criminals and to 24 for the Wheeler et al. white-collar

Table A.5: Age of Onset for Common and White-Collar Criminals

	WHEELER ET AL.[1]		FORST AND RHODES	
	COMMON CRIMINALS	WHITE-COLLAR CRIMINALS	COMMON CRIMINALS	WHITE-COLLAR CRIMINALS
Onset Age First-Time Offenders	—	35	30	41
Onset Age Repeat Offenders	—	24[2]	20	27

1 Adapted from Table 4 in Weisburd, David, Ellen F. Chayet, and Elin Waring, *Crime and Delinquency*, 36(3):350. Copyright © 1990 by Sage Publications. Reprinted by permission of Sage Publications.
2 Based on offenders with three or more arrests.

criminals. The common criminals with prior records in the Forst and Rhodes sample have a mean age of first arrest of 20. For the 60 percent of white-collar criminals whose first offense was the criterion offense, the average age was 41. As measured by arrests, most white-collar offenders truly are "late starters."

If white-collar offenders are often late starters, are they also late stoppers? When and how does desistance take place in white-collar criminal careers? What little is known about desistance in white-collar crime comes from a recent study by David Weisburd and Elin Waring (2001). They took the original Wheeler et al. data set and supplemented it by adding data from the "rap sheets" that the FBI keeps on all offenders. Weisburd and Waring recorded information about all arrests for ten years after the date of the offenders' original criterion offense.

We must use caution in drawing conclusions about white-collar criminals and desistance from the Weisburd and Waring study. As they note, questions about desistance are always difficult to answer with certainty. We can never be sure, except in the case of death, that the last crime we have observed is the last one an offender will ever commit. This is the problem of censoring. After the data-collection period ends, our view of offenders and their activities is censored. However, compared to recidivism studies, in general, the ten-year follow-up period in this study is relatively long. It seems safe to assume that offenders who have not been rearrested for ten years really have desisted.

What we learn from Weisburd and Waring about desistance is that white-collar offenders do not follow the patterns typical among street criminals. Street criminals usually "age out" of offending by the time they reach their thirties. In the Weisburd and Waring sample, however, the average age of desistance for white-collar offenders who had any arrests after the criterion offense is 43. Close to half (47 percent) of the white-collar offenders who reached the age of 50 by the end of the study had been arrested after age 50. With a longer follow-up period, the percentage of new arrests would go up (Weisburd and Waring 2001, 37). Ten percent of the offenders who made it to age 70 had arrests in their eighth decade of life. Overall, compared to common crime samples, a larger proportion of white-collar offenders appear to continue offending late in the life course (Weisburd and Waring 2001, 38).

The causes of desistance from white-collar crime probably are not the same as those for desistance from street crime. Street offenders may quit some types of crimes simply because as they get older they do not have the energy and agility to carry out certain offenses, such as robbery and burglary, anymore. In a sense, their opportunities to offend decline with age. This explanation does not seem to fit in the case of white-collar crime because the offenses are not physically demanding and because opportunities for white-collar crime may actually increase with age. As offenders grow older, they may move into more trusted occupational positions and hence have more opportunities to take advantage of their employers or others.

Another explanation often given for desistance from crime involves changes in informal social control. Street offenders appear to be most likely to desist when they establish strong informal social bonds to family or work. But white-collar offenders are much more likely to already have these bonds when they commit their offenses. So, it seems unlikely that an increase in informal social control contributes to desistance from white-collar crime.

Weisburd and Waring (2001, 41) speculate that the most likely cause of desistance from white-collar crime may be the cognitive changes associated with aging. As they reach and pass middle age, white-collar offenders, like other offenders, may come to the realization that time is passing them by and that they don't want to risk wasting any more of their remaining time in trouble with the law. The hard-driving executives who are willing to do anything for company and career may have a change of heart as they enter their fifties. Even the relatively small risk of incarceration that goes with white-collar crime may strike older offenders as an unacceptably high risk to take.

Criminal career researchers have devoted considerable attention to the matter of specialization in offending. Specialization exists when offenders commit the same type of crime repeatedly, whereas versatility means that offenders commit a wide variety of different types of offenses. Most research on specialization finds little evidence for it (Wolfgang, Figlio, and Sellin 1972; Kempf 1987; Farrington, Snyder, and Finnegan 1988). Most offenders appear to exhibit considerable versatility in their offenses (Gottfredson and Hirschi 1990). Indeed, Gottfredson and Hirschi (1990, 91) consider the evidence against specialization to be overwhelming.

Although the evidence against specialization in the careers of ordinary street offenders is strong, white-collar offenders may be different. Unlike many common crimes, white-collar crimes often require that one have special skills or hold a particular occupational position in order to commit the offense. It takes effort and persistence to learn how to commit some white-collar crimes or to secure the occupational niche necessary for the offense. White-collar offenders may have to invest more time and effort in their offenses than do common criminals. Hence, they have more motivation to capitalize on this investment by specializing in particular offenses than common offenders.

Table A.6: Specialization Among White-Collar Criminals

	PERCENT
Wheeler et al. Data	
Chronic Offenders with Prior Arrests for White-Collar Crime[1]	34.0
Forst and Rhodes Data	
White-Collar Criminals with Prior Arrests for White-Collar Crime	28.0
Types of Offenders in the Forst and Rhodes data	
One-Time Offenders	61.0
White-Collar Specialists	7.0
Generalists	32.3

1 Adapted from Table 5 in Weisburd, David, Ellen F. Chayet, and Elin Waring, *Crime and Delinquency*, 36(3):342–55. Copyright © 1990 by Sage Publications. Reprinted by permission of Sage Publications.

In support of this line of reasoning, in one of the few studies to compare white-collar and common offenders, Benson and Moore (1992) found evidence for greater specialization among white-collar offenders. In the Wheeler et al. data, over one-third of the white-collar criminals with prior arrests had at least one other arrest for a white-collar crime (Weisburd et al. 1990). As indicated in Table A.6, in the Forst and Rhodes sample of whitecollar criminals, 28 percent of the repeat offenders had at least one prior arrest for a white-collar crime.

With the Forst and Rhodes data, it is possible to track offending patterns relatively closely. Using prior arrests, we can identify three types of criminal career patterns: "one-time offenders," "generalists," and "white-collar specialists." One-time offenders are those who have no other arrests besides the one for the criterion offense that brought them into federal court. They make up 61 percent of the sample. Generalists make up 32.3 percent of the sample. These are individuals who have prior arrests that are primarily for non-white-collar offenses (see Table A.6).

Deciding where to draw the line between generalists and white-collar specialists is an arbitrary undertaking. Clearly, someone whose arrest record contains a smorgasbord of offenses ranging from check kiting to illegal drugs to spousal abuse is a generalist. Equally clearly, someone who has been repeatedly arrested for stock fraud can be considered a specialist. But what about someone whose arrest record consists mainly but not exclusively of white-collar offenses? For example, should a person who has three arrests for securities fraud and one for drunk driving be considered a specialist in white-collar crime or a generalist? There is no consensus on this point.

If we say that at least half of a person's arrests must be for white-collar offenses before we can call him or her a specialist, then relatively few offenders specialize in white-collar crime. In Table A.6, the persons categorized as specialists are those who have prior arrests in addition to the criterion offense, with at least half of their total number of arrests being for white-collar offenses. Prior arrests for embezzlement, fraud, corporate crime, and "other white-collar offenses" were classified as white-collar offenses. By these criteria, white-collar crime specialists constitute only 7 percent of the sample. Weisburd, Waring, and Chayet (2001) also found some evidence of specialization in their reanalysis of the Wheeler et al. data, but not a lot. Their analyses suggest that the likelihood of specialization depends on the type of white-collar offense. Persons whose criterion offense was securities fraud appeared to be most likely of all the white-collar offenders to specialize exclusively in white-collar crime (Weisburd and Waring 2001, 47). Overall, both the Wheeler et al. and the Forst and Rhodes data indicate that it is not unusual for white-collar criminals to have prior experience with white-collar type crimes, but it is also not unusual for them to have prior experience with other types of crime, too.

The results on the prior criminal records of white-collar offenders mirror what we learned about their social characteristics. They both coincide with and diverge from the popular image of the white-collar offender. They agree with the popular image in that as a group the white-collar offenders clearly are much less criminal than the common street crime offenders. Yet, they diverge from the popular image of the white-collar offender as a one-shot offender, someone who has only made one mistake in life. Once again, whitecollar offenders appear to be not exactly what we expected.

FAMILY BACKGROUND AND EDUCATIONAL TRAJECTORIES

Thus far, we have learned that in adulthood white-collar criminals occupy distinctly different social locations in American society than street criminals, and they have distinctly different criminal trajectories. To what extent do these social and criminal differences stem from earlier experiences in the life course? In other words, do white-collar and common criminals end up in different places as adults because they started out in different places as children?

Life course researchers have devoted considerable attention to the effects of family background and early childhood socialization on later criminality. Early childhood socialization experiences are considered crucial either for preventing or for failing to prevent later deviance and criminality. However, there has been "no significant effort to link white-collar crime to family background or abnormalities in early socialization" (Coleman 1987).

The Forst and Rhodes data set has four measures of family background that provide a glimpse of the early years of white-collar criminals. These measures tell us if the defendant "was raised in a family environment," "had family members with a criminal record," "was an abused, neglected or abandoned child," and if the "parents or guardians had difficulty providing the necessities of life." Because we have the same data on the sample of common criminals, we can explore whether the individuals in the two samples began life in the same or different kinds of family environments.

Table A.7: Family Background and School Performance for White-Collar and Common Criminals

	COMMON CRIMINALS	WHITE-COLLAR CRIMINALS
Family Background		
Raised in a Family Environment	96.0%	95.9%
Abused or Neglected as a Child	17.9%	6.3%
Raised in Poverty	24.6%	15.3%
Criminal Family Members	18.6%	6.2%
School Performance		
Poor Academic Performance	52.4%	25.0%
Poor Social Adjustment	44.8%	20.9%

Note: Data are from the Forst and Rhodes sample.

As Table A.7 shows, the vast majority of white-collar and common criminals begin life in some type of family environment, but this environment is much more likely to be a troubled one for common criminals. Just under one-quarter of the common criminals (24.6 percent) come from poverty-stricken families in which the parents had difficulty providing the necessities of life. In contrast, only 15.3 percent of white-collar criminals come from deprived backgrounds. Common criminals are almost three times as likely to have been abused or neglected as children as white-collar criminals (17.9 to 6.3 percent, respectively). They are also three times as likely to come from families with criminal members. White-collar and common criminals are likely to begin life in different places.

The statistical gap between white-collar and common offenders widens in school. Indeed, by the time they are in school, the two groups can be clearly distinguished. Two measures in the data set rate the defendant's "overall academic performance in school" and "overall social adjustment in school." Table A.7 shows that about half of all common offenders had below-average or poor academic performance and social adjustment in school, while only a quarter of white-collar offenders had the same problems. By the time they are in school, half of the common criminals already appear to be following trajectories slanting toward trouble and difficulty. In contrast, the percentage of white-collar offenders with below-average academic performance or social adjustment in school is much smaller.

CONVICTION AS AN EVENT IN THE LIFE COURSE OF WHITE-COLLAR OFFENDERS

In earlier chapters, we learned that involvement in crime and delinquency often has collateral consequences, particularly when offenders become entangled with the criminal justice system. John Hagan and Alberto Palloni (1988) have argued that we should think of crime as an event in the life course that has ripple effects throughout offenders' lives. For common criminals, the most detrimental collateral consequences involve educational failures that reduce occupational opportunities.

Because white-collar offenders start their criminal careers at much later ages than common offenders, the collateral consequences of crime are different for them. For juvenile delinquents, involvement in crime and the criminal justice system may prevent or delay them from making certain age-graded transitions in education and employment on time. Failure to make these transitions on time has detrimental consequences in the form of cumulating disadvantages. It "knifes off" future occupational opportunities and leads to a reduced standard of living (Sampson and Laub 1990; Moffitt 1993). White-collar offenders, however, tend to be much older when they first become entangled with the criminal justice system. By the time they are first arrested and convicted, most have already finished school and have welle-stablished occupational trajectories. For white-collar criminals, involvement in the justice system does not knife off future opportunities as severely as it seems to do for street criminals. Unlike juvenile delinquents, white-collar criminals already have acquired human capital and a comfortable standard of living before they become ensnared in the justice system.

There are few studies that investigate the collateral consequences of involvement in white-collar crime. Those that are available suggest that the severity of the consequences of exposure as a white-collar criminal depend on the class status and occupational position of the offender. For example, Benson (1984) investigated loss of socioeconomic status (SES) among a small sample of individuals convicted of white-collar crimes in a U.S. federal court. He compared the offenders' SES at the time of the offense, at the time of conviction, and at times after conviction. The results indicated that loss of SES is not spread evenly among the white-collar criminal population. Professionals, such as doctors and lawyers, and individuals employed in the public sector or in licensed occupations are much more likely to lose SES than private businessmen or those employed by private businesses (Benson 1984). As the time from the point of conviction lengthened, however, nearly all of the white-collar criminals eventually regained their former level of SES.

Although one might assume that the more serious the crime you commit, the more likely you are to suffer negative labeling and collateral consequences, this does not appear to be the case for white-collar criminals. Indeed, the more serious the white-collar crime, the less likely the offender is to lose his or her job after being caught (Benson 1989). For some white-collar criminals, their class positions seem to protect them from collateral consequences, such as job loss. Individuals who hold managerial or employer positions are less likely to lose their jobs than are workers (Benson 1989). For example, analyses of the Wheeler et al. data revealed that among the offenders in the sample, those who committed antitrust and securities fraud offenses were most likely to be owners or officers of companies. These offenders also committed the most serious offenses with respect to the number of persons victimized and the amount of money lost during the offense. The typical bank embezzler, on the other hand, is an employee who commits a less serious offense. Yet, antitrust and securities fraud offenders were much less likely to lose their jobs after their offenses were discovered than bank embezzlers (Weisburd et al. 1991). Less than 5 percent of the antitrust offenders and less than 15 percent of the securities fraud offenders were fired or left their jobs after the offense was discovered. Far fewer bank embezzlers escaped so unscathed; over three-quarters (76.8 percent) of the bank embezzlers lost their jobs after their offenses came to light.

Considered in light of the evidence reviewed in earlier chapters, these investigations of white-collar criminality suggest that position in the class structure influences the collateral consequences of crime throughout the life course. Among juvenile delinquents and young adult criminals, collateral consequences are more serious and persistent for ethnic minorities from the lower classes than they are for white middle-class delinquents. Among whitecollar criminals, the collateral consequences of crime are more serious for employees and workers than they are for owners and managers.

WHITE-COLLAR CRIME AND THE LIFE COURSE RECONSIDERED

The analyses presented here indicate that the individuals who are convicted for violating federal white-collar crime statutes come more from the middle than the upper social classes. This result must be viewed with caution, however. Because our analyses are based on samples of convicted offenders, they can tell us nothing about those who avoid conviction in the first place. It may be that upper-class offenders are simply better at avoiding conviction than middle-class offenders. After all, upper-class offenders have more money to use to hire top-notch legal defense teams, and good white-collar crime lawyers make sure that their clients keep away from courtrooms (Mann 1985). But the relationship between class status and legal sanctioning is complex, and the ability of upper-class individuals to avoid criminal prosecution is not simply a matter of money (Shapiro 1984; 1985). To explore this issue fully is beyond the scope of this book. So, we will have to be satisfied with noting that what we have learned thus far about white-collar offenders and the life course represents only a small part of the story that will eventually be told.

Although they do not fit the classic stereotype of the white-collar offender, the theoretical significance of middle-class offenders should not be ignored. They are not powerful business executives, but neither are they marginalized lower-class outsiders. Their trajectories in crime do not fit either the life-course persistent or adolescence-limited patterns identified by Moffitt (1997). On the other hand, neither do they resemble the powerful corporate executives popularized by Sutherland (1949) and others. So, where do they fit in criminological theory, and how may life course theory be applied to them?

White-collar offenders do not appear to follow the conventional trajectories in crime identified by life course theory. Their official offending careers start relatively late in life, when they are more or less securely ensconced in the middle class. It is possible, of course, that they start breaking the law much earlier than their official records indicate. However, because white-collar crimes tend to involve an occupational position, it is unlikely that they were committing white-collar crimes as teenagers. In the various social domains of adult life, most white-collar offenders appear to follow conventional trajectories. Early precursors of antisocial behavior or early hints of trouble in the life histories of typical white-collar offenders are hard to find. For most of these individuals, their offenses appear to come out of nowhere. Their crimes do not appear to be part of longstanding patterns of antisocial conduct, nor do they appear to be deeply rooted in a troubled family background. With respect to the life course approach, these patterns do not coincide with the typical image of trajectories in crime. They also suggest that theories that rely on latent personality traits (Gottfredson and Hirschi 1990; Moffitt 1993) are not appropriate for explaining white-collar crime. White-collar crime appears to be a function of adult life experience rather than the outcome of an antisocial personality or a troubled family background.

Regarding crime during adulthood, life course researchers have focused on identifying factors that distinguish those who stop offending from those who persist. Persistence in offending is thought to be caused either by an underlying propensity toward crime or by the narrowing of legitimate opportunities that results from the stigma associated with involvement in crime, or both. To explain desistance, Sampson and Laub (1993) proposed an age-graded theory of informal social controls. Transitions that increase informal social controls in adulthood, such as getting married or finding a good job, are hypothesized to lead to desistance from crime. Because onset into offending in adulthood is assumed to be very rare, life course researchers have ignored this pattern. However, as the data presented in this chapter demonstrate, most white-collar offenders do not begin to offend until they are well into adulthood. From the perspective of life course theory, how can this pattern of late starting be understood?

Part of the explanation lies in the occupational nature of white-collar crimes. Because opportunities for many white-collar crimes arise out of occupational positions, only individuals in certain occupations can commit certain types of white-collar offenses. Access to these positions is usually limited to individuals who have completed schooling and are accordingly in their twenties or thirties. Access to these jobs also tends to be limited to individuals who do not have prior criminal records. Hence, the first-time white-collar offender will tend to be older simply because only older individuals can get the jobs that provide opportunities for white-collar crime. This explanation accounts for the age distribution of white-collar offenders, but it does not explain why particular individuals choose to commit whitecollar offenses. Many other individuals have similar opportunities but do not offend.

Travis Hirschi and Michael Gottfredson (1987) argue that those who take advantage of white-collar crime opportunities are those with low self-control. Criminal propensity theorists take essentially the same tack. But there is something unsatisfying with these sorts of explanations. How could someone have enough self-control to get a good job but not enough self-control to resist taking advantage of the criminal opportunities the job presented? Why do some people hold occupational positions for long periods of time before committing their first white-collar offense? If criminal propensity is a stable personality trait, then why don't white-collar criminals take advantage of the opportunities presented by their occupational positions immediately? That they don't take immediate advantage is suggested by the late age at which most first-time white-collar offenders are arrested. The average age of onset is around 40, an age at which it is safe to assume that most people have been in an occupational position for some time. If low selfcontrol or high criminal propensity does not explain white-collar crime, then we have to look elsewhere.

The life course perspective directs our attention to trajectories in other domains of adult life that may trigger involvement in white-collar crime, such as family life and occupation. Interviews with white-collar offenders indicate that some see themselves as responding to emergencies in family economic circumstances when they decide to become involved in whitecollar crime (Rothman and Gandossy 1982; Benson 1985a; Daly 1989). Women appear more likely to become involved in white-collar crimes for family reasons than men (Rothman and Gandossy 1982; Daly 1989).

For other individuals, changes in motivational stressors that arise out of one's occupation are implicated (Weisburd et al. 2001). For example, a sudden downturn in business revenues may force a small businessperson to resort to unlawful means to keep the business afloat (Benson 1985a). A building contractor interviewed by Benson thought he was going to lose his business because of a cash-flow problem. He conspired with his accountant to set up a check-kiting scheme and explained his involvement this way:

> I was faced with the choice of all of a sudden, and I mean now, closing the doors or doing something else to keep that business open.... I'm not going to tell you that this wouldn't have happened if I'd had time to think it over, because I think it probably would have. You're sitting there with a dying patient. You are going to try to keep him alive.

> (Benson 1985a, 598)

Individuals who work in large corporations are subject to a complex combination of microfactors related to their occupational careers and macrofactors related to the structure and culture of the organizations within which they work. At times, these factors may exert pressure on individuals and make corporate offending a rational response (Simpson, Paternoster, and Piquero 1998). For example, persons convicted of antitrust violations sometimes claim that in their industries technical violations of antitrust laws are just part of doing business. Consider these explanations of bid rigging from a public building contractor:

> It was a way of doing business before we even got into the business. So it was like why do you brush your teeth in the morning or something .... It was part of the everyday .... It was a matter of survival.

> (Benson 1985a, 591)

> All you want to do is show a bid, so that in some cases it was for as small a reason as getting your deposit back on the plans and specs. So you just simply have no interest in getting the job and just call to see if you can find someone

to give you a price to use, so that you didn't have to go through the expense of an entire bid preparation. Now that is looked on very unfavorably, and it is a technical violation.

(Benson 1985a, 592)

These white-collar offenders appear to be responding to perceived problems in their lives or businesses (Weisburd et al. 2001). From the perspective of life course theory, the key point is that some white-collar crimes do not reflect continuity in behavior but rather discontinuity. They are not part of a pattern of antisocial conduct. Their causes are rooted not in the unfolding of innate developmental tendencies, but rather in contemporaneous circumstances of offenders' lives.

Section Four

Experiencing Aging, Facing Death

> Everything begins, develops—if animal or vegetable, breeds—then fades away: *everything*, not just humans, animals, plants, but things which seem to us eternal, such as rocks. Mountains wear down from jagged peaks to flatness. (Athill, 2014)

We often hear the period of nearing death described as "the end of life," a phrase that a former editor, Diana Athill, refuses to use because she believes death is "a part of life" (Athill, 2014). We live in a society where most people shudder at the thought of aging or dying. Within this cultural context, this last section of the book covers the topics of growing older and approaching death. Aging and dying, as in prior phases of the life course, are influenced by time and place.

The conception of aging from the life course perspective is such that different cohorts of people cannot be assumed to grow up and grow older in the same way. Elder (1994) writes that "... differences in birth year expose individuals to different historical worlds, with their constraints and options" and that "[i]ndividual life course may well reflect these different times" (Elder, 1994, p. 5). The following studies presume cohort differences, which people often refer to as generational differences, as in differences between the baby boom generation, born between 1946 and 1964, and the so-called "greatest generation," born around 1920 and growing up during the Great Depression era (Brokaw, 1998).

Kotarba (2013) adopts a symbolic interactionist approach to the self and the life course in his qualitative study. He focuses on the process through which individuals become their own selves by giving, refining, and reinterpreting meanings to the course of life. He adds that music, in this process of becoming, offers symbols with which to help define and reinterpret the identities of individuals over time. Among adult fans of rock 'n' roll, for example, maintaining their interest in the music provides stability and therefore helps secure the sense of self. Kotarba (2013) goes on to discuss how baby boomers' love of rock 'n' roll can help create and nurture their sense of self as romantics, parents, and grandparents. Over time, the rock idiom may continue to serve as narrative resources for understanding the aging self of the boomer.

Hampshire and her associates (2008) report the results of extensive fieldwork in a refugee camp in Ghana where Liberian families settled down. The researchers focus on changes in these long-term refugees' intergenerational relations upon describing the conflict in Liberia that made Liberians escape to other countries in West Africa. The traditional intergenerational relations in Liberia are based on deference to elders, who have power over the process of youth's transition to adulthood by controlling labor and marriages. Young men would often bear a lot of debt in order to have wives and land. With its temporary economic boom followed by a downturn, many men in the country experienced a brief period of economic independence from elders, only to be marginalized again without the means to get married or acquire land. The qualitative data collected in the Ghanaian refugee camp represent the perspective of informants. The authors provide numerous narratives from younger and older Liberian refugees that indicate the erosion of elders' authority during their challenging lives as refugees. Older people lost their economic ability to support the younger ones—many of whom had to grow up early in order to survive and became more resourceful and independent as a result.

Finally, Holloway and Smeeding (2007) address important issues and problems for dying in contemporary society, with the goal of helping the dying and those who care for them. The authors' focus is on health care contexts where dying is most likely to occur in technologically advanced societies. They discuss the philosophies behind the hospice and palliative care movements, elements of good death, end-of-life care along with legal issues that accompany end-of-life care, moral and ethical debates about euthanasia, and the attitudes of health care professionals toward euthanasia. The authors conclude that services for the dying depend largely on the health and social care environment, which are, in the end, governed by legislation and policy.

Cohort effects refer to differences based on cohort membership, and period effects represent the broad impacts of historical events on the population. Cohort effect refers to "the social change that occurs as one cohort replaces another (Quadagno, 2014, p. 30), and period effect represents "the impact of a historical event on the entire society" (Quadagno, 2014, p. 29). Although Kotarba (2013) does not use the concepts of cohort or cohort effect, the baby boom cohorts can be distinguished from earlier or later cohorts based on their special affinity for rock 'n' roll music. Hampshire and her coauthors (2008) do not use the concept of period effect to understand why intergenerational relations are changing among Liberian refugees, but attribute the changes to the historical events that disrupt the lives of both the younger and older generations, albeit differently. Holloway and Smeeding (2007) imply both cohort and period effects by portraying dying experiences in the 21st century as different from a century earlier, when dying was more likely to take place in a family setting. As such, Ryder's (1965, p. 861) recommendation still rings true: "sociologists would be well-advised to exploit the congruence of social change and cohort differentiation."

REFERENCES

Athill, Diana. 2008. *Somewhere Towards the End*. UK: Granta Books.

Athill, Diana. 2014. "It's Silly to Be Frightened of Being Dead." *Guardian*. Retrieved September 31, 2014. (http://www.theguardian.com/lifeandstyle/2014/sep/23/-sp-diana-athill-its-silly-frightened-being-dead).

Brokaw, Tom. 1998. *The Greatest Generation*. Westminster, MD: Random House.

Hampshire, Kate, Gina Porter, Kate Kilpatrick, Peter Kyei, Michael Adjaloo, and George Oppong. 2008. "Liminal Spaces: Changing Inter-Generational Relations among Long-Term Liberian Refugees in Ghana." *Human Organization* 67(1):25–36.

Holloway, Margaret, and Timothy M. Smeeding. 2007. "Dying in the Twenty-First Century," pp. 93–117. In *Negotiating Death in Contemporary Health and Social Care*, by M. Holloway. UK: Policy Press.

Kotarba, Joseph A. 2013. "The Self and the Life Course," pp. 113–124. In *Understanding Society through Popular Music*, by J. A. Kotarba. New York: Routledge.

Quadagno, Jill. 2014. *An Introduction to Social Gerontology*, 6th Ed. New York: McGraw-Hill.

Ryder, Norman B. 1965. "The Cohort as a Concept in the Study of Social Change." *American Sociological Review* 30(6):843–861.

The Self and the Life Course

By Joseph A. Kotarba

T he notion of *life course* is important to a particularly sociological perspective on people and their behavior. In general, sociologists believe
that people are only partially shaped by their biological and genetic
capacities. Instead, our self and how we approach social life are constantly
shaped by events and experiences that happen all the way through life.
We change constantly if not occasionally dramatically. The concept of *life
course* holds that socialization is a lifelong process (Furstenberg 2003).
Accordingly, our appreciation for and use of popular music are a dynamic
process that does not end when we become adults.

Social scientists have traditionally focused on popular music experiences
among young audiences. The focus has been on pop music specifically as a
feature of adolescent culture and, therefore, of teenagers' everyday life experiences. As Simon Frith (1981) noted in his famous sociological text, *Sound
Effects*, rock music has been fundamental to the experience of growing up
ever since the end of World War II. Similarly, sociologists have demonstrated
increasing interest over the years in rock and pop music as an indicator of
dramatic changes occurring in the social and cultural worlds of teenagers.
We can trace this interest at least as far back as David Riesman's (1950) classic examination of the emergence of the *other-directed* personality in post-
WWII American society. The new middle class was marked by a weakening
of parental control, a preoccupation with consumption, and a shift in the
meaning of leisure resulting in the masses—the lonely crowd—desperately

trying to have fun. The time was ripe for the emergence of a youth culture defined by what have come to be known as pop and rock music.

The popular music industry that drives rock and pop continues to expand dramatically—beyond multi-billion dollar annual sales, globalization, CDs, MP3 technology, and the internet. Yet, lay and scholarly observers have generally ignored or underplayed an important element of social and cultural change: rock and pop are no longer limited to, nor solely the possession of, teenagers. The original generation of rock fans—the baby boomers—are now parents and, in some cases, grandparents. The music and musical culture they grew up with has stayed with them, becoming the soundtrack of North American cultures.

The aim of this chapter is to survey the many ways rock and pop pervade the everyday lives of adults in North American society. In commonsense terms, we examine what happened to the first, complete generation of rock fans: the baby boomer generation now in late middle age. We argue that rock 'n' roll music continues to serve as a critical meaning resource for its adult fans as they continuously experience the becoming of self throughout life. To better understand how music works throughout the life course we begin by discussing in some depth the concepts of self, identity, and the life course itself.

SELF, IDENTITY, AND THE LIFE COURSE

The self is probably the most important concept for all qualitative sociologists. Yet, it is often used improperly or confused with the concept of identity. Before we proceed to examine the empirical material unique to this chapter, let us discuss in some detail these important ideas. And let us begin with the self. The self, as the word itself suggests, is a reflexive object. Think, for example, of its common use in expressions like: "I hurt myself." When you hurt yourself you direct attention (the realization that you are in pain) to you as an object. In doing so you are both a subject (knower and feeler, in this case) of your action, and an object (known and felt). You are a subject in the sense that you are the one who is mustering attention and directing focus, and you are an object in the sense that such attention is focused on you. In doing so, George Herbert Mead (1934) tells us, you are *minding* yourself. It is by minding that indeed we create a sense of self. We mind our self into being by, for example, engaging in internal conversations (e.g. thinking about oneself), monitoring our sensations, experiencing feelings about the self, and so forth. The "doing" of all these things is the "doing" of the self. The self, in other words, is a constant process, a way of "selfing" ourselves into being as a result of our actions as a subject (the "I"), and as an object of our actions (the "me").

Identity refers to something different. An identity is a typification of self, either imposed upon an individual by others (*social identity*) or adopted by self (*personal identity*). For example, if others view me as a punk rocker and treat me as such, my social identity is that, indeed, of a punk rocker. Others could treat me as a punk rocker even in spite of the fact that I carefully distinguish my identity among available punk styles (and identities) and identify myself as a hardcore punk rocker (my personal identity). An identity can be more or less stable across social settings. For example, my youth friends may have always identified me as punk rocker for all my life, but if one evening I were to attend a grindcore concert and enjoy it, I may very well, at least for that evening, identify myself as (and be identified by other concert attendants as) a grindcore fan. We can refer to these momentary identities that we take up and shed on a regular daily basis as *situational identities*. So, for example, despite our more enduring social and personal identities, on any given day we can have situational identities such as bus-rider, grocery-shopper, pedestrian, etc.

The discussion above highlights the processual nature of self and identity. Think of the self as a molecule of water. A molecule of water is made up of two components: hydrogen and oxygen. A self is similarly the result of the combination of two components: the "I" and the "me." A molecule of water is always in flux throughout its life. When suspended amidst clouds and then falling from the sky, it assumes the identity of a rain drop; when frozen up high in the mountains, it has the identity of an ice crystal; when melting and flowing down the mountain, it has the identity of river water; and when merging with the ocean, it assumes the identity of sea water. Now, of course a molecule of water has no reflexivity (and no personal identity), but from this example you can at least see that its life is a never-ending process and that throughout this process it assumes different identities in light of the settings it inhabits. The same can be said of the self: throughout the life course an individual assumes different social, situational (and also personal) identities as a result of the fluidity of life and the social "pools" with which we come into contact. To the concept of the life course we now turn.

A *life course* is a patterned temporal trajectory of individual experiences. Some scholars, notably social psychologists and psychologists, like to identify objective and universal stages typical for all individuals. Interactionists and constructionists are instead less interested in determining fixed stages and more in examining how individuals assign meanings to their progression through life. In the words of Clair, Karp, and Yoels (1993: vii) their focus is more precisely on "how persons occupying different locations in social space interpret and respond to repeated social messages about the meanings of age." Reflecting on the contribution of these authors, in an influential overview of the concept and research on the life course sociologists Holstein and Gubrium (2003: 836) write:

> (1) age and life stages, like any temporal categories, can carry multiple meanings; (2) those meanings emerge from social interaction; and (3) the meanings of age and the course of life are refined and reinterpreted in light of the prevailing social definitions of situations that bear on experience through time.

As you can obviously see, the life course is therefore about the becoming of self: the fluid process through which we acquire new and diverse roles, social identities, and personal identities. Music, we argue, provides a set or symbolic resources for the definition and reinterpretation of these identities: through music we continuously self ourselves into being. But, how, precisely, do we do so?

THE BECOMING OF SELF

The existential sociological concept of *the becoming of self* is a useful guide in seeking the sociological answers to this question. Existential social thought is heavily derived from and very close in nature to symbolic interactionism. A difference is that existential sociology views the self: "as a unique experience of being within the context of contemporary social conditions, an experience most notably marked by an incessant sense of becoming and an active participation in social change" (Kotarba 1984: 223). The incessant sense of becoming is a reflection of the contemporary need for the individual to be prepared to reshape meanings of self in response to the dictates of a rapidly changing social world. The well-integrated self accepts the reality of change and welcomes new ideas, new experiences, and reformulations of old ideas and experiences that help one adapt to change (Kotarba 1987).

The idea of *becoming* is one of the most important ideas in existentialist thought across disciplines because it places responsibility for fashioning a self on the individual. Whereas Jean-Paul Sartre (1945) argued dramatically that we are condemned to be free and to choose who we are to become, Maurice Merleau-Ponty (1962) insisted more moderately and sociologically that we must ground our becoming-ofself in the real world in order to cope effectively with it. Thus, an effective strategy for becoming begins with a foundation of personal experience and the constraints of social structure, while evolving in terms of the resources presented by culture. We argue that middle-aged North Americans work with a self built to some degree on the meanings provided by the rock 'n' roll idiom, and they continue to nurture the self within the ever-present cultural context of rock 'n' roll.

Douglas (1984) notes that there are, in fact, two analytically distinct stages of becoming-of-self with which the modern actor contends. The first is *the need to eliminate or control threats to the basic security of self* (e.g., meaninglessness, isolation from others, shame, death). Although existential psychotherapists like Yalom (1980) argue that chronic insecurity—or neurosis—is pervasive in our society, Douglas argues sociologically that it is more common for the sense of security to vary biographically, situationally, and developmentally. In general, adults try to shape everyday life experiences in order to avoid basic threats to the self. Basic threats to the adult self in our society would include divorce, the loss of a job, the loss of children (e.g., the empty nest syndrome), illness, disability, and poverty. The second stage of becoming-of-self involves *growth of the sense of self*. Growth occurs when the individual seeks new experiences as media for innovative and potentially rewarding meanings for self (Kotarba 1987). It is through growth, or self-actualization as it is often referred to today, that life becomes rich, rewarding, full, and manageable.

Accordingly, adult fans nurture their interest in and experience with rock 'n' roll music for two reasons. On the one hand, keeping up with the music and the culture that were so important to them when growing up helps them maintain *continuity* with the past and thus solidifies the sense of self security. On the other hand, working hard to keep rock 'n' roll current and relevant to their lives helps adults grow as parents, as spiritual beings, and as friends.

The concept of the *existential self* tells us that the experience of individuality is never complete; the answer to the question "who am I?" is always tentative. In the postmodern world, the mass media—including popular music—serve as increasingly important audiences to the self. The *self* is situational and mutable (Zurcher 1977). One can be various selves as the fast-paced, ever-changing, uncertain postmodern society requires. In the remainder of this chapter, we provide a working inventory of the various ways adults self themselves into being. These are experiences of self common in everyday life, closely related to roles and social and personal identities, and predicated by or embedded in rock 'n' roll culture.

THE E-SELF

As the rock 'n' roll fan ages, many of the attractive aspects of the earlier self become increasingly difficult to maintain. There is a tendency for youthfulness, energy, risk-taking, appearance, sensuality, and other aspects of the adolescent or young-adult self to become either less available or less desirable. Our culture does, however, provide the resource of an image of social identity that resonates with the affluence of middle age, as well as with the continuing need to establish status/self-esteem. The *e-self* (or electronic self) refers to an experience of individuality in which the affective and philosophical self-resources of rock 'n' roll media are displaced or at least supplemented by the increasingly technological and commodified aspects of the media. For the middle-aged fan, what you play your music on can be at least as, if not more, important than what you play.

Middle age results in less concert attendance and more music experience in the comfort of home, automobile and, for the energetic, on the jogging trail. A quick reading of *Wired* magazine (October 2004), which is geared toward the affluent and technologically-interested middle-aged person, discloses the strategy of marketing rock 'n' roll to its audience. There are ads for sophisticated cell phones that allow the consumer to "keep rockin' with your favorite MP3s." The promotion for "THEWIREDAUCTION," on eBay which benefits a children's foundation, includes a "limited edition series precision bass guitar signed by Sting" among other high-end music items. The ad for the Bose Music intelligent playback system highlights "its unique ability to listen to the music you play and learn our preferences based on your likes, dislikes, or even your mood at the moment." There are numerous ads for satellite radio systems and the luxury SUVs that include them as standard equipment.

Such marketing sometimes resonates with the adults it targets. George is a 51-year-old, Anglo electrical engineer who just installed a satellite radio system in his Lexus sedan. He sees two benefits of his musical purchase: "I don't have to mess with CDs or radio anymore. I get to play only the music I like to hear ... There are stations dedicated just to '80s heavy metal. Cool." George has effectively eliminated the hassles of concert crowds and debates over musical tastes with peers. High technology puts his e-self in control of his musical environment. George can experience his music with the aura of cultural independence affluent adults seek.

THE SELF AS LOVER

A significant aspect of the continuous popularity of rock 'n' roll music is its use in helping make sense of others, especially in intimate relationships. Numerous observers have correctly identified the sexist messages present in rock (e.g., McRobbie 1978). A postmodern existentialist view, however, highlights the fact that rock 'n' roll music displays an open-ended horizon of meaning for its audiences. What a rock 'n' roll music performance means is largely a function of the situation in which it is experienced and the particular self-needs of the audience member (Kotarba 1994a). As time passes, the rock 'n' roll audience matures, biographies evolve, men's and women's relationships change, popular music commodities come and go, cultural themes available through the media advance, and we would expect the actual lived experience of popular music to change.

A particular self-need of the mature rock 'n' roll fan is to interpret *romantic* phenomena. This can happen two ways. First, fans can (re)interpret music to fit romantic needs. In Joe's autobiographical writing as a rock 'n' roll fan (Kotarba 1997), he described the way he used Dion's 1961 classic song "Runaround Sue" to account for the way a girl back in eighth grade rejected his very timid show of affection in favor of that of a more aggressive, older teenaged boy. Like the Sue in the song, Joe's Sue was a *bad* girl and he was merely a victim of her wiles. Twenty-five years later, at a class reunion, he used the same song as the basis for a conversation with the same Sue. They laughed about the silliness of those elementary school days, but Joe's heartbeat jumped a bit when she admitted that she really did like him back then but was too shy to tell him!

Second, fans can gravitate towards music that can be perceived as romantic. Autobiographically speaking (Joe), "Smokey" Robinson and the Miracles' "Tracks of My Tears" was a constant play on my 45 rpm record player in 1965 when it put comforting words to yet another heartbreak in my life. I would not have been drawn as much to this new record if I did not have a personal need for its plaintive prose. In general, fans gravitate towards music that fits their everyday life concerns.

Baby boomers use rock 'n' roll materials for a range of romantic purposes. They use music (e.g., CDs and DVDs) as birthday and Christmas gifts. They use music to help them appreciate other media such as films and television. One of the more interesting romantic uses of rock 'n' roll music is the *our-song* phenomenon, in which a musical performance serves to define a relationship. Our-songs are clearly not limited to baby boomers. Pre-adolescents, for example, commonly choose songs that remind them of a boy or a girl, but are often too shy to disclose this fact to the other, as we have seen!

For mature rock 'n' roll fans, the our-song can function at least two ways. First, it provides meaning for benchmark events in the relationship. Shirley is a 52-year-old, Latina sales person who is a big Los Lobos fan. She builds anniversary activities around one particular song she and her husband both enjoy:

> We fell in love with "Nadie Quiere Sufrir" at a Los Lobos concert when we were still just dating. It is a very pretty waltz that actually comes from an Edith Piaf song … I make sure the CD (with the song) is in the car when we drive to (our anniversary) dinner. He bought me the CD for our anniversary a few years ago … Oh, I guess it just makes us feel young again.

Second, the our-song can help the person feel like a lover. As couples age and perhaps find themselves feeling and acting less romantic over time, the our-song can function as a quick emotional fix. Rob is a 58-year-old, Anglo executive who has maintained a serious relationship with Tommy, a 47-year-old artist, for about fifteen years. Their song is Queen's "Bohemian Rhapsody:"

> There will never be another Freddie Mercury. It was really special to have our own gay rock icon … I surprise Tommy by playing "Bohemian Rhapsody" now and again. Tommy is still thrilled that I remember it … Why? Well, it's one of those songs that make you feel good, to feel that you can be gay and a rocker at the same time … I like doing things for Tommy. We are just so busy with our careers, 'makes us feel like an old married couple!

Needless to say, the popular music industry is aware of the market for rock 'n' roll goods and services. One of the more recent examples is the advent and growing popularity of rock 'n' roll cruises. Carnival Cruise Lines offers the following "rock 'n' roll Cruise Vacation" in an on-line ad:

> What could be cooler than a seven-day Caribbean cruise with legendary big-hair 1970s/80s rockers Journey, Styx and REO Speedwagon? Well … we'll reserve comment. But, if your idea of a totally awesome vacation is a seven-day cruise with legendary big-hair 1970s/80s rockers Journey, Styx and REO Speedwagon, you're in luck.

Interactionist sociologists—as you can glean from the above—are not only interested in what individuals experience throughout life course, but also in "how the life course is interpretively constructed and used by persons to make sense of experience" (Holstein and Gubrium 2003: 841). In order to construct meaning, Holstein and Gubrium tell us, we utilize *narrative resources:* tools for building, shaping and re-shaping, and making sense of the becoming of self. Music is a narrative resource. By employing narrative resources and constructing a sense of self endowed with a feeling of continuity and growth we engage in *biographical work* (ibid.).

THE SELF AS PARENT AND GRANDPARENT

As we have shown in Chapter 1, the impact of rock 'n' roll on one's self as parent is possibly the most pervasive aspect of the personal rock 'n' roll biography. Baby boomers grew up experiencing music as a major medium for communicating with parents. Managing music illustrates one's skill at parenting, as well as one's style of parenting.

There is a greater tendency among parents—apparently across ethnic groups and social classes—to manage rock 'n' roll as though their teen-agers are children who need to be nurtured and protected rather than as adolescents who must be controlled, sanctioned, and feared. Mass media-generated images of obstinate if not rebellious youth generally ignore the reflexive relationship between teenagers and their parents. Parents then respond to the identities they helped create by controlling, criticizing, sanctioning, and punishing their teenagers for living out their rock 'n' roll-inspired identities—responding to them as if they were autonomous, responsible adults.

This *congenial* style of being a parent appears to extend into the next cycle of life: that of grandparent. As Mogelonsky (1996) and other family researchers have noted, grandparents have a tendency to interact with their grandchildren in ways very similar to the ways they interacted with their own children. If pop music was an important feature to them as parents, it will be the same as grandparents. What changes, of course, are styles of music, music technology and the moral context of pop music. Frank is a 61-year-old retired public school teacher who has two grandchildren: 17-year-old Bobby and 11-year-old Denise. Bobby has been easy to please with musical gifts and experiences. Just as he did with his own son thirty years ago or so, Frank has given Bobby birthday and Christmas gifts of music, but according to current styles: iTune gift cards, an iPod mini, and tickets to a Radiohead concert. However, Frank will not share musical experiences with Bobby because:

"Bobby listens to a lot of rap, and I just cannot stand that stuff." Denise presented other kinds of difficulties. In addition to a Carrie Underwood CD she wanted for Christmas, she begged Frank for tickets to see Hannah Montana in concert at Reliant Stadium in Houston. Her father told her that the family could not afford tickets, so she strategically asked her doting grandpa. Frank's response was "how can I tell my little girl no?," but the task of actually getting tickets was monumental:

> I heard that all tickets sold out in about ten minutes. I went online and couldn't get in for almost a half-hour. I actually drove down to the Reliant box office later that morning, and it was the same story. I then went on-line to eBay and paid $400 for two (nose) bleeds ... You're old enough to remember when concert tickets were ten bucks at the door. Man, how things have changed, but I promised her.

THE SELF AS BELIEVER

As we have seen, baby boomers' early experiences of rock 'n' roll music were complex. They learned to love, play, dissent, and through the idiom. They also experienced spirituality (Seay and Neely 1986). In adulthood, the spiritual dimension of rock 'n' roll continues to impact the self as believer. The lyrics and mood created by such performers as Van Morrison (*Astral Weeks*) and U2 (*The Joshua Tree*) provide baby boomers with non-sectarian yet religion-friendly soundtracks. New Age music, such as that produced by Windham Hill, functions the same way.

Rock and pop music have also had a direct influence on spirituality by helping shape organized religious ceremonies and rituals to fit the tastes of the adult members. For example, Catholic baby boomers grew up at a time when the Church, largely as a result of the Vatican II Council, encouraged parishes to make use of local musical styles and talent. Witness the emergence of the rock 'n' roll mass in the 1970s. Today, the very popular style of praise and worship music, with its electronic keyboard and modern melodies, is infiltrating Catholic liturgy.

An integral segment of the self-as-parent is moral if not religious or spiritual socialization. Rock and pop function as mechanisms for teaching religious beliefs and values in many families, whether or not rock is compatible with the particular family's religious orientation. For mainstream Protestant denominations, rock 'n' roll increasingly fits with the faith. Take, for example, the success of Jars of Clay—a soft rock Christian band—or Creed, an edgier and equally spiritual ensemble. In these cases too, we can see how music functions as a resource selected by fans and made meaningful in their building of a sense of identity.

THE SELF AS POLITICAL ACTOR

Rock 'n' roll music serves as a soundtrack for the situations in which baby boomers perceive themselves as political actors. rock 'n' roll can add both atmosphere and meaning to political events. For example, New York punk poet and singer Patti Smith performed a concert in Houston on March 28, 2003—right at the beginning of the war in Iraq. The concert was originally scheduled simply to support an exhibit of her art displayed at the Museum of Contemporary Arts. The audience was overwhelmingly middle-aged people, dressed up in their jeans and long (hippie) skirts. Through conversations with numerous fans after the concert, it was clear that they *enjoyed* the concert. Patti Smith's poetry and songs (e.g., "People Have the Power") gave them a relevant and identifiable venue for sharing their overwhelmingly negative *feelings* about the war.

Families also use rock and pop to relay a sense of political history to their children. For example, every year on Memorial Day in Houston, various veterans' organizations sponsor a concert and rally at the Miller Outdoor Theater. Most of the veterans present fought in the Vietnam and Gulf Wars, two wars for which rock 'n' roll served as the musical soundtrack. Most of the veterans bring their children to the event. Among all the messages and information available to the kids is the type of music popular during the war. A popular band regularly invited to perform is the Canadian band Guess Who, whose "American Woman" was a major anthem among soldiers. Joe has observed fathers explaining the song to their teenaged and preteen children, who would otherwise view it as just another of dad's old songs. The fathers explain that the song had different meanings for different men. For some, it reminded them of girlfriends back home who broke up with them during the war. For others, the title was enough to remind them of their faithful girlfriends back home. For still others, the song reminded them of the occasions when they were sitting around camp, smoking pot and listening to any North American rock 'n' roll songs available as a way of bridging the many miles between them and home. In Houston, Juneteenth and Cinco de Mayo activities function much the same way for African-American and Hispanic families, respectively. In summary, rock 'n' roll music is vital to maintaining a sense of the political self because many baby boomers learned their politics—and how to be and feel political—from Country Joe McDonald (and the Fish), Jimi Hendrix, and the Grateful Dead.

CONCLUSION

We have described several contemporary experiences and manifestations of self to illustrate the ways the rock idiom has remained a major cultural force in the life course of mature fans. There are obviously other experiences. Furthermore, these experiences are not limited to fans. Rock music is also a preeminent aspect of the musician's self who performed rock music many years ago, and who continues to perform. These musicians redirect their careers in directions more comfortable if not more profitable. Kinky Friedman comes to mind. He was a Texas-based band leader in the 1970s (The infamous Texas Jew Boys). He now performs acoustically in small clubs, while managing a very successful line of men's clothing and authoring popular mystery novels. As time passes (Kotarba 2002b), rock 'n' roll provides narrative resources for the aging self's biographical work. In interviews Joe routinely hears respondents note how the recent deaths of middle-aged rock 'n' roll artists, such as Robert Palmer and George Harrison, are disturbing because these afflictions may be more the result of aging than the excessive lifestyles associated with the premature deaths of artists such as Janice Joplin, Jimmy Hendrix, and Jim Morrison. It will be interesting, then, to see the various ways in which baby boomers draw upon the rock idiom as they move beyond middle age. For example, what new meanings will aging boomers attach to the rock idiom? What place will rock have in the grandparent–grandchild relationship? Attending to such questions will highlight the role that music plays in the ongoing becoming-of-self.

Liminal Spaces

Changing Inter-Generational Relations among Long-Term Liberian Refugees in Ghana

By Kate Hampshire, Gina Porter, Kate Kilpatrick, Peter Kyei, Michael Adjaloo, and George Oppong

INTRODUCTION

While young people have been shown to be particularly vulnerable in situations of conflict and forced migration, it has also been increasingly recognized in recent years that they can exhibit remarkable resilience and ability to overcome adversity when faced with new and changing situations. However, where this is the case, the relationships between older and younger people may be reconfigured and generational categories blurred. In this paper, we present an emic perspective of changing inter-generational relations among long-term Liberian refugees in the Buduburam settlement camp in Ghana, focusing on the social implications of disruptions to "normal" life course chronology.

THEORETICAL BACKGROUND: CHANGING INTER-GENERATIONAL RELATIONS IN REFUGEE SITUATIONS

Conflict and the various disruptions associated with forced migration are widely considered to affect children and young people disproportionately (Machel 2001; Berman 2001). The negative impact of conflict on young people can be heightened when they are conscripted into armies, which has been widespread in Liberia and other conflicts in Africa (Human Rights

Kate Hampshire, Gina Porter, Kate Kilpatrick, Peter Kyei, Michael Adjaloo, and George Oppong, "Liminal Spaces: Changing Inter-Generational Relations among Long-Term Liberian Refugees in Ghana," *Human Organization*, pp. 25–36. Copyright © 2008 by Society of Applied Anthropology. Reprinted with permission. Provided by ProQuest LLC. All rights reserved.

Watch 1994). However, a growing literature finds that young people affected by war and displacement can act positively as agents in overcoming adversity. Boyden (2003) suggests that children and young adults often adapt to disruption and the demands of change more easily than elders. Young people may be better able to take up new livelihood opportunities during times of conflict and social change, and to interact with personnel from aid agencies (Vincent and Sorenson 2001). Chatty and Hundt (2001) found that young Palestinian refugees coped with conflict and displacement though mobilizing diverse social support systems (family, friends, and formal and informal youth groups), as well as engaging in religious and political activism. Swaine and Feeny (2004) show how, during the Kosovo conflict, adolescent girls took active steps to pursue their own wishes and needs (despite considerable obstacles) which helped them to make sense of their situations.

Conflict and displacement frequently lead to the transformation of young people's roles and responsibilities. Boyden et al. (2002) noted that children and young people caught up in conflicts in South Asia often took on increased productive responsibilities, as well as being involved directly in armed struggle. Young people might also assume the role of carers for elders. Hinton (2000:206) found high levels of child-to-parent support among Bhutanese refugees in Nepal, which were critical in keeping families and communities together: "far from being passive recipients of support, [children] were active in promoting social cohesion."

Such transformations may have important consequences—both positive and negative—for inter-generational relations. Hinton (2006) argues that, by supporting their parents, Bhutanese children developed an increased sense of self-worth and respect, while Mann (2004) suggests that adopting care-giving roles toward elders enables young people to establish a role for themselves in the community and to become adults.

Conversely, older people may feel that their own ability to contribute to the well-being of their family and community is undermined through such transformations. The new roles of young people may be seen as threatening to social norms that condition relations of authority and respect between young people and their elders, as well as wider social values (Boyden et al. 2002). Swaine and Feeney (2004:83) argue that, in relation to the conflict in Kosovo, "resilience...often carries a high price. Young people may find themselves disagreeing or even in conflict with parents and other adults...some of the girls had assumed roles that challenged traditional hierarchies. ..they often faced cultural and social resistance." Vincent and Sorenson (2001) find that young displaced Sri Lankans took on the role of mediators between the displaced communities and external aid agencies, which some elders saw as threatening and undermining social traditions. Similar fears from elders about loss of authority, and "losing" their youth to an alternative set of values, are expressed in Kaiser's (2006) study of a refugee settlement in Uganda.

Experiences of conflict and exile may lead to the shifting of generational categories and boundaries. "Youth" and "adolescence" are ambiguous, culturally contingent categories. Often, "young people" are defined by what they are not (i.e. neither children nor fully adults) rather than what they are (Women's Commission for Refugee Women and Children—WCRWC 2000). Youth can thus be seen as a liminal state—a negotiable period of initiation into adulthood. Utas (2003) argues that young Liberian ex-combatants find themselves caught between modernity and tradition, with neither offering a satisfactory path to adulthood. As such, many continue to define themselves as "youth" well into their thirties and beyond. The only path remaining for many young men was use of their "warrior" status, leading to performances of hyper-violence and hyper-masculinity (such as rape and violent killings) as initiation into adulthood.

Several commentators (Kibreab 2004; Harrell-Bond 2000; Turner 2004; Agier 2002) have argued that refugee camps can be seen as loci where background processes of social change are telescoped or catalyzed, where aspects of modernity can quickly become rooted, and which may generate spaces for new identities, roles, and relationships to be negotiated. The liminal spaces between childhood and adulthood can provide new opportunities within the context of refugee camps. Turner (2004, 2006) describes some young Burundian Hutu refugees in Tanzania as becoming "liminal experts," taking advantage of the dismption of the traditional order and establishing themselves as leaders in the refugee camp, as NGO/agency workers, and as businessmen. The exploitation of liminality may allow young people to undertake roles and activities traditionally denied to them, but is by definition simultaneously a process of exclusion from traditional community identities. Kibreab (2004) argues that this can also be linked with the pursuit of livelihood activities that are illegal or risky in other respects.

Changes in gender roles interact with inter-generational relations among displaced communities, since exile can have differential impacts on the ability and pathways available for young men and women to achieve full adulthood, and on their authority within households and wider communities. Conflict-related displacement often leads to changes in gender relations, with women commonly taking on increased economic responsibilities (El Bushra et al, 2002), resulting sometimes in increases in power, political participation, and autonomy for women (Sideris 2003, working in Mozambique). Leach (1992) found that, among Liberian refugees in Sierra Leone, women were better able to integrate into local livelihood strategies than men. Frequently, however, the implications of displacement for gender relations are more ambiguous. Based on his work in Tanzania, Turner (2004) argues that the presence of United Nations High Commission on Refugees (UNHCR) and aid agencies in the refugee camp have led to men feeling that their role as husbands/providers has been usurped by external agencies. As a result, existing gender ideologies are strengthened as male refugees attempt to reverse this situation: men still make the decisions while women carry the brunt of the workload.

Social changes resulting from conflict and displacement may thus be highly ambivalent. While much research supports the idea that changes in young people's roles and aspirations can create serious inter-generational tensions, several studies point to the continued importance of inter-generational support for both youth and elders. For example, Farwell (2001) found that the support of grandparents and other elders was critical in helping young exiled Eritreans to deal with crisis and to normalize their experiences. Similarly, Turner (2006) notes considerable ambivalence toward the changing values regarding youth and elders among Burundian refugees. In what follows, we explore ideas of liminality and ambivalence in relation to changing inter-generational relations among long-term Liberian refugees in the Buduburam Settlement in Ghana.

SOCIAL AND HISTORICAL CONTEXT: CONFLICT AND INTER-GENERATIONAL RELATIONSHIPS IN LIBERIA

The conflict that led to Liberians fleeing to Ghana and other West African countries began in December 1989, although it had its roots in the last 150 years of Liberian history. Since Liberia's founding in 1821 as a colony for freed slaves, and subsequent independence in 1847, political and economic control remained almost exclusively within the hands of the Americo-Liberian elite (descendants of ex-slaves). In 1980, Samuel Doe (a junior level indigenous military officer) led a successful military coup. A number of further coup attempts in the 1980s led to widespread ethnic conflict throughout the country. By the official end of Liberia's war, in 1996, there had been some 200,000 casualties and approximately 750,000 refugees as well as 1.4 million internally displaced persons (IDPs) (out of a pre-war population of 2.8 million). In 1997, Charles Taylor was elected president, but the troubles in Liberia continued. The United Nations (UN) imposed sanctions on Liberia in May 2001, and later that year, fighting erupted in the north; by mid-2003, rebel forces controlled roughly two-thirds of the country. In August 2003, Taylor resigned and went into exile in Nigeria. The rebel groups signed a peace agreement and a large UN-controlled peace-keeping force arrived. Despite this, fighting continued in many parts of the country in 2004, but by the end of 2004 considerable disarmament had been achieved. Elections were held in October 2005, and in January 2006, Ellen Johnson-Sirleaf was sworn in as Liberia's new president (and Africa's first woman president). Since then, Liberia has been relatively peaceful, but the task of reconstruction and reintegration of refugees and IDPs remains considerable. (For a fuller review of the conflict, see Dick 2002a, 2002b; Richards et al. 2005.)

A substantial literature suggests that tensions in inter-generational relations have characterized Liberian society in recent decades. Indeed, these have been blamed by many as being a major cause of the conflicts in Liberia and Sierra Leone (Richards 2005; Ellis 1999; Utas 2005). This contrasts with the views expressed by most Buduburam camp inhabitants—both young and old—who described inter-generational relations before the conflict as relatively harmonious, and particularly as conforming to idealized views of how parents should support their children.

Ethnographic accounts of "traditional" Liberian society (particularly northwest Liberia) describe a pattern of strongly deferential relations between youth and elders, reinforced by a number of structural factors that made it very difficult for young men to assert themselves as full members of society (gaining a wife and means to support themselves economically) without becoming indebted to the older generation (Bledsoe, 1976; 1980a). Bledsoe (1980b) describes traditional Kpelle society as being based on a "wealth in people" system, in which both women and land were monopolized by elites of elders, supported by the institution of polygyny. The widespread system of patronage led to a very stratified society, in which most young men were obliged to enter into patron-client relationships (both within and beyond their own lineages).

In order to marry, men (or their families) had to compensate their wives' families either through payment of bride-wealth, through bride service, or political patronage (Bledsoe 1976). Young men typically depended on older family members to help with bride-wealth payments, thus creating dependency on them, or became indebted to their in-laws through bride service. Either way, young men were seen as "wife borrowers" who then had to spend years repaying "debts" incurred to their own kin, in-laws, or other patrons (Bledsoe 1980b). As Bledsoe (1980b: 79) put it, "Young men are in a bind: either they indebt themselves to older people in order to acquire women, or they forego the chances for advancement that marriage and the control of women bring."

The rituals associated with the initiation of young men and women into secret societies (Poro for men, Sande for women) also helped to maintain inter-generational relations based on fear and deference (Bledsoe 1980b; Ellis 1995; Rich-ards et al. 2005). In northwest Liberia, initiation into secret societies is a critical part of transition to adulthood for both men and women, who are considered marriageable only after initiation. Bledsoe (1980b:71) argues that Poro and Sande elders control both the production and the reproduction of initiates, who are obliged to work for the elders in exchange for protection in a system closely resembling wardship or clientship, and that the deference to Poro and Sande elders becomes a lifelong obligation.

Although rather less has been written about other areas and ethnic groups in Liberia, it is generally accepted that the problems faced by young men (particularly those from non-elite families) in gaining access to wives and land without incurring long-term debts of obligation were widespread throughout the country (Handwerker 1973; Ellis 1999; Utas 2005). Utas (2005) notes that many young men were thus destined to remain bachelors for life. In summary, in traditional Liberian society, elders controlled the labor and marriage prospects (and thus entry into adulthood) of most young men and women.

The late 1950s and 1960s saw an economic boom in Liberia, affecting in particular urban areas. This led to what Ellis (1999:287) describes as a "modest social revolution," whereby young men and women were able to obtain salaried employment and thus some independence from elders and patrons. Bledsoe's account (1976), based on fieldwork in 1974, describes the effect of "modernisation," in which new economic opportunities were leading to a breakdown in the "control of people" system, and enabling young people to escape the control of elders. For young men, who now had the opportunity to earn money required for bride-wealth independently, this led to reduced obligations to both their own elders and in-laws. Although young women had less access than men to many forms of wage labor, many were also able to achieve some degree of financial independence through small-scale trading and sexual liaisons, which afforded them more choice than before over when and whom to marry, with many electing to remain single for extended periods of time (Bledsoe 1976, 1980b).

However, the economic boom proved to be unsustained and the late 1970s and 1980s saw an economic downturn with less salaried employment available (Ellis 1999). Utas (2005: 150) argues that, in urban and semi-urban areas, this had a major impact on youth relations:

> An ever-growing number of young people in urban/semi-urban environments were excluded even from the possibilities of becoming adults. Possibilities to participate in the wage economy diminished and education ceased having any importance. With this crisis looming, many young men lost even the possibility to establish themselves as adults, by building a house, or getting married—even though they continued to become fathers of children for whom they could not provide. Chronologically, they outgrew youth, but socially they became 'youthmen.'

Utas and others have argued that the frustration of youth was central to the onset on conflict in Liberia (and Sierra Leone), with the wars representing part of a "youth revolution," in which marginalized young people (men in particular) resorted to violence as a means of overturning traditional relations between young and old: "Enlistment in the armies, in the first place, was envisaged as a move away from the margins and into the centre of society—a means of integrating into society, even if by force" (Utas 2005:151). Richards's (2005) work with former young combatants from rural areas paints a similar picture, suggesting that lack of access to jobs, land, and wives were the primary motivating factors for many to fight: "'We joined the RUF willingly.. .the main reason was lack of job... and lack of encouragement for youth.'" (2005: 578; see also Peters and Richards 1998).

Richards et al (2005) suggest that inter-generational tensions are now a strong feature of conditions in Liberia, not least in the context of reconstruction activities and free labor demands, particularly for men. The militias continue to be fed there by large numbers of young people no longer able or willing to integrate within a traditional social system based on family land and social deference.

THE BUDUBURAM REFUGEE SETTLEMENT

The Buduburam Refugee Settlement was established in 1990. In order to accommodate the great influx of Liberian refugees, the Ghanaian government made land available at Buduburam in Gomoa District, some 35km west of Accra. The majority of Liberians were settled in Buduburam, while smaller numbers went to live in the much smaller Krisan camp in Senzulle (Western Region) and some in Accra and other towns (Dick 2002a, 2002b). Material assistance was provided under the UNHCR's administrative direction, in partnership with a variety of NGOs. This included provision of food rations, tents for shelter and, in the following years, educational assistance and vocational training.

After the 1997 elections, the situation in Liberia was deemed safe for return. UNHCR shifted its focus from humanitarian support to voluntary repatriation and, by June 2000, all UNHCR assistance to Liberian refugees had been withdrawn, as part of UNHCR regional policy (Dick 2002, b). However, the vast majority of Liberians decided to remain at Buduburam, and the early 2000s saw further influxes of refugees as the conflict in Liberia re-intensified. By January 2005, the UNHCR reported a total of over 41,000 Liberian refugees and asylum seekers resident at Buduburam (UNHCR Ghana 2005). To our knowledge, there are no official recent statistics on the ethnic composition of Buduburam residents, and among the refugees themselves ethnic identity is very much downplayed. All of the main ethnic groups in Liberia are represented by our research participants, with no one group dominating, and Buduburam refugees come from all parts of Liberia. Refugees in Buduburam tend to come disproportionately from the urban middle classes, particularly from Monrovia.

In July 2002, the UNHCR re-established a presence at Buduburam. Today, the UNHCR is not giving individual humanitarian assistance, with the exception of aid to "vulnerable" groups such as children and the elderly, but is engaging in community-level support, working toward self-reliance. Current UNHCR support includes the provision of medicine and equipment to the clinic, as well as collaborations with UNICEF to try to improve the water and sanitation situation, and with The Christian Council of Ghana to provide education and vocational training. Additionally, refugees in Buduburam have formed a large number of community-based organizations, including many that are youth-based.

Spatially, the Camp is divided into twelve zones. Just beyond the entrance to the camp is the main square, surrounded by small stalls held by petty traders. Around the main square are the principal public amenities, including the camp clinic and the Welfare Council offices. The two main streets leading from the square are lined with small shops, stalls, bars, video clubs, and Internet cafes and next to the square are football and basketball fields, which are frequently in use. All zones are ethnically mixed. In addition to the official camp zones, there are four "Gaps": areas within the camp but outside of the officially recognized organization of the camp. The Gaps are inhabited mostly by young people: largely former combatants who arrived without their parents or adult family members.

Buduburam refugee settlement can thus be seen as constituting a space marked by "layered sovereignty" (Turner 2005:330). Buduburam is situated within Ghanaian sovereign territory and falls within the jurisdiction of the local Ghanaian traditional chief, but the UNHCR and associated NGOs have de facto sovereignty of the camp, controlling distribution of food and basic services, and imposing curfews. The Gaps lie officially within the boundaries of UNHCR jurisdiction yet, within the Gaps, normal rules of camp behavior become suspended, and activities that would not be condoned elsewhere (drug use, gambling) are tacitly tolerated. Thus, the Gaps can be seen as "pockets of sovereignty outside the reach of UNHCR" (Turner 2005:332). As we shall see, it is the Gaps that represent the most extreme manifestation of challenges to spatial gerontocracy within the camp.

GENERATING EMIC PERSPECTIVES: A REVIEW OF METHODS

Intensive fieldwork was conducted in Buduburam Refugee Settlement from January to May 2005. After initial work with one of the UK researchers, this was mostly conducted by three experienced Ghanaian researchers (two academics, one from a youth-focused NGO), with substantial support from the Welfare Council and other camp inhabitants.

The aim of the fieldwork was to generate emic perspectives on social change, as seen by the refugees. A multi-method qualitative approach was adopted in order to facilitate crosschecking and tria ngu lation of data and to increase reliability. The definition of youth was left deliberately unspecified, in order to elicit local interpretations and meanings. It emerged that youth is a contingent category, and that the experience of conflict and becoming refugees has shaped such social and generational categories.

Nineteen focus group discussions were held, twelve with groups of young people and seven with elders (Morgan 1997). Groups were composed of six to ten people and were in most cases homogeneous with respect to generation and gender, but were ethnically mixed (as noted above, ethnic identity is downplayed among the refugees, with different ethnic groups living side by side). Thirty individual interviews were conducted: ten semi-structured interviews with young camp inhabitants, eight life history interviews with older Liberians, and twelve key informant interviews with representatives of camp-based organizations and local government. In addition, two Senior Secondary School students kept 24 hour photo-diaries, using disposable cameras, and one other kept a detailed daily diary for two months. The three Ghanaian researchers participated in daily life and took detailed field-notes in the form of an ethnographic diary based on detailed observations (Geertz 1973; Sanjek 1990).

All interviews and focus groups were conducted in English, and were fully transcribed and coded for topics (Miles and Huberman 1994). Subsequent analysis used grounded theory: theory generated from the data rather than imposed on it (Glaser and Strauss 1967). The coded data were searched for emergent patterns, using a series of validity checks (Miles and Huberman 1994). Throughout the research process, regular meetings were held with a small consultative group of key stakeholders and camp residents. Additionally, two workshops were held for camp inhabitants, which enabled people to comment on, and make changes to, the findings and analysis.

Data generated from the narratives represent transformed reality: rather than an objective real-time account of changes, they represent participants' own analysis of social change. Thus, this paper presents an emic perspective of changes in inter-generational relations, which, as we shall see, does not always correspond with ethnographic accounts of pre-conflict Liberia.

Ethical Issues

This study was given ethical approval by the Durham University Ethics Advisory Committee. There are clearly serious ethical implications of conducting research with young people who have lived through conflict and displacement, in particular the possibility of re-evoking emotional and psychological trauma and falsely raising hopes and expectations. These concerns were discussed at the consultative group meetings before research commenced, and mitigating steps were taken. The researchers explained very clearly to participants at the outset the scope and remit of the project, making it clear that we were not in a position to solve people's problems directly. However, routes to appropriate counseling facilities were established and publicized.

LIFE IN BUDUBURAM REFUGEE SETTLEMENT

Without exception, our informants, both young and old, pointed to the day-to-day difficulties experienced by those living in Buduburam. Since the withdrawal of UNHCR humanitarian support in the late 1990s, many refugees struggle to meet basic needs. Because they are not Ghanaian citizens, Liberian refugees in Ghana have few rights and limited access to services. Many complained that they cannot work formally outside the camp without a work permit, which is very difficult to obtain. Only a few well-qualified Liberians such as nurses and teachers obtain work within the camp. Almost all livelihood activities consequently take place in the informal sector, mostly within the camp. The major problems identified by young people were: very limited educational and livelihood opportunities, high living costs (accornmodation, education, healthcare, food, water, and sanitation), insufficient external support, and loss of family members.

A substantial proportion of camp residents (estimated at about 20% by some informants) were receiving regular remittances from family abroad, particularly the United States. Those lacking adequate remittances were more likely to be pushed into risky and illegal livelihood strategies. (It should be noted that Gomoa is one of Ghana's poorest districts and that poverty and livelihood insecurity are also commonplace among local Ghanaians.) This context of widespread economic insecurity and difficulties in meeting basic needs experienced by the majority of refugees underpins many of the tensions and ambiguities in inter-generational relations that we now describe.

YOUTH AS A SOCIAL CATEGORY AND TRANSITION TO ADULTHOOD

There is a strong ambivalence about the transition to adulthood in the camp. On the one hand, because of the economic situation, young people are obliged to assume economic responsibilities associated with adulthood at an earlier age than they might have done in Liberia. The transition to adulthood can be quite sudden, as in the case of a young woman, who told us, "I was fifteen and my father had no resources to support three children, so I started being an adult." This was a commonly expressed view: "Even a 12 year old girl is not a youth because of the things she has to do to survive in the camp here," explained one young man, while another told us, "Children on the camp.. .are forced to be men at a tender age, going for food, paying for school fees..."

One the other hand, because it is almost impossible for most people ever to provide adequately for a family, there is a sense that full adulthood is delayed indefinitely. In other words, there is an increasingly protracted "in between" period, of being neither a child nor a full adult, able to participate fully in social and domestic life. This feeling of indefinite liminality underpins many of the difficulties expressed by camp inhabitants about the relationships between the generations. Moreover, the boundaries between youth and adulthood have become increasingly blurred in both directions, with some elders saying that they have, at least in part, lost their adult status.

In Buduburam, "youth" as a social category, defined not by chronological age but by inability to achieve full adult status (Utas 2003), has assumed a great importance in camp life. There is a strong generational "youth" identity, based on camaraderie and mutual support. "We live as a group," said one young man. Young people identify strongly with America, and in particular, with black American youth culture: "Most of our youth dress like Americans, and play their songs too," remarked one older woman. Many in Buduburam receive remittances from family in the United States, and living in America represents an important aspiration for most young people: "On the camp, you feel connected to America, you have a friend or relative there," said a young man, whose friend agreed: "Most people plan to go to America."

CHANGES IN INTER-GENERATIONAL ROLES AND RELATIONSHIPS

There is a strong consensus in the camp (across generations and ethnic groups) that conflict and exile have resulted in major changes in inter-generational relations and often increasing inter-generational conflict. Many aspects of the process of becoming and being refugees are seen to have affected how young people and elders relate to each other: the experience of the war itself, family separation during flight from Liberia, the experience of poverty, and loss of livelihoods in the camp.

One of the most widely expressed concerns, both of young people and elders, was the inability of parents, and the older generation more widely, to provide materially for their children, and the impacts of this on social authority. There were many accounts of inter-generational role reversals within the household, in which children were now providing for parents, rather than the other way round, with elders becoming increasingly dependent on youth incomes for their own survival. Many of the livelihood opportunities on the camp are seen to be more accessible for young people than for elders, including sex work (often in the form of women making a living from "gifts" from boyfriends), heavy manual labor, and violent crime such as armed robbery.

Moreover, young people typically learn the skills needed to access Internet facilities, enabling them to maintain ties with friends and families abroad (and even create new Internet-based relationships) more effectively than elders, and thus to receive remittances.

Accounts of young people supporting themselves, and their families, materially were widespread among both young and old:

> Now the 16 year old girls are supporting their parents, and the parents don't ask them where they get the money, because they need it. It was different before the war. (young woman).

> Now a 50 year old man may be depending on a 20 year old boy, because he gets remittances from the USA. (young man).

> Back home, we didn't have the system of young people working—the parents were responsible for their upkeep, but here you can't provide for them, (elderly man).

It was the widespread view of camp inhabitants, both young and old, that the apparent economic role reversals had led to a breakdown of the usual relationships of authority and respect between young and old. "On the camp, the young people are not respecting older people. If you call a young person to offer some advice, they will insult you—they will shout, 'Is it your concern?'" explained an old woman—a view echoed widely in interviews and focus groups. "We respected the old people [when we were young] and even stooped before them when we greeted them. Now they stand far away and shout hello," bemoaned another older woman, whose friend agreed: "When we were growing up, we were obedient to our parents and older people but not now."

Interestingly, these views were as widespread among young people as they are among the elders. "Before the war, there was much respect in Liberia," said a woman in her twenties. "Young people were respectful and afraid of vices in the presence of their parents and older people. Now things have changed."

The breakdown in respect and authority is generally blamed on parents' inability to support their children materially. One old woman explained in a focus group:

> Initially as people came here with their children, there was respect and parents were able to control their children. But as conditions deteriorated and started getting harder,... th ings changed and the respect got lost because you can't feed your children. The children go out for food themselves. The respect has been eroded. You can't even reprimand someone's child.

> Other focus group participants agreed:

> Our children are not listening to us because they can't get what they want from us.

> If your child is doing what you don't want, they shout back that they are doing things for themselves to support themselves.

Another focus group exchange, among a group of elderly men, echoed similar sentiments:

> We can't support our children here. The children are not respecting their parents because parents can't support them.

> Because of the inability of the parents to support their children, the respect is gone. Once you can't feed them adequately, they won't listen to you.

> I had 100% control of my children in Liberia. But in the camp, I can't buy a shoe for them. How can I control them?

> To be very frank, the respect for the youth to the old is very limited because the older people can't care for them.

There was almost complete consensus among our interviewees that, before the conflict, flows of material support had been from elders to youth, and that this fundamental change in economic relations underpinned the breakdown of elders' authority. Notably, the consensus on this spanned all generations and ethnic groups.

The idea that, in traditional Liberian society, elders provided for the younger generation is at least partially supported by the ethnographic literature presented above (Bledsoe 1976; 1980a; b; Ellis 1999; Richards 2005; Richards et al. 2005; Utas 2005). Elders (own kin, in-laws, and other patrons) provided the means (bride-price, land, political protection) for young men to progress to adulthood. However, this came at a price, with young men becoming indebted to their elders and saddled with long-term obligations of labor and social deference. According to these accounts, it was the young people who were the main laborers, with their labor and income controlled by elders, via a variety of patron-client type relationships. What seems to have changed in recent times is not who was working, but who was *controlling* youth labor and income.

However, most researchers claim that this had already begun to change well before the conflict, with the rise of wage labor in the 1950s and 1960s. According to Bledsoe (1980b) and Ellis (1995), among others, this gave both young men and women more economic independence from elders, which in turn led to the gerontocratic relationships of social authority beginning to break down. Further changes came with the economic downturn since the late 1970s, which reduced opportunites for wage labor and led to increasing frustrations of youth (Ellis1995; Utas 2005).

The reasons for the apparent partial mismatch between refugees' narratives and ethnographic accounts are not clear. One explanation is that the ethnographic accounts, based largely (although not exclusively) on rural, north-west Liberia do not represent the range of social contexts from which the Buduburam refugees come. In particular, social relations in urban, middle-class areas, from which many in Buduburam come, are likely to have been rather different from those in more rural areas.

However, as noted above, there was a surprising degree of consensus across generations, ethnic groups, and geographical backgrounds in how people described the changes in economic relations and the effects on inter-generational relations of social authority. It is likely that the refugees' narratives constitute a constructed, shared version of social norms and changes, and that discourses of breadwinning and authority are a reflection of emotional loss and more general dissatisfaction rather than an accurate, real-time account of social changes. Whichever is the case, such discourses hold great sway within the camp and profoundly affect how both young and older people view their current situation.

It was not just perceived economic role reversals that had led, in the refugees' view, to a breakdown of inter-generational relations of authority and respect. Experience of the conflict itself has played an important role. Involvement of young people in the war is seen to have contributed to changes in their relations with elders. "This has happened because of the war," said one old man, "The younger people don't respect the older people. In the war, there were child soldiers commanding adults." This theme was echoed by other older people. "During the war, children had guns, so they had power over older people," explained one elderly man. Perhaps the most vivid account came from another elderly man, who said, "My own son told me he has a war face. He is about 18 years old. He said that if I touch him, he will show me his knife." The relationship between the war and inter-generational tensions is almost certainly two-directional. While elders were often quick to blame young people's role as combatants for the perceived breakdown in inter-generational relations, most commentators have argued that inter-generational conflict was a major contributing factor to the war (e.g. Utas 2005: 151; Richards, 2005).

The most extreme manifestation of the breakdown in inter-generational relations is in the four "Gaps": youth ghettoes, consisting mostly of young men, embracing a culture based strongly on Rastafarian identity. Many of those living in the Gaps are ex-child combatants, who fled Liberia and arrived in Ghana alone. Based largely on our observational data, it appears that, within the Gaps, new forms of support and reciprocity have developed, in the absence of families and elders. Although typically criticized by other refugees as representing a breakdown of the moral order, the systems of social support are highly sophisticated and appear to be very effective. Those living in the Gaps have largely opted out of inter-generational relations altogether, preferring to create relationships based on Active intra-generational kinship (for example, referring to each other as brother and sister). This resonates with work done by Utas (2003; 2005) in urban squatter communities in Liberia, in which unrelated young people have replaced family relationships with kinship-type relationships of solidarity, authority, and respect, between themselves.

REVERSALS IN LIFE-COURSE CHRONOLOGY

One of the most striking features of the changes in inter-generational roles and relations described above is how life-course chronology has become disrupted and, in some cases, reversed. Many elders are, in their own terms, losing their adult status through becoming obliged to depend on their children for support. This dependence entails considerable loss of autonomy, as the following focus group exchange between elderly women demonstrates:

> My daughter from London sends me money and gives me instructions as to what to use the money for. She is making decisions for me.

> This is exactly what is happening. They decide what the money should be used for. My daughter sends $50 and dictates for us how long the money should last, and what we should eat and buy.

In an even more explicit manifestation of reversals in life-course chronology, the rapid development of "youth culture" within the camp, and increasing idealization of youth has led some older people to adopt aspects of youth culture. This is driven partly by economic necessity. In order to attract "boyfriends," whose "gifts" might be critical for economic security, some older women feel under pressure to appear young and so dress accordingly, as well as adopting other aspects of "youth culture" and engaging in "immoral behavior" typically associated with younger women. "Presently, some older people dress like girls to attract the men," remarked a woman in a focus group. Her friend recalled a particular incident: "An older woman was dressed revealing parts of her body and I was looking surprised…" This was a common theme in focus groups, as was the ignominy of older women competing with younger women for boyfriends. "A mother and daughter may be chasing the same man," said one elderly woman, whose friend pointed out, "There is a case of a mother and daughter each having a child from the same man."

But it is not only economic necessity that drives some older people (in particular women) to adopt aspects of youth culture and dress. Many believe that old age is no longer valued, while youth is prized. Addressing someone as an old woman or man used to be seen as a mark of respect; now some see it as an insult, as one older woman explained: "Some old women now refuse to be called old women. You want to give them respect by calling them old woman but they are angry."

Such behavior, which appears to violate the normative codes for inter-generational relations, attracts the criticism of young and old alike. Young people criticise the older generation for reneging on their responsibilities to provide appropriate role models: "Old women now wear the same things as young women—apuskeleke [revealing dresses]. Some old women wear these dresses because they want to get younger. But it shouldn't be so—they should set good examples." (young woman)

Likewise, elders are sometimes criticized by young people for failing to take seriously their responsibilities to educate and discipline their children. Elders are accused of placing economic necessity above social responsibility and teaching their children appropriate behavior:

> In Liberia, the older people were taking care of the family. They were well-dressed and we emulated them. But on the camp they are doing all sorts of dressing and some older people even advise the youth to go out and bring money [through immoral or illegal activity], (young woman). Some of the parents encourage the youth to go out and bring money and they don't care how they get the money, (older man).

In some senses, the experience of living in the refugee camp prevents (nearly) everyone in Buduburam from achieving or maintaining full adult status. Harrell-Bond (2000) argues that refugee camps should be seen as "total institutions," in a similar way to prisons or mental hospitals, in that they are depersonalizing and controlling. Turner (2004) describes the ways in which the UNHCR and external agencies become symbolically identified as father/husband/patriarch, and refugees as helpless babies/children/women. Most Liberian refugees, young or old, are dependent on someone else (UNHCR, friends and relatives abroad, churches) for a living. Thus life as a refugee plays a part in both the indefinite extension of a liminal period of youth, in which young people feel ill-prepared to assume the full social responsibilities of adulthood, and simultaneously in the infantilization of older people.

AMBIVALENCE IN INTER-GENERATIONAL RELATIONS

It is, perhaps, because both young people and elders share the frustration of not being able to fulfill the social responsibilities of adulthood that inter-generational relations are more ambivalent than might appear at first sight. While conflict and blame are certainly part of the discourses used to describe changes in inter-generational relationships of authority, there is also considerable sympathy for the situation in which members of other generations find themselves, combined with a strong sense of shame and guilt that more cannot be done to ameliorate the situation. And while it is very common for people to talk about inter-generational differences and conflict, there is also a strong sense that everybody, young or old, is in the same boat and suffering from the same problems.

It would thus be wrong to portray all inter-generational relationships as fraught with difficulty and mutual hostility. Although parents are often unable to provide materially for their children, many young people interviewed expressed the importance of advice and emotional support provided by elders in their families and the wider community, demonstrated by this focus group exchange between young women:

> My mother is old, so she can't provide for us, but every time she is thinking about how we are doing.

> My mother advises me, she directs me for a good future. She knows 1 am going through difficulties.

> The old people have experience. They can counsel you and give you the encouragement to continue in life.

> They encourage us that this is not the end of life.

Older people also provide practical support in times of trouble. One young man explained, "We go to older people when we have problems with the police... in every legal issue we need matured people." Moreover, many youth recognize and appreciate the efforts that their parents and grandparents go to in order to provide them with school fees and other material support. One young woman explained, "My grandmother sells bread and my mother sells water. They paid the fees to complete the SSS [Senior Secondary School]." As well as turning to older relatives, Welfare Council members (elders) provide both formal and informal support to young people.

In turn, while many elders are critical of young people's attitudes and lack of respect for their parents, they understand and are extremely sympathetic for their plight, exemplified by the following exchange in a focus group of women elders:

> If I were a younger person in this camp where my parents don't support me financially... it would be difficult. It is more difficult to be a youth now in this camp [than it was for us when we were young].

> Some too are frustrated. Their parents are dead, so they decide to live their lives anyhow.

This sympathy is recognized by many of the younger people such as the young man who said in one focus group, "The older people will continue to feel for us because we need to do something to support them. The older people will feel for us because these acts [stealing, selling drugs, prostitution] were not done in Liberia for the sake of making a living."

Even in the Gaps, which appear to represent the extremes of breakdown of "normal" social relations and traditional gerontocracy, these have been replaced by transformed forms of social support and obligation. Again, there are parallels here with Utas's (2005) account of a group of young men living in a ghetto in Monrovia. Utas described the group as "part of a subculture much at odds with mainstream society" (2005:143). However, they were still embedded in longstanding social practices and relations, although transformed, with wartime friends replacing family networks, and retaining a place (albeit on the lowest echelon) in patron-client relations. Similarly, Turner (2005:325) notes that, among Burundian refugees in Tanzania, "although the norms and hierarchies of Burundi are not reproduced in the camp, they certainly are renegotiated."

One of the Gaps even has a father figure—an older man living in the Gap, to whom the youth defer for important decisions. He was immediately nominated by the Gap youth to represent them at our project workshops (although by living in the Gap, the old man had effectively forfeited any place or rights in mainstream camp society).

More generally, there is a deep ambivalence, felt by youth and elders, about the change toward a youth-oriented culture, and a sense of longing for a more stable (although perhaps illusory) past, in which "proper" relations of youth deferring to elders were maintained. Again, in another context, Turner (2006:776) described in Tanzania "...a constant struggle between orthodox and heterodox opinion, between longing for the moral order of yesterday and striving for the opportunities created in the camp."

INTERACTIONS BETWEEN GENDER AND INTER-GENERATIONAL RELATIONS

Apparent changes and ambivalence in inter-generational relations must also be understood within the context of gender relations within the camp. Entry into adulthood can mean different things for young women and men, and is marked by different transitional events. It was broadly agreed that boys stay "younger" for longer than girls, who may be forced toward adulthood more quickly, often by becoming pregnant. Teenage pregnancy was widely recognized by the refugees to be a serious and widespread problem in the camp. Motherhood is seen as one defining "adult" characteristic, propelling many adolescent girls into at least partial adulthood, while young men who become fathers are able to reject or ignore this responsibility. However, while motherhood opens the door for young women to achieve adult status and recognition, it can simultaneously close off avenues to economic independence by curtailing opportunities to work or study.

Both men and women thought that young women have more avenues for economic gain open to them than do men, through personal charm and sexual liaisons (never mentioned as an option for men). Several young men observed that, "The smile of a woman can get her help." In other words, earlier entry into partial adulthood for women is not only precipitated by pregnancy, it is facilitated by the possibility of commercial sex work (or informal liaisons). However, partial economic autonomy gained in this way may cut off routes to fuller and more sustainable economic autonomy, as noted above, and other social attributes of adulthood, such as "respectability," may be also compromised. The physically risky nature of this strategy was widely acknowledged, with harassment, rape, and other forms of violence against women common in the environs of the camp (Kreitzer 2000; N'Tow 2004).

It is worth noting that many young Liberian women seek sexual relations with older men (both Liberian and Ghanaian), an arrangement that bears resemblance to the "traditional" practice of older men controlling the sexuality of younger women in Liberia, and another indication that not all of the traditional relations of inter-generational power and authority have been overturned. Likewise, the practice of young women (married and unmarried) taking on lovers (sometimes several at a time), often for financial gain, has been reported by Bledsoe (1980b:92-93) in "traditional" Kpelle society.

The perception (real or not) that sexual liaisons can afford women possibilities for economic autonomy not open to men also feeds into the sense that traditional relations of authority expressed through gendered power relations are being challenged. Bledsoe (1980b) notes that, in traditional Kpelle society at least, women were always under the economic and legal control of men. There is a consensus that, in Buduburam, women have more resources at their disposal than men. This is seen as undermining the adult status of some men relative to women, and is highly threatening to male roles and ideas of masculinity, as these life history accounts demonstrate:

> Men feel ashamed that women are doing all the providing and that we can only loaf around" (44 year-old man). Before 1989, men were the heads of households…My father was the breadwinner and my mother was supporting…[On the camp] there is no employment for men, only menial jobs such as construction. Women are mainly the breadwinners. This has a psychological effect on the men—they feel helpless. (48 year-old woman).

Conversely, the accounts of elders adopting youth dress and culture, thus compromising their adult status, were almost exclusively confined to women, for whom appearing to be young was seen to be a crucial attribute for attracting potentially profitable sexual relationships.

CONCLUSIONS

As in other cases reported in the literature, refugees in Buduburam descibed substantial shifts in inter-generational roles and relationships in the camp. In particular, interviewees, both young and old, pointed to changes in the economic roles associated with young people and elders, which they believe have led to the re-shaping of inter-generational relations of authority and respect. Perhaps more significantly, the boundaries between different generational categories (childhood, youth, adulthood) appear to have shifted and become blurred. Youth has become an indefinite period of liminality (Utas 2003), in which people are forced to leave childhood behind at an earlier age, due to the need to take on economic responsibilities, but are never quite able to enter full adulthood. At the same time, life in Buduburam has led to an erosion of the adult/elder status of many, leading to disruptions, and even reversals, in life-course chronology. However, refugees' perceptions of changes in inter-generational relations are complex and ambivalent (Teo et al. 2003). While new conflicts and blame play a major part, refugees recognize many commonalities between youth and elders. There is the feeling of being "all in the same boat," particularly because, in effect, everyone is prevented from achieving or maintaining full adult status in their own terms.

Clearly, these changes are not purely the result of the conflict and forced migration. As Kaiser (2006) observes, based on work in a Ugandan refugee camp, displacement is neither a necessary nor sufficient cause of inter-generational tensions, which are a very common phenomenon in rapidly developing societies. However, she goes on to suggest that "it is likely that the experience of exile and the new opportunities it has made available to the younger generation are contributory factors" (ibid. :200). Agier (2002) has compared refugee camps with cities, in representing a melting pot within which social relations become re-shaped and certain forms of identity become subsumed under new forms.

As noted above, inter-generational relations have been changing rapidly in Liberia at least since the 1960s, and many have argued that the frustrations of marginalized young people were a major cause of the Mano River conflicts (Ellis 1999; Richards 2005; Utas 2005). Similar kinds of changes and tensions in inter-generational relations have also been documented by Utas (2003, 2005) among those who remained in Liberia during the conflict. Thus, the relationship between social change and civil conflict in Liberia should be seen as a dialectical one, and unraveling cause and effect in the post-conflict setting is far from straightforward.

Nonetheless, our interviewees clearly saw the refugee experience in general, and the reversals in economic opportunities in particular, as a major driving force behind social change and increasing inter-generational tension. Clearly, their narratives represent a transformed version of reality, and may be tinged with a nostalgic, rosy view of the past (Ellis 1999). In the context of having been through very traumatic experiences during the conflict and living in a refugee camp, it is likely that people need to construct a story that enables them to make sense, on a collective basis, of what has happened to them. In Buduburam, this appears to involve downplaying ethnic difference and the construction of a harmonious set of pre-conflict social relations. Blame for what has gone wrong is thus shifted away from those in the camp to an external "other." However, whether or not refugees' narratives represent an objective account of social change is relatively unimportant. What matters is that they represent a commonly accepted discourse among camp residents about the nature of the conflict and inter-generational relations, which is likely to endure and affect post-conflict reconstruction and rehabilitation.

While some young people may have benefited from greater freedom and new opportunities, there is little doubt that the perceived changes have had very negative consequences for many others. This is important because inter-generational support and solidarity can play an important role in enabling people (both young and old) to cope with life as refugees (Farwell 2001; Chatty and Hundt 2001). In Buduburam, elders provide practical and emotional support, which helps young people to make sense of their situations within a cultural framework of reference. A breakdown of inter-generational relations, itself in part the consequence of young people's capacity for social resilience, also thus has the potential to undermine that capacity.

In the context of the camp, thought needs to be given to how elders can be helped to come to terms with the inevitable loss of status and authority that comes with living as a refugee, and to how they might be able to derive new forms of social status, without having to resort to mimicking youth behavior. This might involve, for example, directing particular livelihood opportunities toward older people, or having more formalized systems of emotional support and advice between elders and youth. UNHCR (2000) and HelpAge (Knight 2001) have drawn attention to the value of older refugees as resources for guidance and advice, and as transmitters of culture, skills, and crafts, but this needs stronger conversion into practical policies of support. At the same time, we need to consider the needs of young people, in particular how to enable easier transitions to adulthood that are less risky than many of the current ones.

In the longer term, there are major implications for the process of rehabilitation and re-integration of refugees into Liberian society. This has been recognized by other commentators. Utas (2005:51) contends that, for a large proportion of Liberia's young ex-combatants, for whom the war seemed to be an opportunity to overturn social relations that kept them marginalized, "re-marginalisation, not re-integration, remains the only reality." Richards et al. (2005) argue that central to the process of reconstruction in Liberia should be a series of measures to address the marginalization of rural youth, such as widening access to land and enforcing new marriage laws which diminish elders' control over young women.

Finally, it is important to recognize that, although young long-term refugees often demonstrate a strong degree of resilience and resourcefulness, there is sometimes an important price to be paid in terms of personal and social consequences, many of which are felt to be negative by the refugees themselves. While the shift toward a more positive view of refugees as agents with important resources and capacities is to be welcomed, this must be coupled both with a realistic assessment of the policy and support context within which refugees find themselves, and with an analysis of the likely impacts of refugee coping strategies on both their own health and well-being, and on wider social relations within their communities.

REFERENCES

Agier, Michel
2002 Between War and the City: Towards an Urban Anthropology of Refugee Camps. Ethnography 3(3): 317-341.

Berman, Helene
2001 Children and War: Current Understandings and Future Directions. Public Health Nursing 18(4): 243-252.

Bledsoe, Caroline
1976 Women's Marital Strategies among the Kpelle of Liberia. Journal of Anthropological Research 32(4): 379-389.
1980a The Manipulation of Kpelle Social Fatherhood. Ethnology 19(1): 29-45.
1980b Women and Marriage in Kpelle Society. Stanford, Calif: Stanford University Press.

Boyden, Jo
2003 Children under Fire: Challenging Assumptions about Children's Resilience. Youth, Education and Environments 13(1). http://colorado.edu/journals/cye (accessed December 15, 2007).

Boyden, Jo, Jo de Berry, Thomas Feeny and Jason Hart
2002 Children Affected byArmed Conflict in South Asia: A Review of Trends and Issues Identified through Secondary Research. RSC Working Paper No. 7, January 2002, Oxford: Refugee Studies Centre.

Chatty, Dawn and Gillian Hundt
2001 Lessons Learned Report: Children and Adolescents in Palestinian Households: Living with the Effects of Prolonged Conflict and Forced Migration. Refugee Studies Centre, Oxford University.

Dick, Shelley
2002a Liberians in Ghana: Living Without Humanitarian Assistance. New Issues in Refugees Research, Working Paper No. 57.
2002b Responding to Protracted Refugee Situations: A Case Study of Liberian Refugees in Ghana. Geneva: UNHCR Evaluation and Policy Analysis Unit.

El-Bushra, J, A, El-Karib and A. Hadjipateras
2002 Gender-sensitive Programme Design and Planning in Conflict-affected Situations. London: Agency for Cooperation and Research in Development (ACORD).

Ellis, Stephen

1995 Liberia 1989-1994: A Study of Ethnic and Spiritual Violence. African Affairs 94(375): 165-197.

1999 The Mask of Anarchy: The Destruction of Liberia and the Religious Dimension of an African Civil War. London: Hurst and Company.

Farwell, Nancy

2001 'Onward Through Strength': Coping and Psychological Support among Refugee Youth Returning to Eritrea from Sudan. Journal of Refugee Studies 14(1): 43-69.

Geertz, Clifford

1973 The Interpretation of Cultures. New York: Basic Books.

Glasser, Barney G. and Anselm L. Strauss

1967 The Discovery of Grounded Theory: Strategies for Qualitative Research. New York: Aldine.

Handwerker, W. Penn

1973 Technology and Household Configuration in Urban Africa: the Bassa of Monrovia. American Sociological Review 38(2): 182-197.

Harretl-Bond, Barbara

2000 Are Refugee Camps Good for Children? UNHCR New Issues in Refugee Research, Working Paper 29, August 2000.

Hinton, Rachel

2000 Seen but not Heard: Refugee Children and Models for Intervention. In Catherine Panter-Brick & Malcolm Smith (eds) Abandonned Children. Pp: 199-212. Cambridge: CUP.

Human Rights Watch/Africa

2004 Easy Prey: Child Soldiers in Liberia. September 1994, New York: Human Rights Watch.

Kaiser, Tania

2006 Songs, Discos and Dancing in Kiryandongo, Uganda. Journal of Ethnic and Migration Studies 32(2): 183-202.

Kibreab, Gaim

2004 Refugeehood, Loss and Social Change: Eritrean Refugees and Returnees. In Philomena Essed, Georg Frerks, and Joke Schrijvers (eds) pp. 19-30. Refugees and the Transformation of Societies: Agency, Policies, Ethics and Politics, Oxford: Berghahn Books.

Knight, Lesley-Anne

2001 Emergencies and Aging: A Position Paper. London: HelpAge International.

Kreitzer, Linda

2000 Reflections on Research among Liberian refugees. FMR 8 August 2000. http://www.fmreview.org/text/FMR/08/04.htm. (December 29,2007).

Leach, Melissa

1992 Dealing with Displacement: Refugee-Host Relations, Food and Forest Resources in Sierra Leonean Mende Communities during the Liberian Influx, 1990-01. IDS Research Report no. 22, April 1992, Brighton: IDS

Machel, Grar,a

2001 The Impact of War on Children. LTN1CEF/UNIFEM

Mann, Gillian

2004 Separated Children: Care and Support in Context, *In* Jo Boyden and Joanna de Berry (eds.) Children and Youth on the Front Line, pp. 3-22. Oxford: Berghahn 2004.

Miles, Matthew B. and A. Michael Huberman

1994 Qualitative Data Analysis. Newbury Park, Calif: Sage.

Morgan, David L.

1997 Focus Groups as Qualitative Research. Thousand Oaks, Calif.: Sage.

N'Tow, Saah Charles

2004 How Liberians Live on the Camp at Buduburam in Ghana. The Perspective, Atlanta, Georgia, June 14th 2004. http://www.theperspective.org/2004/june/buduburamcamp.html (accessed December 29, 2007).

Peters, Krijn and Paul Richards

1998 Why We Fight: Voices of Youth Combatants in Sierra Leone. Africa 68(2): 183-210.

Richards, Paul

2005 To Fight or to Farm? Agrarian Dimensions of the Mano River conflicts (Liberia and Sierra Leone. African Affairs 104(417): 571-590.

Richards, Paul, Steven Archibald, Beverlee Bruce, Watta Modad, Edward Mulbah, Tornorlah Varpilah, and James Vincent

2005 Community Cohesion in Liberia: A Post-war Rapid Social Assessment. Washington DC: World Bank, Social Development Department, paper no. 21, January 2005.

Sanjek Roger (ed)

1990 Fieldnotes: The Makings of Anthropology. Ithaca, N.Y.: Cornell University Press.

Sideris, Tina

2003 War, Gender and Culture: Mozambican Women Refugees. Soc Sci Med 56: 713-24.

Swaine, Aisling with Thomas Feeney

2004 A Neglected Perspective: Adolescent Girls' Experiences of the Kosovo Conflict of 1999. *In* Jo Boyden and Joanna de Berry (eds) Children and Youth on the Front Line, pp. 63-86. Oxford: Berghahn 2004.

Teo, Peggy, Elspeth Graham, Brenda S.A. Yeoh and Susan Levy

2003 Values, Change and Inter-generational Ties between Two Generations of Women in Singapore. Ageing and society 23; 327-347.

Turner, Simon

2004 New Opportunities: Angry Young Men in a Tanzanian Refugee camp. *In* Philomena Essed, Georg Frerks, and Joke Schrijvers (eds) Refugees and the Transformation of Societies: Agency, Policies, Ethics and Politics, pp. 94-105. Oxford: Berghahn Books.

2005 Suspended Spaces—Contesting Sovereignty in a Refugee camp. *In* Thomas Blom Hansen and Finn Stepputat (eds) Sovereign Bodies: Citizens, Migrants and States in the Postcolonial World, pp. 312-332. Princeton and Oxford: Berghahn Books.

2006 Negotiating Authority between UNHCR and 'The People'. Development and Change 37(4): 759-778.

UNHCR

2000 UNHCR Policy on Older Refugees: Older Refugees a Resource for the Community. Geneva: Health and Community Development Section, UNHCR.

UNHCR Ghana

2005 Statistical Report of Asylum Seekers and Refugees in Ghana, 01 January 2005.

Utas, Mats

2003 Sweet Battlefields: Youth and the Liberian Civil War. Uppsala University Dissertations in Cultural Anthropology, Uppsala, Sweden: Uppsala University.

2005 Building a Future? The Reintegration and Remarginslisation of Youth in Liberia. In Paul Richards (ed) No Peace, No War: An anthropology of Contemporary Armed Conflicts pp. 137-154. Athens: Ohio University Press.

Vincent M. and B.R.Sorensen (eds)

2001 Caught Between Borders: Response Strategies of the Internally Displaced. London: Pluto Press.

WCRCW (Women's Commission for Refugee Women and Children) 2000, Untapped Potential: Adolescents Affected by Armed Conflict. WCRCW: New York, January 2000.

Dying in the Twenty-first Century

By Margaret Holloway and Timothy M. Smeeding

INTRODUCTION

C ontemporary dying presents a series of questions for the dying person, their family and the professionals who attend them. These questions are embedded in complex ethical debates which have legal, medical, ideological, philosophical and religious ramifications. This situation arises from two features of modern life—the fact that medical advances allow us to control, to a great extent, both the manner and moment of death, and a concern for human rights, which constantly seeks to balance the rights of the individual with the wider interests of society. Woven through are a number of subsidiary issues which pose their own sets of questions. When is a person effectively dead? How do we determine capacity and incapacity and who should take 'life and death' decisions on behalf of a person deemed incapable of making their own? How do we determine quality of life? Are some lives more valuable than others when it comes to allocating resources or making treatment choices? Do a person's wishes and choices voiced at one point in time have currency when the situation changes? These and many more questions about the relationship between life and death face individuals and families in their personal lives and professionals in their daily work. All too frequently individuals find themselves surprisingly ill-prepared when confronted with a particular dilemma, despite increasing public debate, fuelled by some high-profile cases.

Margaret Holloway and Timothy M. Smeeding, "Dying in the Twenty-First Century," *Negotiating Death in Contemporary Health and Social Care*, pp. 93–117. Copyright © 2007 by Policy Press. Reprinted with permission.

The ongoing demographic changes discussed in Chapter One have resulted in many of these issues seeming to crystallise in the care of older people. These are separately discussed in Chapter Six. However, they are by no means confined to dying in old age. Life support technologies are available to keep accident victims alive in states where once they would have died. Babies born prematurely are nurtured through survival into growth, but frequently with big questions hanging over their present and future quality of life. Sensitive issues surrounding organ donation and transplants have to be dealt with in situations of emotional stress and haste. Overall, the seemingly elastic boundary between life and death can make the enormity of a decision which is irreversible feel overwhelming. The shock of the cold finality of death is felt even when it is an event which was planned and prepared for.

For a long time it seemed that discussion of the ethical questions underlying and surrounding our technologically sophisticated medical and healthcare systems lagged behind the realities of practice. Not only did this leave patients and families adrift as they struggled with decisions put to them, it left doctors in particular, but other front-line healthcare professionals also, vulnerable in law and frequently feeling themselves to be on the horns of a dilemma, or personally compromised. What became evident is that the law is a blunt and mistaken instrument for resolving these dilemmas in practice and as a society we cannot afford to ignore them. Fortunately, while it cannot be claimed that we have arrived at all the answers, or indeed that there are any 'answers' in some situations, there is now an accumulating public and professional debate to inform deliberations and guide practice in the particular instance. Stimulated by the hospice movement, we also have some notion that there are better and worse ways to manage dying, and palliative care has pushed forward its approach to the former. The challenge is how to bring together philosophies, ideologies and pragmatics of care which contain within them contradictions.

PHILOSOPHIES AND ETHOS OF CARE

We have seen in Chapter Two how the prevailing ethos in contemporary health and social care systems may be inimical to the development of quality care for people who are dying. The development of palliative care has been driven by a core philosophy which has to do with a focus on the whole person. This has been translated into objectives that now have international currency in both the developed and the developing worlds.

Hospice and palliative care

The World Health Organization (WHO) now defines palliative care as:

> an approach that improves the quality of life of patients and their families facing the problem associated with life-threatening illness, through the prevention and relief of suffering by means of early identification and impeccable assessment and treatment of pain and other problems, physical, psychosocial and spiritual. (World Health Organization, 2007).

The WHO statement goes on to stress the need for integrated care delivered by a multidisciplinary team and that palliative care strikes a balance between lifeaffirming and prolonging treatments and the acceptance of dying as a normal process.

The palliative care movement has grown out of the hospice movement, whose mission was originally driven forward through a philosophy of care which had four key points:

- attention to individual detail
- control of pain
- helping people to live until they die
- supporting the dying individual in a community of faith and hope (Saunders, 1990).

Hospices have stayed essentially true to this mission and all that it implies. For example, the St Christopher's hospice in South London (founded by Cicely Saunders) declares its mission as follows:

> St Christopher's exists to provide skilled and compassionate palliative care of the highest quality … St Christopher's care extends beyond the treatment of physical symptoms to consider the support, emotional, psychological, spiritual and social needs of our patients, their families, children, friends and carers. (www.stchristophers.org.uk)

This translates into an approach which aims to 'open up' dying. For staff this may involve confronting their own fears about dying in order that there are no emotional and psychological obstacles to continuing communication with the dying person. An emphasis on communication is a key aspect of hospice care and can be seen as a direct response to the cultures of 'closed awareness' (see Chapter Three) observed in hospitals in the mid-twentieth century, and still today in some instances (a recent Californian study found that families' experiences of communications with hospital doctors was 'one of interruption, inconclusion and marginalisation' [Russ and Kaufman, 2005, p 120]). There is concern that staff, family and friends should not 'cut the dying person off' prematurely, but stay in communication with them right to the end. As we shall see later in this chapter, there can be tensions between the objectives of staff to keep the patient fully engaged and in control of their life, and the wish of the dying person and their family for sedation. Although symptom and pain control are central tenets of hospice care, it is recognised that pain is not just physical, and that some symptoms are much more difficult to control than others. The notion of 'staying with the pain' alongside the dying person, including emotional, psychological and spiritual pain, is embedded in the hospice philosophy of care—'total care for total pain'. So too is attention to individual wishes, such as a last trip, or hairdo, which are not a treatment necessity and may even be risky in terms of the patient's illness. They may, however, be important to the person's sense of wholeness and wellbeing and a valuable way of showing continuing investment in what remains of their life. Alongside this continuing maintenance of hope in the person, hospices acknowledge the losses experienced and anticipated by the dying person and their family and offer counselling and support beforehand and bereavement support after.

Such care is demanding of individual staff to offer and sustain at all times, and such a broad mission is increasingly difficult for voluntarily funded organisations to continue to pursue, especially when it cannot be justified in terms of easily measurable outcomes. It was shown in Chapter Two how the prevailing culture in health and social care is leading hospices to concentrate on the practical detail of palliative care. Increasingly, it is necessary to build the evidence base for aspects of hospice care which are not so easily demonstrated but which lie at its heart. For example, a large survey in the US of spouse survival rates post-bereavement suggested that the support offered through hospice care might attenuate the known mortality risk for bereaved spouses, particularly widows (Christakis, 2003). The case studies which form the basis for Chapter Eight, taken from current practice, illustrate some of these tensions, and at various points in this book there is discussion of how the hospice mission may at times be failing or distorted in some aspects. Nevertheless, hospices remain a potent force championing quality services and dignified care for people who are dying.

One way in which their role is changing in the shifting context of end-of-life care is analysed as 'managing the boundaries' between life and death. No longer do people just enter hospices in order to die, nor is the provision of hospice services confined to the building. Nevertheless, it is argued that hospices continue to create that liminal space in which people may make the transition from life to death (Froggatt, 1997). If this is to be facilitative it must not be undermined by poor transfers between services, where the energies of the dying person become dissipated in coping with discontinuities in care between different providers (Woods et al, 2006). As noted earlier, the move to make hospices into a fully integrated part of the health and social care network is a key element in the current agenda.

The extension of its philosophy and practice into all healthcare settings is currently the main thrust of palliative care, with calls for such care to be seen as a basic human right (Harding, 2006). The public health agenda which this implies—in terms of government policy, including ensuring universal availability of drugs for pain and symptom control, professional training, and raising public awareness—is being particularly promoted in countries hit by the HIV pandemic. However, there is continuing evidence that much still needs to be done in the developed world to make good palliative care available in hospitals, despite the setting up of specialist units. Until palliative care principles permeate the health and social care system, people at the end of life will remain vulnerable to experiencing insensitive care, ignorant of their total needs and the most appropriate ways of meeting them. Initiatives like the Liverpool Care Pathway for dying patients (Ellershaw et al, 1997) aim to disseminate the good practice of hospices and specialist palliative care units more widely, but its proponents acknowledge that transforming the 'culture' is difficult (Jack et al, 2005; Twomey et al, 2007). The House of Commons Health Committee, concluding its report on palliative care, emphasised the need to address social attitudes to death and dying if the culture in which dying takes place, and the care which is provided, are to change (HC Health Committee report, 2003–04).

Religion and spirituality

The hospice movement has emphasised spiritual care from the outset as part of a holistic approach which treats the whole person in their total context. Yet it is still claimed that much end-of-life care is 'spiritually barren' (Fetzer Institute, 2003). Across the range of palliative and end-of-life care, it is possible that both perspectives are true. Even within hospices, recognition of the existence of spiritual need and spiritual pain at the end of life is not matched by the same level of understanding about how to identify this need within the individual patient, or how to respond to it. This is despite the fact that a considerable amount of research has been conducted, in nursing in particular, aimed at trying to define spirituality and assess spiritual need.

The situation is complicated in western, secular societies by the fact that in the professional literature attention has been focused on distinguishing 'religion' from 'spirituality', a distinction which is often lost on lay people (McSherry, 2007). Lay people do, however, recognise that facing death causes most people to grapple with some of the 'bigger questions', although the extent to which these are significant and how big the question is, will vary enormously (Lloyd, 1997). Moss suggests that spirituality is 'what we do to give expression to our chosen world view' (Moss, 2005, p 60), which places it into a wider frame than definitions such as the search for meaning which may have little to distinguish them from humanistic counselling (Holloway, 2007) or what others might term social or psychological needs (Kellehear, 2000). Kellehear distinguishes 'situational', 'moral and biographical' and 'religious' needs as commonly featuring in discussions of spirituality in contemporary palliative care, observing, however, that each of the two former categories may be overlaid with 'religious desire' in the individual. Situational needs, he suggests, are concerned with meaning and purpose, moral and biographical needs are largely relational and concerned with harmony and reconciliation, whereas religious needs address all these through belief in a divine entity and purpose.

The secular caring professions have been concerned to distance themselves from any association with institutional religion in their interest in spirituality, the suggestion appearing to be that in so doing they would alienate non-religious persons who nevertheless have spiritual needs—and the common observation of nurses in palliative care, who perhaps spend the most time directly with the dying person, is that 'everyone' has spiritual needs. Palliative care professionals in northern Europe and Australasia have tended to pay little more than lip-service to their role in this less defined spiritual care. In southern Europe there may be strong identification with the religious foundation of the hospice with 'spiritual care' delivered through this medium and the distinction between religion and spirituality may be of no importance. Only the US, generally recognised to be a much more religious society than the UK or other northern European countries, has seen the active development of spiritual care functions among secular professionals, with the emergence of what some have dubbed 'surrogate chaplains' (Paley, 2007).

This 'spiritual but not religious' distinction belongs to the mainstream 'postChristian' cultures of the west. It exists alongside a growing interest in palliative care in facilitating the religious requirements of 'other' religions, particularly those of ethnic minority families. This mostly takes the form of describing the rituals and sacraments important in the particular faith and making suggestions about how palliative care professionals can work alongside the family and their religious adviser. For example, emphasis is placed on the importance for Buddhists of a peaceful environment at the point of death, in which the 'transfer of consciousness' may take place with the dying person's sense of well-being enhanced as they focus on their death and rebirth. This suggests many things for the behaviour of healthcare professionals in the days and hours leading up to the death and immediately after death has occurred. For example, they should minimise disturbances, such as routine checks and avoid unnecessary noise, such as pagers going off whilst attending to the patient. The body should be left in place for as long as possible after the death (Dinh et al, 2000; Barham, 2003; Smith-Stoner, 2005).

Belief in karma, that one's deeds in one existence determine the state into which one is reborn, implies that all should be done for the Hindu to make the death 'good', since past misdeeds may be redeemed through the mode of dying. For some Hindus this may include the patient endurance of suffering, pain relief not being requested; the imparting of wisdom to surviving members of the family (katha); and the avoidance of food and drink so as to purify the body and avoid contaminating symptoms such as incontinence (Gatrad et al, 2003). Being in a state of preparedness is essential and the completion of social, psychological and emotional tasks—such as setting one's affairs in order, saying goodbye to relatives—belong to this spiritual preparation. Where some aspect of the death is 'bad karma', it is the sacred duty of relatives to try to undo its effects through rituals and good deeds (Firth, 2005). Thus, healthcare practice which obstructs or denies the opportunity for the Hindu patient to have their own 'good death' may have lasting implications for the family. In Islam, a number of detailed rituals are proscribed (Ross, 2001). These centre around beliefs about the relationship between the body and spirit, and the soul as the unique mix of both in each individual. In death, the soul is released from the body to commence its passage into the spiritual realm. It is important not to violate the body in any way as this may lead to contamination of the soul, but organ harvesting is allowed once death has occurred, since the preservation of life is a sacred goal. The Jewish tradition, meanwhile, places greater emphasis on the obligation to heal, which implies both that the patient should cooperate with medical procedures advised by their doctor, and that relatives, friends and healthcare providers should attend to the social, emotional and spiritual needs of the person who is dying. Creating a community in which the individual's dying might take place, and avoiding isolating the patient if at all possible, should therefore be the objective of good palliative care (Dorff, 2005).

The point that is in danger of being lost when the focus is on the rites and rituals of a particular religious tradition is that for committed adherents of any religious faith—including Christians—death is an event of deep spiritual significance and dying is imbued with spiritual meaning. These meanings may be experienced positively or negatively, and every professional, not just the chaplain or religious adviser, contributes to that experience by their attitudes and behaviour. The existence of spiritual pain and existential distress or despair are beginning to be recognised as significant, as much for the religious person as for the non-religious (Parker, 2004). Parker describes the core phenomena of existential distress as hopelessness, helplessness, powerlessness, loss of a sense of control and a sense of meaninglessness. Spiritual pain, however, may further personal growth and ultimately be an enriching experience (Burton, 2004).

This may affect the carer of someone who is dying as much as the dying person. A study in America described informal carers as accompanying the dying person 'through the existential challenges of the transition to the unknown' (Pearce et al, 2006, p 755). This study found that where their spiritual experience was a positive resource on which to draw it contributed to feeling that they could bear the pain and burden of their situation and sometimes derive spiritual enrichment from it. Where they experienced their situation as being abandoned or punished by God, or implying that God was powerless, however, they were more likely to find their situation burdensome and sometimes unbearable. In a survey of hospital social workers and chaplains which I undertook in the early 1990s, 86 per cent said that they recognised spiritual pain in the dying and bereaved people they worked with but the social workers as a whole did not see themselves as having any part to play in spiritual care (Lloyd, 1997).

The existence of untreated depression is a significant factor to be taken into account in any end-of-life decision making. However, there is a balance to be achieved between appropriate psychiatric care and seeking to medicalise something—existential despair—which defies medical solution (Parker, 2004). An alternative is to see connecting with the spiritual meanings of the other person as an essential part of sensitive care, regardless of the specific belief position of the individual patient, relative or worker. Such an approach is transcultural, in that it seeks to access the strengths and resources both within the other person and within a tradition which has meaning for them (Holloway, 2006a).

The good death

At the heart of palliative care a concept has developed which has come to be referred to as 'the good death'. The origins of the term are twofold. First, as is often pointed out in discussions of euthanasia, the Greek translates as 'good death', literally meaning dying 'well' or painlessly. However, as Kellehear (1990) has pointed out, there is also another Greek word used to describe a good death, in which the emphasis is on dying according to a socially acceptable and prescribed pattern. The 'art of dying well' predates the modern articulation and historically was built around some quite opposite values, including the value of suffering and the rewards of sainthood (Walters, 2004). In its reaction against the common experiences of dying in the modern, impersonal hospital, geared to cure rather than care, the hospice movement took the notion of pain relief and comfortable dying and combined it with social, psychological and spiritual objectives to arrive at a model for dying which was 'good'. Thus the notion of the 'good death' which has gained widespread currency in contemporary palliative care has accommodated both meanings in the original Greek through a reaction against all that was bad about modern dying. This may be one reason why ideas of good and bad dying have become somewhat stylised among healthcare professionals, with all the problems that imposing a 'right way' to die may have in terms of responding to individual patient need (Lloyd, 1995; Jones and Willis, 2003; Walters, 2004). Furthermore, this idealised picture may belong more to palliative care than to the wider society, since few studies have been undertaken which actually gathered the views of patients and their families (McNamara et al, 1994; Mak and Clinton, 1999). Payne et al (1996) found that while staff tended to pursue a policy of 'open awareness', encouraging a situation in which the patient was conscious and in control of their dying, patients themselves were most concerned about a pain-free death.

Nevertheless, by the early 1990s a consensus had emerged in the literature and in healthcare practice about what constituted 'the good death'. There are a number of elements which appear to have international and cross-cultural acceptance:

- to die at peace, with one's affairs in order;
- to be free from pain;
- to die in a place of one's choosing;
- to be surrounded by and reconciled with loved ones;
- to be treated with respect and afforded dignity.

These were elaborated upon in 1999 in the UK by an Age Concern study group, which produced twelve principles:

1. to know when death is coming, and to understand what can be expected;
2. to be able to retain control of what happens;
3. to be afforded dignity and privacy;
4. to have control over pain relief and other symptom control;
5. to have choice and control over where death occurs (at home or elsewhere);
6. to have access to information and expertise of whatever kind is necessary;
7. to have access to any spiritual or emotional support required;
8. to have access to hospice care in any location, not only in hospital;
9. to have control over who is present and who shares the end;
10. to be able to issue advance directives which ensure wishes are respected;
11. to have time to say goodbye, and control over other aspects of timing;
12. to be able to leave when it is time to go, and not to have life prolonged pointlessly (Debate of the Age Health and Care Study Group, 1999).

The flurry of responses which appeared in the pages of the *British Medical Journal* (*BMJ*) after it published these principles underlined the fact that, while few disagreed with these principles as aims, we have rather less control over death than they might appear to suggest. A debate in the *BMJ* three years later also argued that undue weight is placed on some aspects of care and others, such as mental health needs and psychological care, are ignored (Prigerson et al, 2003). The notion of personhood, discussed in Chapter Three under the category of 'personal death', is at the heart of the good death but becomes implicit rather than explicit the more criteria are defined. These discussions illustrate the complexity of applying, in practice, those key objectives of contemporary health and social care of personcentred care which affords dignity, choice and control to the individual.

Bradbury asks, 'For whom is a death good?', and argues that we have multiple representations in our society of both good and bad deaths and contemporary ideas do not necessarily accord with those of previous generations (Bradbury, 2001, p 59). For example, when infant and child mortality rates were high, these deaths could be deemed 'natural' by comparison with contemporary developed societies where death of a child is viewed as 'untimely'. This did not mean that such deaths were seen as 'good', or as the preferred outcome. The same can be said of deaths of children in the developing world, where aid workers and television images testify to the grief of parents at the loss of every child, even though they might struggle to feed and care for them, and deaths of children are shockingly commonplace. Bradbury distinguishes three types of good death: the sacred, the medicalised and the natural. The sacred is located in a belief system which sees death as the gateway to a better existence; the medicalised is one which is controlled through medical intervention; the natural is one which occurs without such intervention and, according to Bradbury, unexpectedly—for example, dying in one's sleep. Another very common contemporary idea is that a natural death is one which occurs when one has reached the end of one's natural lifespan. Bad deaths, by definition, occur when the opposite circumstance prevails. So, bad ways to die are when the individual takes himself or herself out of the hands of God by committing suicide; or evil appears to prevail as in murder; or pain and distressing symptoms are not well controlled; or the death is in some way untimely, occurring as a result of accident or there is 'unfinished business' and/or the individual is unable to prepare.

Bradbury touches on the fact that the complexities of contemporary dying mean that the types tend to get mixed up. It is worth pursuing this if we are to better understand and respond to the needs of diverse people and situations. First, since almost all deaths are medicalised to some degree and, as the next section makes clear, significant and multiple ethical issues are raised by the possibilities created by medical intervention, it is most likely to be the accommodation reached between medicalised death and the beliefs about death and dying held by the individual and family that will determine whether or not this is a good death for them. So, for example, someone who wishes for a 'natural' death in their sleep may adjust this concept to include terminal sedation. Someone with strong religious faith, who believes that life and death are in the hands of God, may be grateful for the best of medical intervention but accommodate suffering and untimely death as part of 'God's plan'. I vividly recall a Muslim woman whose baby had been stillborn, being uncomprehending of the suggestion that it might help her to talk about her feelings, because her baby's death had been 'Allah's will'. A narrative may be constructed which sees the death as good because it touched the lives of others, carrying within it creative and regenerative possibilities for other people (Maudlin, 2001); because learning to accept rather than control death is spiritually transforming (Peterson, 2000; Crosby, 2004); because the baby born with a congenital disorder had reached the end of her natural lifespan and was ready to die (Guthrie, 2000).This mother reflects, from a non-religious position, a number of these ways of concluding that her baby had died a good death:

> 'In this whole process of life and death for *baby* it just wasn't meant to be … I feel that she was actually given to us for a reason, but that she was actually only meant to live for ten and a half months, but in that time, the effect she had, not just on us, but on other people was, well, astounding.' (Lloyd, 1996, p 302)

These ways of understanding the good death expand the concept from the physical process of dying and the moment of death. It is possible that they can accommodate features of 'bad' deaths—such as symptoms which cannot be well controlled—because meaning is ascribed to and emphasis placed on other aspects. Within the established model of the good death, delivered through good palliative care, such deaths are hard for patients and staff to accommodate, because both may have expectations which are disappointed. Lawton (1998) in an ethnographic study of hospice care, observed that increasingly hospices may be used to accommodate those patients whose symptoms are such that they cannot be contained in community palliative care. Her study suggested that this 'dirty dying' transgresses all the boundaries which our vision of 'dying well' has erected, leading to staff separating these patients off from others for whom they can better achieve a good death. If this picture were to become widespread—and there are some suggestions that it is (Bowling, 2003; Kalbag, 2003)—we should have a situation in which, ironically, hospices are contributing to the sequestration of death, not only within the wider society, but also within themselves.

There are further problems in promoting this idealised type of the good death. It belongs to a western philosophical model which gives primary emphasis to the individual and their medical care. The uncritical application of the value of autonomy is problematic. By definition, the person who is near death must rely on someone else to maintain control according to their wishes on their behalf. Dying with dignity is as much about having one's vulnerability respected as it is about exercising autonomy. Grogono (2003) advocates appointing an 'amicus mortis', a trusted friend or relative, but not everyone has such a person available. Second, it has taken repeated efforts to remind healthcare providers that respect for different cultural and religious practices as well as belief systems has to underpin this medical care and affect its mode of delivery (Neuberger, 2003).Walter suggests that different models of the good death emanate from different societal and cultural norms, but that these in turn relate to three factors; the extent of secularisation; the extent of individualism; and the length of time it takes to die (Walter, 2003). Campione argues that in Italy religious, materialistic-biological and 'personalistic' concepts of the good death are intertwined—not necessarily in each individual death, but in the social context in which dying is managed (Campione, 2004).

We have as yet little empirical evidence to test Walter's assertion.What we have, suggests a surprising degree of consensus concerning core elements across quite different societies. For example, a study in Uganda identified the desire to die at home, to be free from pain and other distressing symptoms, to experience no stigma (this appears to relate to the high levels of death through HIV/AIDS), to be at peace and to retain a degree of autonomy whilst having one's needs met (Kikule, 2003). Two studies of Chinese people, one undertaken in Hong Kong and the other in the UK, suggested that pain and symptom control and a physically 'comfortable' death were a priority as well as not being a burden on family; this led in the UK to a preference for not dying at home. However, relational aspects were also emphasised—knowing that one's family relationships were intact, with children and grandchildren established and happy, and to have them around the bedside; knowing that one had completed one's business in life and the spirit could be released peacefully (Quality Evaluation Centre, City University of Hong Kong, unpublished survey results; Payne et al, 2005). However, these summary findings tell us little about what may in practice be crucial differences and important contributory factors to a good or bad death. For example, Walter cites the example of Hindus' wish to die lying on the floor, in accordance with their beliefs, and not liking to ask for this to be facilitated in western medical care; food is both medicine and comfort in Chinese culture and it is important for family members to provide certain foods for the sick and dying person; Chinese migrants prefer not to die at home because, unlike the ancestral home, 'home' is a transitory abode inhabited by the spirits of strangers; African languages and aboriginal peoples do not distinguish between 'secular' and 'religious' and spiritual care is an assumed part of dying well. The complex web of cultural assumptions and imperatives which may lead to a particular individual death being deemed 'good' is illustrated by the story told by Elizabeth Grant of a woman dying of cancer in sub-Saharan Africa. Paradoxically to the western mind, this woman expressed the wish to die when in hospital with her pain controlled and receiving good physical care, where earlier, experiencing terrible pain and deprivations at home, she had declared herself content to rest on God's timing (Grant, 2003).

What is clear is that the notion of the good death has to expand to deal with the fact that the majority of contemporary deaths in the developed world take place over a period of time, as people live with life-threatening illness or slow degenerative con- ditions. Thus, the focus is gradually shifting from the original model of hospice and palliative care towards end-of-life care which aims to provide quality for individuals in the 'dying phase' of life.

End-of-life-care

Evidence of the increasing numbers of people dying from a range of life-threatening conditions, particularly in old age, is widening the remit of care for the dying. Health and social care is beginning to recognise that good care for many people with chronic, disabling conditions is also good end-of-life care, and the proven tenets of palliative care, developed in the main around cancer patients, should be transferred into other care settings.

The policy context and initiatives for this were discussed in Chapter Two. At the heart of this initiative is to increase choice about their care for all people at the end of life and to ensure that those choices are respected wherever possible (Institute of Medicine, 2001; NHS, 2006). This is in the light of information that most people do not die at home even though just over half in the UK, US and Australia are reported as expressing the wish to do so (Fried et al, 1998; Higginson et al, 1998). The picture is actually rather more nuanced than these figures would suggest and the complexities surrounding the making and sustaining of choices are discussed in Chapter Six.

Nevertheless, there is growing interest in the making and implementing of choices concerning end-of-life care and the tools which might be available to assist with this. Behind this lies the question of incapacity, that in the event of becoming incapable of making and/or expressing their views, individuals may wish to make them known in advance of that situation. Not unnaturally, given that people are living longer but with increasing physical and mental debility, much of the debate among care providers about the facilitation and implementation of such expressions relates to older people. The focus of attention here tends to be on directives to withhold treatment (including the wish not to be resuscitated), although more recent emphases are on a positive care planning approach. The issues and evidence in the context of older people's care are discussed in Chapter Six. The high-profile cases, raised periodically in the media, tend to feature younger adults with seriously debilitating, degenerative diseases, who may wish to put in place a request for physician-assisted suicide and to identify the point at which they wish this to be activated. Where this challenges the legal position in a particular country, or moves into a 'grey area', the case is taken out of the patient and healthcare professional arena and into the courts.

The legal status of these tools varies from country to country. However, the general drift is as follows for the UK:

- *Advance directives or living wills*: both terms are currently in use. These documents allow the individual to express their wishes about specific medical interventions, commonly concerning 'do not resuscitate' (DNR) orders and artificial hydration or nutrition. They may be combined with designating 'power of attorney' to someone else to make, or instigate, these decisions for the person completing the original directive.
- *Enduring power of attorney*: under legislation in the UK about to be implemented, power of attorney is extended from financial and property matters to cover all aspects of the health and social care of a person deemed 'incapable' of making decisions for themselves.
- *Advance care planning*: this is carried out between the service user and the care provider(s). It is likely to become a crucial part of long-term care provision in the twenty-first century as a means of facilitating user choice.

The gathering of evidence concerning the use of such measures is so far in its early stages and the focus has tended to be on the care of older people and limited to health-care directives. This evidence specific to older people is considered in the next chapter.

The wider use of more holistic advance care planning procedures is still in its infancy. Young adults with life-threatening illnesses, for example, have been found to have little knowledge of advance directives or planning (Pendergast, 2001). However, some factors can be highlighted generally which have relevance for the management of dying in the community.

Making the point that most advance care planning takes place far too late and often in the hospital or office, thus effectively excluding seriously ill people and their relatives from playing an active part in the planning process, an American study piloted and evaluated the use of social worker-facilitated discussions in the home with people in receipt of home care, of whom 29 per cent were under 65; each had been diagnosed as having a life-threatening illness with a life expectancy of up to two years. A key goal of the intervention was to honour service user wishes concerning the site of their end-of-life care; this was achieved in the majority of cases, with 70 per cent of those who died during the study period being cared for at home as they had wished. The researchers highlight two important factors contributing to this success: emphasis was on the communicative process between worker and service user, rather than the exercise of patient autonomy; and the intervention was offered to people identified by the community nurse, who understood their individual history, circumstances and illness progression.

Haley et al (2002) also emphasise the importance of advance care planning taking place within the family and intimate relationships. They make the point that two groups are particularly vulnerable to inappropriate decision making and receiving unwanted care if the present emphasis on individual autonomy and legal status continues to override other considerations. Ethnic minority groups may feel their cultural sensitivities, including how decisions are taken within the family, are ignored. Partners without legal status (such as is frequently the case in same-sex partnerships) may be excluded, despite the fact that they may be intimately involved in care-giving in the home and their emotional investment greater than that of other persons who might be consulted as 'next of kin'.

A final point about advance directives and living wills is that, unlike advance care planning, they are often located in controversial and ethically disputed terrains. They may also involve established and relatively uncontentious procedures (except for some religious groups) such as organ donation, where the individual opts to forgo life-prolonging treatment and choose to donate organs. Advance directives are in themselves opposed by some religious groups on the grounds of individuals attempting a degree of control which does not belong to them, either in terms of their own life or in relation to the actions of others (O'Connor, 2005). These are the questions to which we now turn.

EUTHANASIA AND ASSISTED DYING

In contrast to the palliative care approach which seeks to maintain and sustain the dying person as comfortably as possible at the end of life, a number of interventions have emerged where the objective is to hasten or bring about the person's death. These may involve the person alone, the person assisted by a friend or relative, a doctor acting on the wishes of the patient or the wishes of next of kin where the person themselves is incapable of giving consent, or, more rarely, the medical team acting on their professional judgement after seeking an external ruling on the matter. Both the legal position and extent to which these options are practised are unclear and vary between countries. Switzerland is credited with having been the first state, since 1942, to allow assisted suicide, provided that the helpers are 'disinterested' persons, although it is suggested that relatives of seriously ill patients are now asked to sanction euthanasia (Gardner, 2003). Significant attempts have been made in the western world in the last decade to legislate for the circumstances, constraints and procedures under which such practices might be carried out: the 1996 Rights of the Terminally Ill Amendment Act, Northern Territory, Australia; the Oregon Death with Dignity Act; the legalising of euthanasia and physicianassisted suicide (PAS) in Holland in 2002; the legalising of euthanasia by doctors but not PAS in Belgium in 2002. Evidence of actual practice is increasingly emerging and there are recent important legal initiatives, such as the Joffe 'assisted dying' Bill in the UK.

A good place to start in tackling this subject is to define the terminology. Problems arise in dissecting the issues when terms are used to mean different practices. The UK House of Lords report (HL, 1993–94) points out how the use of some terms, such as 'passive euthanasia', has been misleading and arrives at the following definitions:

- *euthanasia*—originally meaning a gentle and easy death, now used to mean a deliberate intervention to end a life where the patient's condition is terminal and their suffering 'intractable';
- *withdrawing treatment; not initiating treatment; treatment-limiting decision*— preferred to 'passive euthanasia' and used to refer to a medical decision not to give treatment necessary for the prolonging of life;
- *double effect*—the administration of treatment to relieve pain or severe distress where the likely consequence is that it will hasten death;
- *voluntary euthanasia*—brought about where the patient requests their own death; *non-voluntary euthanasia*—where the patient does not have the capacity to understand what euthanasia means and therefore to either request it or withhold consent;
- *involuntary euthanasia*—where life is terminated for someone who does have the capacity to make a request or give consent but has not actually done so;
- *assisted suicide*—where someone capable of making the decision to end their life desires this but is physically unable to bring about their death without assistance;
- *physician-assisted suicide*—which occurs when that help is given by a doctor, for example providing a lethal dose of a drug;
- *terminal illness*[1]—a progressive illness which will inevitably result in death within a short period of time;
- *irreversible condition*—a condition which is not progressive, often present at birth, and does not necessarily lead to death;

- *chronic progressive disease*—where deterioration is inevitable but may not of itself bring on death;
- *persistent vegetative state*—absence of cognitive, behavioural, verbal, or purposive motor responses over a period of not less than 12 months, with no evidence of other voluntary motor activity.

Certainly it is euthanasia which is the word most likely to raise public interest and rouse passions, although as can be seen from the above definitions, specific interventions may seem to merge in practice (for example, physician-assisted suicide and voluntary euthanasia, despite the fact that the amended Joffe Bill insists that a clear distinction must be drawn between them). Phrases such as the 'right to die' have become sloganised and concepts such as 'dignity in dying' appropriated by opposing camps. The issues are discussed in terms of three debates (although the arguments similarly merge): the moral-ethical debate; religion and euthanasia; and palliative care and euthanasia.

The moral-ethical debate

The philosophical case for euthanasia stems from a privileging of the principle of autonomy, that an individual has an absolute right to determine that they wish to die. This can be suicide at any point in life or voluntary euthanasia when the suffering in one's life becomes intolerable or it is anticipated that it will become so. More recent articulations of the 'right to die' add to it the 'responsibility to die'. From a philosophical standpoint this will be limited to a narrow range of specific situations in which one's death is imperative in order to serve the greater good, even that the greater good may be jeopardised otherwise. The example often cited is the suicide of a captured soldier lest he reveal secrets under torture which may lead to the deaths of many others. There are also vestiges of this thinking in 'hero' stories where one person sacrifices him/herself in order to make it more likely that others will survive (for example, an injured member of a climbing expedition party). While some utilitarian philosophers do extend this principle to a moral obligation to remove oneself when one's continuing existence is too much of a burden on society, others are much more cautious about the responsibilities and obligations surrounding the question of interconnectedness, pointing out that the individual who contemplates ending their life also has responsibility for the potential distress this may cause their loved ones (Nuyen, 2000). This is especially the case where the relative or friend is asked to assist in the act bringing about the death or in creating the circumstances in which it might take place.

The philosophical case 'for' is countered by a philosophical case against—although Nuyen suggests that the case against has become remarkably muted, the question of to what extent euthanasia should be legalised and institutionalised having taken over (Nuyen, 2000). Principally, the privileging of individual autonomy is challenged. Williams asks why autonomy should carry any more weight than the principle of the sanctity of life, and suggests that to give autonomy such moral authority infers that society is composed wholly of consenting adults (Williams, 1996). However, Harris takes issue with a privileging of the sanctity of life which fails to distinguish between existence, per se, and the lives of persons. Harris believes the case for euthanasia rests on respect for individuals who embody personhood, which he describes as a critical appreciation of one's own existence. If such a person wishes to die, Harris believes, it is both an arrogance and a tyranny to frustrate that desire (Harris, 1995).

However, others argue that if the case for euthanasia rests ultimately on the individual's right to choose to die, then there is no case for those people who have lost the capacity to exercise that choice, whatever their condition (Finnis, 1995). The case against is filled out by discussion of the question of intent, where the argument is put forward that the *moral* argument against euthanasia as a form of 'intentional killing' does not extend to the use of drugs where death occurs as an unintentional, although likely, side effect, or the declining of life-prolonging treatment because its impact is, in itself, undesirable. However, it does extend to the withdrawal of treatment or care, with the intent to bring about death (Finnis, 1995). Harris argues that there is no moral argument against such actions where personhood has been lost, suggesting that were an individual in a persistent vegetative state to have earlier completed an advance directive outlining their wish to be kept 'alive' whatever their condition, this would have no moral precedence over other 'critical interests'—including that health service resources might be put to better use.

A significant angle within the philosophical debate concerns the ethical obligations of doctors. The Hippocratic oath is usually taken as the starting point, with there being general agreement that doctors have a duty to sustain life and refrain from intentional killing. However, it is argued that both the particulars of individual cases (Meilaender, 2005) and the presence of competing moral duties—such as to relieve suffering—lead to the conclusion that no one moral position can be taken to be absolute or to always override another (Seay, 2005). From this standpoint there is no reason to try and distinguish between letting someone die, physician-assisted suicide, or double effect (Huxtable, 2004), because each privileges a different moral duty—refraining from intentional killing, the ending of suffering, or the relief of suffering such that death is likely. Indeed, Frey (2005) argues that it is the moral context of how we see the alternative—for example, allowing this child in this condition to die—which determines the morality of the action (or inaction). Despite the apparently irreconcilable philosophical positions on euthanasia, Meilaender (2005) argues that there is considerable consensus on some critical starting points when it comes to the application of moral ethics:

- We do not believe that 'biological life' must be preserved at all costs.
- We combine adherence to first principles with forming judgements about particular cases.
- Each life is of equal value and our aim should be to preserve rather than to end it.
- Respect for human life implies caring for the individual life in such a way as to allow that there may be a greater good than the continuation of that life in some circumstances.

Religion and euthanasia

The straightforward religious position, as represented by all the world's major religions, is that it is not for human beings to decide the moment of their own, or another's, death. This does not mean that compassion should not be shown for human suffering, including the mental and spiritual anguish of the person who takes their own life for whatever reason. This principle did, however, lie behind the ruling until 1961 in the UK that persons who had committed suicide could not be interred in consecrated ground. Conscientious objectors who refuse to fight in war on religious grounds are applying the same principle. The majority position in the Christian and Muslim religions, however, is that a just war and/or a soldier's duty are special circumstances in which other principles take precedence. Euthanasia, on the other hand, is generally considered wrong by religious thinkers. The positions of the major faiths were summarised thus in *USA Today* following the passing of the Oregon Death with Dignity Act:

> CATHOLIC: 'We are encouraged, if our end is to be loving, to examine how can we do that best. I don't love someone best by saying, "There are no possibilities for you, no hope or meaning …" Who am I to say that?'—the Rev. Kevin Fitzgerald.

> PROTESTANT: 'The New Testament teaches that we are to model ourselves on Christ. I'm not really to live for myself. I'm to live for the glory of God and the life of others'—bioethicist C. Ben Mitchell.

> JEWISH: 'You are given a self when you are born, but you can't willfully destroy it. You can refuse to prolong dying or to deepen the pain with interventions. But (suicide) ends all possibility of human flourishing'—Laurie Zoloth, medical ethics professor.

> MUSLIM: 'Islam rules (suicide) out. The trend is to accept your destiny as God-given destiny. Suffering is not regarded as evil, and there is faith that God … helps people to endure pain and suffering'—Abdulaziz Sachedina, religion professor.

> BUDDHIST: 'There are famous Buddhists in history who have committed suicide, but by far most Buddhist ethicists would say this is unacceptable. A doctor who assists someone in dying is called the "knife-bringer"'—Paul Numrich, author of *The Buddhist Tradition: Religious Beliefs and Healthcare Decisions.*

> HINDU: 'You and I cannot take our lives into our own hands. It is regarded as a form of ego. This ego keeps you in bondage in the cycle of reincarnation'— S. Cromwell Crawford, author of *Hindu Bioethics for the 21ˢᵗ Century.*

(*USA Today*, 5 October 2005)

However, there is something of a debate around suffering, compassion and healing through death. A widely held view is that medical interventions which are no longer bringing any benefit but merely prolonging life may be withdrawn or withheld, but aggressive use of painkillers or other deliberate acts to bring about death are wrong (Gushee, 2004). The distinction is made in Catholic theology between impermissible intended consequences and those which are permissible because while the consequences are not intended they can be foreseen (the doctrine of 'double effect'). There are four conditions imposed: the action itself must not be inherently wrong (for example, administering analgesics); the intention must be to produce the good effect (for example, the drugs are administered for the relief of pain); the good effect must not be brought about via the bad effect (for example, pain should be relieved before and without death occurring); the good effect must outweigh the bad (for example, relief of suffering was the primary outcome). Some take this line further and argue that resisting death when one's time has come (including through disease) is also wrong (Hatzinikolaou, 2003); indeed death should be welcomed and seen as the healer (Grad, 1980).

Mohrmann, as a paediatrician and medical ethicist, argues that religion has paid scant attention to children as beings and hence to their rights and our responsibilities towards them. She suggests that these can only be discharged when seen in the context also of the needs of those who care for, and about, children. Thus, the suffering of parents must also be taken into account when determining benefit of treatments, particularly where the benefits are uncertain (Mohrmann, 2006).

Islamic guidance for healthcare professionals is connected to the principle of beneficence, whereby positive actions to prevent or remove what is bad or harmful and to promote what is good or beneficial are required; the direct termination of life, however, must be left in the hands of Allah (Rassool, 2004). Within Chinese culture, there is agreement between Confucianism, Buddhism and Taoism that life should be cherished as a natural process but not be attached to; adherents are likely to be opposed to active euthanasia but comfortable with the notion of 'letting die', the natural process therefore taking over (Chong and Fok, 2005). In Israel, the context is complex, combining both the Jewish Orthodox tradition with a political context which favours communitarianism over individual autonomy and is sharply mindful of its twentieth-century history at the hands of the Nazis. The Israeli Patient Rights Law (1996) requires all cases of 'informed refusal' of medical treatment to be referred to an ethics committee in which the religious interest may be outweighed by others (Leichtentritt, 2002).

Palliative care and euthanasia

One of the most intense debates has been between advocates of euthanasia and palliative care specialists. The position originally taken by the latter was that good palliative care, with adequate relief of pain and other distressing symptoms, more or less obviates the demand for euthanasia—or, to put it another way, that the policy emphasis should be on making good palliative care available and accessible to all, rather than looking to legislate for euthanasia. However, it is now recognised that some palliative care patients do nevertheless request a hastening of their death and that doctors in palliative care face the dilemma over double treatment effect as much as elsewhere.

In 2001, the European Association for Palliative Care (EAPC) established a Task Group to advise them on euthanasia and physician-assisted suicide. The Task Group published a position paper (Materstvedt et al, 2003) alongside 55 responses from academics, clinicians, practitioners and researchers from 32 different countries. This published debate represents the most significant airing of the issues to date. One of the important things it establishes is that the musings of philosophers about definitions, moral boundaries and moral duties are not simply abstract conceptualisations; they are reflected in the thinking of clinicians and practitioners as they struggle with real-life dilemmas (Campbell and Huxtable, 2003). The position paper itself is succinct and acknowledges the deeply divided views while generally rejecting voluntary euthanasia (on which it focuses) as being able to sit alongside palliative care. There is some empirical evidence for this view: a New York study showed that healthcare professionals in a cancer centre who were more inclined towards assisted suicide had correspondingly less knowledge about symptom management (Portenoy et al, 1997). However, evidence from the Netherlands about the effect of provision for euthanasia on palliative care practice is said to be contradictory (Hurst and Mauron, 2006).

In an editorial reviewing both the EAPC Task Force paper and responses to it, Campbell and Huxtable conclude that both the theoretical underpinnings for arriving at a particular conclusion on euthanasia, and evidence about the effects on palliative care of new legislation, require considerably more investigation. Although not highlighted by the editorial, important points about the cultural context of palliative care, including the extent to which there is a culture in which diagnosis and care are discussed with the patient and/or the family, are made by contributors. Greater clarity of definition and consensus concerning the use of these definitions are highlighted as essential. In particular, without open discussion of the relationship between motivation and intent, of patient competence and incompetence, and of the determining of a 'terminal' condition and the notion of 'mercy killing', clinicians and practitioners in palliative care settings will continue to be dogged by uncertainty and ambiguity. A useful contribution to this clarification exercise is contributed in a paper from Switzerland, which argues for a number of values held in common by advocates of voluntary euthanasia (VE) and assisted suicide (AS), and palliative care. Four shared underpinning values are identified: the importance of reducing suffering; a concern to maintain a focus on the dying *person* rather than biological entity; the importance of the patient retaining some control at the end of life; an acceptance that death is not always the worst thing to happen (Hurst and Mauron, 2006). However, as the authors point out, it is how these values are understood in practice where differences remain and need further exploration. For example, compassion is interpreted by palliative care to mean 'staying with' the patient's pain (understood holistically) even as one seeks to relieve it, whereas advocates of VE/AS view this as itself the compassionate act. They acknowledge that some positions, such as whether the value of individual autonomy ever overrides the principle of not ending human life, may be irreconcilable. So too may the conflict between the physician's right to autonomy and the duty of care which respects the patient's right to make decisions about their own quality of life.

Clearly, the legal position in most countries makes it difficult to gather empirical evidence, and conclusions drawn are affected by methodological issues—were patients screened for depression, for example? What are the ethics of undertaking a prospective study with a patient, set alongside the impact of the death on relatives if undertaking a retrospective study? What is the effect of relying on staff accounts as to whether or not a patient has requested euthanasia or physician-assisted suicide? Nevertheless, the evidence appears to show that remarkably few requests are made for euthanasia by patients in palliative care (Kristjanson and Christakis, 2005). Of more recent interest is an exploration of the patient characteristics and experiences which lead, or might lead, to such requests. High levels of actual or anticipated pain, suffering and perceived diminished quality of life are associated with euthanasia requests or patients identifying that they might wish to have this option (Georges et al, 2005; Johansen et al, 2005). A small qualitative study in Hong Kong also identified high levels of existential distress as being associated with requests for euthanasia and suggested that such requests should not be taken at face value but the spiritual need addressed (Mak and Elwyn, 2005). One further point on which there is agreement is that patients' views appear to fluctuate and there is often ambivalence.

Attitudes of healthcare professionals

A recent survey generating 857 returns from doctors in the UK conducted by Clive Seale discovered that the popular belief that a lot of euthanasia is actually going on under the guise of end-of-life care technologies is actually not the case. The survey asked about voluntary euthanasia, physician-assisted suicide and ending life without an explicit request from the patient; low levels of all three practices were reported, with the UK having lower or similar rates compared with those reported in Belgium, Denmark, Italy, Holland, Sweden, Switzerland,Australia and New Zealand (Seale, 2006). This appears to reflect the attitudes reported in an earlier survey of British geriatricians, in which only 13 per cent said they would be willing to administer active voluntary euthanasia and only 12 per cent willing to provide physician-assisted suicide in some circumstances (Clark et al, 2001). A large survey of Swedish physicians employed in end-of-life settings reported that a third had administered drugs for pain and symptom control in doses likely to hasten death (Valverius et al, 2000).

Another large survey carried out in Hong Kong compared the views of the general public with those of doctors. Doctors were reported to agree in general with passive euthanasia (which they defined as withdrawing or withholding treatment), to be neutral about non-voluntary euthanasia (defined as when the patient cannot give consent through incapacity or coma), but opposed to active voluntary euthanasia.The general public, however, agreed with active voluntary euthanasia but disagreed with non-voluntary euthanasia and was neutral about passive euthanasia (Chong and Fok, 2005). The authors point out that lay persons are likely to be influenced by the Chinese culture which sees pain and suffering as being inflicted on the family as well as the individual, hence there may be a duty to remove this burden from one's relatives, whereas doctors are more likely to be influenced by their professional ethic and duty of care.

The attitudes of nurses have been separately studied. One of the reasons for this is that nurses have the closest day-to-day contact with patients and are involved in giving intimate care. Thus they are both the professional to whom patients and relatives may express their deep fears, anxieties and wishes, and also the one who may be there when they die, including as they 'slip away' under sedation. A nurse may well be the person to whom the patient voices a request for euthanasia (De Bal et al, 2005). One of the things that emerges in studies of nurses' attitudes to euthanasia and associated practices is the stress felt by many in the last stages of a patient's care. This may arise, for example, from feeling left to manage the implementation of decisions taken by others, from experiencing poor communication or differences of opinion with doctors, and from finding the care of a patient on terminal sedation an emotional burden with their therapeutic caring role removed (Morita et al, 2004). Demands for better training for all nurses in both ethics and palliative care (Doolan and Brown, 2004; Verpoort et al, 2004) relate to findings that working in palliative care significantly affects nurses' attitudes to euthanasia. Their greater expression of reservations, however, is significantly influenced by the success of palliative care in affording pain and symptom control (Verpoort et al, 2004). Even experienced palliative care nurses, opposed to euthanasia, are disturbed by the fact that some symptoms are still very difficult to control.

One US study of hospice nurses in Oregon found that once the question of physician-assisted suicide had been raised, the nurses felt increased responsibility to control symptoms completely, as though their ability to keep the patient comfortable was all that stood between them both and failure (Harvath et al, 2006). Some nurses felt that they had inadvertently been drawn into assisting patients with voluntary euthanasia—for example, by assisting them to control vomiting which then enabled them to take a lethal dose. Some nurses expressed regret that when euthanasia was chosen, it removed the opportunity for personal and family growth, spiritual transformation and reconciliation. This is a view clearly echoing the hospice philosophy of helping people to live until they die.

This Oregon study also, unusually, looked at the dilemmas experienced by social workers around euthanasia requests. Considering that social work has a long history of working with seriously ill and dying people, it is curious that the social work literature has largely ignored the issue of euthanasia and the impact that such requests might have on their relationships with dying and bereaved people (Arnold, 2004). The few empirical studies which have examined social workers' attitudes and practices around euthanasia (Ogden and Young, 1998 Csikai, 1999; Arnold, 2004) appear to show that social workers, when asked the direct question, largely reflect the predominant social attitude (for example, North Americans privileged the value of individual autonomy and the majority were in favour of legalising voluntary euthanasia and assisted suicide). But when asked to consider actual scenarios, or recount situations in which they had been involved, they demonstrate greater ambivalence (Leichtentritt, 2002; Arnold, 2004). This is unsurprising. Although they are not directly involved in the medical and physical aspects of care, social workers centre their engagement with dying people and their families on a psychosocial approach, which brings to the fore the effects of the illness and death on the dying person's life as a whole, most especially their relationships. They do this from a value base which prioritises the empowerment of the dying person. Thus it would seem likely that there would be some contradictions in these principles in practice around the question of euthanasia, not least because social work's family and social approach leads it to constantly seek to balance competing needs and rights.

A possible contradiction in the context of end-of-life care lies in social work's commitment to client self-determination and its sustaining role, which more recent articulations have seen as 'maintaining the spirit' (Lloyd, 2002) and palliative care social work has tended to see as the maintenance of hope. Arnold (2004) argues that further research is needed on the sources and meanings of hope in the context of life-threatening illness if social workers are to maintain this role in the current context of end-of-life care. Social work's commitment to antioppressive practice challenges the profession to engage with issues such as advance directives, treatment withdrawal or refusal and treatments to hasten death when performed on patients with diminished capacity or those who are incapable of giving consent. It is suggested that the profession must revise its various codes of ethics to take account of the contemporary treatment context (Mackelprang and Mackelprang, 2005). As with nurses, there are calls for training programmes to address these dilemmas, with the recognition that social workers are woefully ill-prepared for the issues which some service users may bring to the encounter in end-of-life care (Leichtentritt, 2002; Luptak, 2004).

A similar neglect is pointed to in the practice and training of rehabilitation professionals, who, it is argued, have no literature to assist them to grapple in practice with the dilemmas raised by euthanasia questions and genetic counselling programmes (Zanskas and Coduti, 2006). Rehabilitation professionals, such as speech, occupational and physiotherapists, work primarily outside of palliative care. They do, however, work with disabled people and people with long-term conditions of all ages and are at the centre of discussions about the potential for rehabilitation where there is a degenerative condition, or where the potential for recovery from an acute episode, such as a stroke, may be questioned. Both of these situations commonly occur in the frail older person who may be particularly vulnerable and disadvantaged. At the other end of the life cycle, rehabilitation has an important role to play in assisting parents with managing a child with multiple and complex impairments. Thus rehabilitation professionals are working in situations where legal and ethical dilemmas may frequently arise in decision making.

CONCLUSION

Twentieth-century developments in the care of people who are dying emerged out of deep concern about the attitudes and practices prevalent in the western world and entrenched in its hospitals, and the additional suffering which this caused to dying people and their families. Thus the hospice and palliative care movement has been underpinned by a valuing of the individual and philosophy of care which place their comfort and dignity at the centre. This led to a natural desire to define those character-istics which make for a 'good death'. However, that which grew out of the transforming influence of the hospice movement has been in danger of turning into the opposite—a restrictive template which pathologises those whose dying does not conform. In my own work I have referred to this as the 'tyranny' of the good death, appealing for a vision which embraces the 'goodenough-for-me' realities of most people (Lloyd, 1995). It is only as disquiet with reductionist versions of the good death has surfaced that scholarship has returned to the multifaceted roots of the concept. We are beginning to understand how 'dying well' for each individual requires a careful negotiation of these elements such that the dying is personally acceptable and the death has social meaning. Walters refers to this as 'dying with panache', including 'raging into the night' if this is how this person has lived their life and is their authentic death (Walters, 2004, p 408). But increasingly in our society the majority dying—the deaths of the very old—does not obviously have panache and does not fit with what Seale has termed the 'heroic' model of death (Seale, 1995b).

The importance of philosophical debate and the theoretical underpinnings for policy are just beginning to be recognised as crucial to the ongoing development of good end-of-life care and the ethical dilemmas contained therein. These confront practitioners on a daily basis, because one thing which *is* certain is that dying in the twenty-first century is for the most part a managed process. This is one reason why deaths which occur outside of that process are so difficult to accommodate within our ontological frame. Policy in health and social care is notoriously under-theorised and our neglect of the philosophical dimension has been at the expense of considerable ethical discomfort experienced by those people charged with implementing policy and providing hands-on care. When this is end-of-life care, it touches the deepest personal concerns and instincts and is governed by cultural imperatives. Yet although the impor-tance of religious ethic, philosophical standpoint and cultural context are acknowledged and represented in the debates about end-of-life care, technologies and euthanasia, the empirical research is still relatively sparse on the significance of religion, beliefs and culture on the wishes and choices which dying people and their relatives express, or professionals promote.

This chapter has also shown how services for people who are dying are shaped by the overall climate of health and social care. In summary, the key thrusts are:

- to enable people to receive palliative care while remaining at home for as long as they choose, including to die at home if possible;
- to extend the remit of palliative care to non-cancers including the diseases of old age;
- to facilitate individual choice and the full involvement of the dying person and their family in treatment decisions;
- to reach out to minority groups and make mainstream services culturally appropriate;

- to further define and demonstrate in practice the outworkings of the principles of holistic care;
- to make hospices a fully integrated part of the health and social care network.

Some elements and positions in the issues we have discussed are irreconcilable. It is the task of the legislators and policy makers to negotiate a path which is acceptable to the majority and allows minority viewpoints to be respected wherever and as far as is possible. Ultimately, the arguments put forward against the Joffe Bill in the UK in its first incarnation were a mixture of moral, religious and pragmatic (Neuberger, 2006). However, legislation and policy may determine the framework which governs care of the dying, but patients and service users and health and social care practitioners alike contribute their experience and expertise to the environment in which that dying takes place. There remains an acute shortage of specialist palliative care practitioners across the world and this must be addressed. There is also, however, continuing evidence that too many health and social care professionals outside of palliative care are ignorant of the philosophy and practice which constitutes sensitive, culturally competent and quality care for people nearing the end of life. Only so equipped can professionals in all sectors of health and social care negotiate the complex choices and issues involved in contemporary dying – for themselves as well as for those they seek to help.

Key questions for practitioners
1. What have you learnt from this chapter about approaches to the care of people who are dying and how might this affect your work?
2. Do you come across any of the ethical dilemmas discussed here and how do you currently resolve them?
3. Is there anything in the positions discussed here which might help you deal better with your dilemma(s)?
4. Does end-of-life care planning feature in your direct work with service users? If not, why not? Should it?
5. How well does the service in which you work address the needs of people from ethnic minorities?
6. How well does it address spiritual and religious needs?
7. What further knowledge/skills do you need to gain in order to improve your practice with people at the end of life and their families?

Note
[1]But see Chapter Two for discussion of the reduction in 'terminal' diagnoses due to progress in treating malignant conditions.

CPSIA information can be obtained
at www.ICGtesting.com
Printed in the USA
LVHW011907191222
735562LV00005B/33

9 781621 317340